Healthcare Spaces

No.2

Healthcare Spaces

No. 2

Roger Yee

Visual Reference Publications Inc., New York

Visual Reference Publications Inc.
302 Fifth Avenue
New York, NY 10001

Distributors to the trade in the United States and Canada
Watson-Guptill
770 Broadway
New York, NY 10003

Distributors outside the United States and Canada
HarperCollins International
10 East 53rd Street
New York, NY 10022-5299

Library of Congress Cataloging in Publication Data:
Healthcare Spaces No.2

Printed in China
ISBN 1-58471-045-4

Book Design: Priscilla Sue Mascia

CONTENTS

Introduction by Roger Yee 7

Above left: University Health Network, Toronto.
Design firm: HOK.

Above right: Children's Hospital, Omaha.
Design firm: HDR.

Left: Cuthbertson Village at Aldersgate, Charlotte.
Design firm: FreemanWhite, Inc.

Far left: Children's Hospital at Vanderbilt, Nashville.
Design firm: Earl Swensson Associates, Inc.

Introduction

"Shall I supersize it?"

Right: Cleveland Clinic Florida, Naples.

Design firm: Marshall Erdman & Associates.

"Shall I supersize it?" asks the server with a smile that says another heap of French fries might make that triple cheeseburger and supersized soft drink even more satisfying. The everyday tripling of portions pays tribute to a land of abundance and symbolizes America's attitude towards healthcare. The means to good health are available to everyone, but so are a cornucopia of tempting alternatives.

Unfortunately, faith in medicine's silver bullet that cures everything is the ultimate preventative for too many people. Accordingly, healthcare facilities are designed to intervene when chronic bad health habits trigger acute episodes. With over 60 percent of adults and 20 percent of children now overweight or obese,the nation's heathcare institutions are responding by such means as building or renovating emergency departments, cardiovascular centers and children's hospitals.To their credit, these

institutions are also teaching people healthier ways to live. Combining medicine, marketing and design, they are developing such innovative facilities as wellness centers, resource centers and demonstration kitchens where staying fit through healthy lifestyles, education and check ups has never looked or felt so good. Why should healthcare be only for patients?

Obviously, healthcare institutions play complicated roles. That's why the recently completed healthcare facilities on the following pages of Healthcare Spaces No. 2, created by some of the nation's best designers are so inspiring. Working closely together, architects, interior designers and healthcare professionals are successfully establishing patient-centered environments where well being can thrive.

Roger Yee
Editor

Anderson Mikos Architects Ltd.

1420 Kensington Road
Oak Brook, IL 60523
630.573.5149
630.573.5176 (Fax)
dmikos@andersonmikos.com

Anderson Mikos Architects Ltd.

Children's Memorial Hospital
Surgical Short Stay Observation Unit
Chicago, Illinois

Needing additional beds for patients requiring longer second-stage recovery and observation following outpatient surgery, Chicago's respected Children's Memorial Hospital has transformed a tight, L shaped, former outpatient clinic area into a playful, open space, limiting patient transfers to an inpatient nursing unit. Requirements for the 4,000-square foot Surgical Short Stay Observation Unit, designed by Anderson Mikos Architects, reflected its complex nature. Technically an outpatient area, the new facility required many utilities common to recovery beds, along with a pleasant, private environment for patients and families staying up to 23 hours. Consequently, full side walls flank nine open beds for observation and privacy, two fully enclosed beds provide contact isolation, and decentralized supplies and two sub-nurse work stations support one central nurse station in an efficient yet comforting "forest" setting.

Above right: Central nurse station.

Right: Open bed.
Far right: Enclosed bed.

Opposite: Open beds and sub-nurse station.

Photography: Mark Ballogg /Steinkamp/Ballogg.

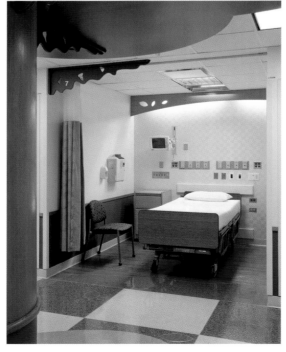

Anderson Mikos Architects Ltd.

Swedish Covenant Hospital
Acuity-Adaptable Inpatient Unit
Chicago, Illinois

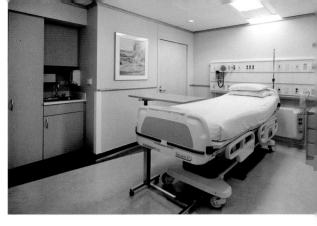

Top right: Acuity-adaptable bed.

Above right: Nurses station.

Below left: Corridor.

Photography: Mark Ballogg/Steinkamp/Ballogg.

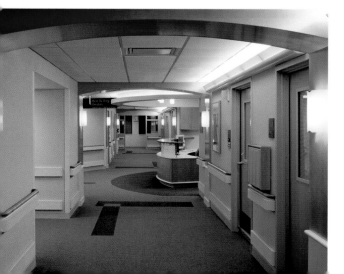

Unpredictable events leave hospitals perennially short of the right kinds of beds. To test an innovative solution to this problem, Swedish Covenant Hospital, an institution founded in 1886 serving north and northwest Chicago, recently collaborated with Anderson Mikos Architects to develop a 10,000-square foot Acuity-Adaptable Inpatient Unit with 56 flexible patient rooms. The concept of an acuity-adaptable bed, based on a footprint that can perform like specific care rooms without imposing their limitations, has sufficient potential that the Illinois Department of Public Health is treating the project as a test case for the state. For all its technicality, the Acuity-Adaptable Inpatient Unit also provides a healing environment. Its warm home-like appearance, incorporating such design elements as maple wood trim, carpet, pilasters, wainscoting, arching soffits, sconces, indirect lighting, and attractive patient room furnishings, assures patients and families regardless of medical acuity. "The new flexible inpatient unit allows Swedish Covenant Hospital the potential to flex inpatient bed needs as dictated by day-to day events", says Saliba Kokaly, Director of Design and Construction at Swedish Covenant Hospital.

Anderson Mikos Architects Ltd.

Hinsdale Hospital
Koplin Family Endoscopy Center
Hinsdale, Illinois

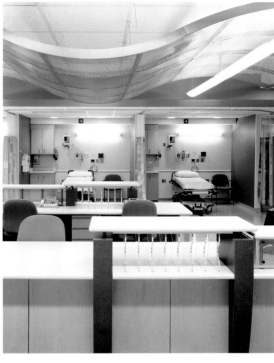

Sometimes a confined area can become an open one in perception only, a familiar challenge to hospital planners and designers that is handled with economy and style at Hinsdale Hospital's new, 8,000-square foot Koplin Family Endoscopy Center, in Hinsdale, Illinois, by Anderson Mikos Architects. Though the floor area allocated to the Center was landlocked and capped by a low ceiling, the design conjures a convincing image of expanding space by using bisecting planes and curves with different colors, materials, textures and lighting sources to break up and obscure the actual boundaries of walls and ceilings. In this carefully studied composition, little things count. Consider two lighting details: Wall-mounted direct/indirect lighting creates a subdued atmosphere in each recovery bay, while direct/indirect lighting at the nursing station plays up the subtle roll of the suspended serpentine ceiling. Offering patients a facility this responsive may seem unusual, but it's a trademark of 459-bed Hinsdale Hospital, a member of Adventist Health System Midwest Region that has been serving the people of Chicagoland for nearly 100 years.

Above left: Nursing station.
Above right: Recovery bays.
Left: Cabinetry detail.
Photography: Mark Ballogg/Steinkamp/Ballogg.

Anderson Mikos Architects Ltd.

Louis A. Weiss Memorial Hospital
South Addition
Chicago, Illinois

Below: Atrium in entrance pavilion.

Right: Entrance pavilion.

Photography: Mark Ballogg/Steinkamp/Ballogg.

How do hospitals feel about growth? Continuing increases in patient volumes recently gave Louis A. Weiss Memorial Hospital, a 369-bed Chicago institution affiliated with the University of Chicago Hospitals that first opened its doors to the public in 1953, a golden opportunity to upgrade its overall physical environment. Following a master plan prepared earlier by Anderson Mikos Architects, Weiss Memorial and Anderson Mikos have completed a 47,000-square foot addition and renovation project that includes a new main entry and lobby, expanded emergency department, admitting, intensive care unit and private physicians' offices, as well as updated mechanical systems. The work has accomplished considerably more than enlarge the Hospital's capacity to handle existing patient volumes. For example, the new emergency department provides patients the proper level of care they need with improved timeliness and privacy, by including a fast-track area for less severe cases and enhancing specialty programs for stroke, chest pain, asthma and pain management. In addition, the new ICU offers highly advanced resources for care of critically ill patients, the new entrance pavilion and its two-story atrium accommodate convenient registration and admitting areas in a setting that is considerably more visible

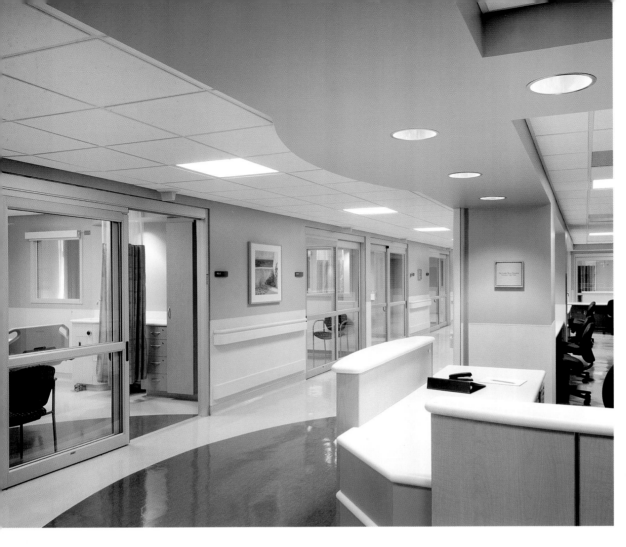

and welcoming than before. The new bypass corridor enables patient areas to be kept separate from public areas, and new parking areas adjacent to the Hospital enhance safety and convenience through better site lighting, landscaping and pedestrian/vehicular circulation patterns. No less important is the new public image established by the award-winning design. While a modern architecture of brick, metal and glass smoothly links the new addition to existing construction, an interior design of clean, fresh tones, light maple veneer, natural lighting and varied man-made lighting, terrazzo flooring, and attractive yet durable furnishings helps reassure patients and families, particularly in the more stressful, high-technology areas. For the more than 600,000 people living in Weiss Memorial's primary service area, which embraces Chicago neighborhoods from Lakeview and Logan Square to Rogers Park and Skokie, the future of health care has become brighter as well as bigger.

Anshen + Allen Architects

901 Market Street
San Francisco, CA 94103
415.882.9500
415.882.9523 (Fax)

1500 4th Avenue
Suite 450
Seattle, WA 98101
206.652.0111
206.749.0176 (Fax)

www.anshen.com
info@anshen.com

250 West Pratt Street
Suite 1000
Baltimore, MD 21201
410.528.7700
410.528.8456 (Fax)

One Olivers Yard City Road
London, EC1Y 1HQ
England, UK
011.44.207.017.3100
011.44.207.017.3101 (Fax)

Anshen + Allen Architects

Contra Costa County Regional Medical Center
Ambulatory Care Clinic
Martinez, California

Above right: Corridor and waiting area.

Right: Entrance.

Below right: Clinical area.

Opposite: Main lobby.

Photography: Bob Canfield.

The recent addition to the Contra Costa County Regional Medical Center campus, in Martinez, California, a 60, 000-square foot, three story Ambulatory Care Center, designed by Anshen + Allen Architects, continues a century of service by making patients feel especially welcome. For example, the attractive, modern and patient-focused facility, which houses specialty diagnostic and treatment clinics for infusion, cardiopulmonology, family practice, dental, ear /nose /throat and audio /vision, is broken into two wings oriented around courtyard gardens, flooding the interiors with natural light and views of landscaping, quiet pools and an existing nearby redwood grove. Each clinic, in turn, is laid out as a standard module to handle different uses, depending on which clinic is in operation. Among the many benefits of this soothing environment are that Cancer Center patients can receive their chemotherapy in a private garden and the glazed public corridor enjoys garden views.

Anshen + Allen Architects

Asian Hospital and Medical Center
Filinvest, Alabang, Philippines

For a nation that has not seen a major new hospital in years, the recent opening of the Asian Hospital and Medical Center, in Filinvest, Alabang, Philippines, has been a revelation. The 710,000-square foot, 250-bed Center, designed by Anshen + Allen Architects with an 11-story inpatient tower linked by a sky bridge to a seven-story outpatient medical office building, powerfully demonstrates the Center's commitment to a healing environment unlike anything the nation has known. Many of the nation's top medical and surgical specialists head its departments, wielding state-of-the-art equipment and supported by carefully trained staff and a patient-centered, holistic environment where families are welcome, two nursing stations on each inpatient floor provide personalized care, and the interior design inspires comparisons with five-star hotels.

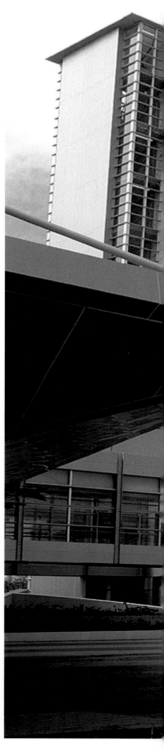

Top: Main lobby.

Above: Patient room.

Right: Lobby detail.

Far right: Tower, MOB and sky bridge.

Photography: Ava Lugtu, Bert and Franz Albert Dimson (exterior).

Anshen + Allen Architects

Intermountain Healthcare
Dixie Regional Medical Center
St. George, Utah

With the recent opening of the new Dixie Regional Medical Center, a 420,000-square foot, 132-bed replacement medical center in St. George, Utah, southern Utah's residents can receive medical treatment locally that sometimes took them 303 miles to Salt Lake City. The initial construction phase, comprising a three-story diagnostic and treatment wing, five-story inpatient tower and four-story physicians' office building, all connected by a concourse with discrete entrances to major services, has been designed by Anshen + Allen Architects to house emergency, surgery, medical and surgical inpatient services, intensive care, imaging, cardiac and pulmonary rehabilitation and out-patient surgery.

Above left: Entrance, diagnostic and treatment wing.

Above right: Diagnostic and treatment wing reception.

Right: Patient room.

Far right: Admissions, inpatient tower.

Opposite: Concourse lobby.

Photography: John Lyndon.

Anshen + Allen Architects

UCSF Children's Hospital
Ambulatory Care Center, Pediatrics Clinic
San Francisco, California

When you receive 50,000 patient visits annually, as University of California San Francisco Children's Hospital does at its Pediatrics Clinic, you have obvious reasons to consolidate and realign previously dispersed clinical services within a flexibly designed modern space. Anshen + Allen Architects transformed a 19,000 sq. foot floor into a patient-friendly and efficient environment. Circulation has shifted inward from the window wall to be replaced by flexible team workrooms, and corridors narrow as they radiate from the core, where waiting and examination rooms cluster. Yet efficiency still leaves room for such playful details as murals, signage, child-scaled furnishings, fiber optics in the ceiling and a floor-to-ceiling blackboard that brings out the kid in teenagers as well as kindergartners.

Above right: Waiting room.
Right: Elevator area.
Far right: Corridor.
Photography: Bob Canfield.

Architectural Nexus Inc.

2150 So. 1300 East Suite 200
Salt Lake City, UT 84106
801.924.5000
801.924.5001 (Fax)
www.archnexus.com

Architectural Nexus, Inc.

Huntsman Cancer Institute Research Hospital
University of Utah Medical Center
Salt Lake City, Utah

Above: Waiting room.

Left: Exterior.

Lower left: Lower level entrance with pedestrian bridge.

Opposite: Interior atrium 3-story structural glass curtain wall.

Illustration: Architectural Nexus 3D Renderings.

To provide cancer patients innovative and effective care in an attractive and comfortable setting, the Huntsman Cancer Institute at the University of Utah Medical Center is developing a striking, 291,143-square foot, seven-level, 50-bed Cancer Research Hospital, designed by Architectural Nexus, on an adjacent hillside site overlooking Salt Lake City. The steep, sloping terrain imposed numerous design challenges that demanded creative solutions, affecting such issues as egress, linear accelerator vaults, cyclotron suite, and dock area. Yet the topography has not prevented the Hospital, which is chiefly oriented towards outpatient oncology, from establishing a light, airy and patient-centered environment for radiation therapy, physical therapy, urgent care, surgical suites, endoscopy services, diagnostic radiology, diagnostic laboratory, pharmacy, inpatient rooms with family sleeping accommodations, inpatient floor showers and restrooms for family members, chapel /meditation room, dining, gift shop and business center. Thus, patients will participate in the development of new treatment protocols for cancer patients in the Intermountain West and throughout the world, knowing they will be sustained by their families in an exceptional facility with such amenities as on-demand food service comparable to that of a fine hotel.

Architectural Nexus, Inc.

Eccles Critical Care Pavilion
University of Utah Medical Center
Salt Lake City, Utah

Right: Waiting area.

Below: Exterior.

Bottom left: Operating room.

Bottom right: Nurses station.

Opposite: Brick, metal and glass curtainwall.

Photography: Dennis Mecham Photography, Paul Richer Images.

The George S. and Dolores Doré Eccles Critical Care Pavilion at the University of Utah Medical Center is a126,136-square foot addition and 19,450-square foot remodeling project, designed by Architectural Nexus, that will simultaneously provide an expanded surgical suite, surgical ICU, same day surgery, and emergency department, and realign buildings on the Medical Center's campus to facilitate orderly growth. Within the Pavilion, the interiors are rearranged and expanded to increase staff efficiency, establish adjacency between functions, and create a patient-centered environment combining hospitality-like furnishings with good wayfinding and landscape

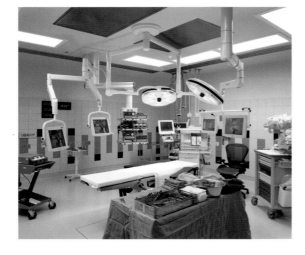

vistas. As a critical component of the Medical Center, the Pavilion has been positioned so the future School of Medicine, due to replace an existing structure slated for demolition due to seismic deficiencies, will be a matching west wing to the Pavilion avoiding a potential chain reaction of displacement among existing buildings.

Architectural Nexus, Inc.

Mercy Regional Medical Center
Durango, Colorado

Although Mercy Regional Medical Center's new, 215,000-square foot, three-level, 82-bed Mercy Hospital, currently under construction in Durango, Colorado, along with a 180,000-square foot medical office building, daycare center, central utility plant and parking, gives little hint of its destiny, the structure is planned to grow by 100 percent while staying fully functional during expansion. The regional health care complex, designed by Architectural Nexus for Catholic Health Initiatives, will evolve into an integrated campus of inpatient and outpatient care for the new, 1,100-acre planned community it serves. A spacious, 2-1/2-story rotunda lobby at the entrance will direct patients and visitors to a nearby chapel and healing garden as well as the various medical areas. In this family-friendly environment, residents of the new community will find attractive furnishings, naturally inspired colors, sensitive lighting, wayfinding cues and artwork along with quality care from the latest addition to a health care system serving southwest Colorado since 1882.

Architectural Nexus, Inc.

Cache Valley Specialty Hospital and Medical Office Building
Logan, Utah

Years of hard work produced a health care choice for the residents of Utah's Cache Valley when the new 51,398-square foot Cache Valley Specialty Hospital and 28,053-square foot medical office building opened recently in Logan, realizing a vision shared by local, independent physicians. The new Hospital, predominantly a same-day surgery facility, includes a 30,000-square foot physicians' practice area along with a six-bed inpatient unit and combined waiting areas. It acknowledges the context of a small community from the start, emphasizing good wayfinding and appropriate aesthetic expression, a point made again and again when patients and families come into the rotunda entry and easily find their way to the treatments they seek.

Upper right: Waiting area.
Above: Rotunda entry.
Photography: Dennis Mecham Photography.

Array
Healthcare Facilities Solutions
Formerly BLM Architects

2520 Renaissance Blvd. Suite 110
King of Prussia, PA 19406
610.775.6430
610.775.6530 (Fax)
www.blm-architects.com

Array

Sacred Heart Hospital on the Emerald Coast
West Destin, Florida

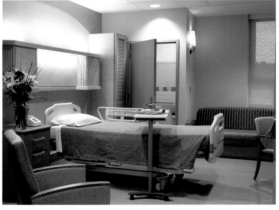

Left: Waiting area along concourse.

Upper right: Patient room at headwall.

Above right: Patient room wall unit.

Opposite: Entrance lobby.

Photography: Joseph Lapeyra.

Sacred Heart Health System, which has served northwest Florida since the Civil War, is reaching out to a growing population with the new, 105,000-square foot, 2-floor, 50-bed Sacred Heart Hospital on the Emerald Coast, in West Destin, designed by Array in association with Gresham Smith & Partners and Caldwell Associates. Working with Sacred Heart's program experts, the design team has developed an upscale, family-friendly and state-of-the-art environment for the West Destin facility, based on a universal room design that accommodates intensive care, step-down and acute care. Patients and families easily find their way along a concourse connecting such destinations as inpatient units, emergency services, imaging, physical therapy, outpatient surgery, diagnostic center, visitor waiting, cafe and gift shop. And while the Hospital is designed for effectiveness, patients, families and staff also appreciate such amenities as resort-style furnishings, indirect lighting, artwork and a beautiful healing garden.

Array

St. Joseph Outpatient Center Bluemound
Wauwatosa, Wisconsin

Above: Nurses station, PACU.

Left: Exterior.

Opposite above: Outpatient entrance.

Opposite below: Reception and waiting area, same day surgery.

Photography: Jim Morrill/JJ Images.

To create a cohesive outpatient facility, incorporating such ambulatory services as urgent care, rehabilitation, women's services, imaging, and day surgery along with a large medical group practice and physicians' offices, Array, in association with Eppstein Uhen Architects, has designed the 210,000-square foot, five-story, limestone and glass-clad St. Joseph Outpatient Center and 1,200-vehicle parking structure in Wawautosa, Wisconsin as a spacious and inviting facility. It's just one example of how the award-winning design for Covenant Healthcare System responds to the site and existing adjacent building, providing separate entrances for ambulatory services and physicians' practices, connecting on grade to the women's pavilion, and extending a second-level pedestrian bridge to the existing parking structure and second-story balcony main entrance. In addition to establishing state-of-the-art facilities in an optimal spatial orientation, the design introduces an upscale environment with residential-style comfort and such amenities as a bistro and a gift shop that are especially impressive in light of a tight schedule that allowed five months for design and ten months and a day for construction. Says Jonathan Flyte, a senior vice president of Covenant, "It really reflects the current status of how ambulatory services should be done."

Array

St. Joseph Regional Medical Center
South Tower, Center for Women and Infants
Milwaukee, Wisconsin

Left: Upper level view of entrance lobby.

Lower left: Cafe.

Bottom left: Patient care floor reception.

Opposite: Entrance lobby.

Photography: Howard Kaplan/HNK Photography.

Over 4,000 babies are delivered annually at St. Joseph Regional Medical Center, in Milwaukee, Wisconsin, which suggests the importance of the 105,000-square foot new construction and 86,000-square foot renovation project to the Center for Women and Infants in the South Tower, designed by Array in association with Zimmerman Design Group. St. Joseph, part of Covenant Healthcare Systems, is proud of its role as Wisconsin's leading birthing center, as well as its largest perinatal center, with the state's largest NICU at 59 bassinets. Thus, the development of new and renovated spaces for the lobby, hospitality facilities, classrooms, chapel, NICU, and such obstetrical services as pre-natal assessment, delivery suite, and ante-partum and post-partum bedrooms, has been seen as an important means of assuring the quality of the Center's services for years to come. Essential to the success of the project has been the extraction of the post-partum component from the main service floor to allow ante-partum bedrooms to expand, the NICU to relocate to a new space, and delivery functions to expand in place. Needless to say, women and their families are also delighted by the new, hotel-like, two-story entrance lobby with grand piano, reception desk, glass-enclosed stair and dedicated elevators, which leads them into a family-friendly environment of elegant, home-like

Array

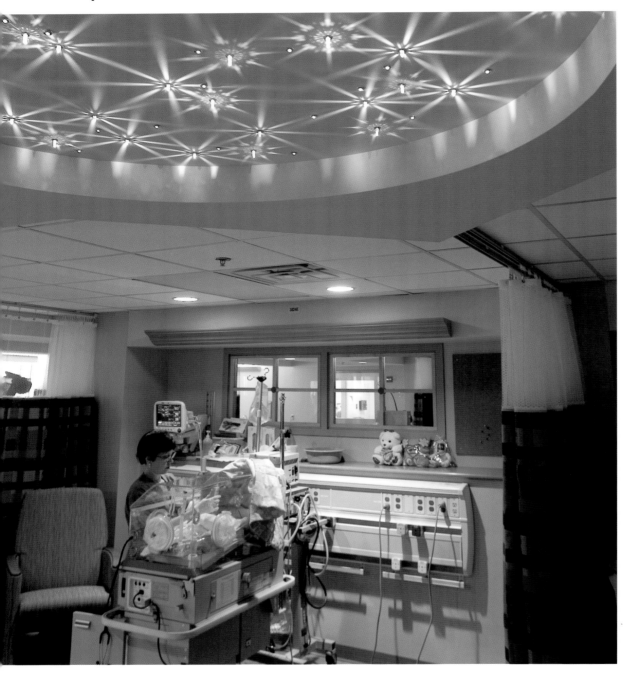

furnishings, soothing colors, natural wood finishes and sophisticated lighting, featuring post-partum rooms with family-comfort zones that can accommodate entire families all constructed without interrupting the deliveries of babies and other vital functions at the Center.

Left: NICU.
Below: Entrance lobby mezzanine.

Bradley-Blewster & Associates

8026 Picardy Avenue
Baton Rouge, LA 70809
225.769.7040
225.769.7065 (Fax)
www.bradley-blewster.com

Bradley-Blewster & Associates

Woman's Hospital and Physician's Tower
Baton Rouge, Louisiana

Renovations and additions involving 237,570 square feet at Baton Rouge's Woman's Hospital, one of the first women's specialty hospitals in the nation, founded in 1968, and Physician's Tower, a medical office building, have vividly updated the facilities as well as added vital capacity. As a result, patient rooms, surgery, day surgery, labor and delivery, laboratory, pharmacy, dietary, nurseries, NICU and ICU have been transformed by the latest technology, enhanced wayfinding, and a comfortable, home-like environment. The parking garage has more parking spaces and a helipad. MOB has two new floors. The handsomely detailed project, designed by Bradley Blewster & Associates reflects the owners focus on patients and their families. Over 7,500 babies are born each year.

Top: Waiting area, surgery.

Left: Labor delivery, patient room, Woman's Hospital.

Right: Cafe, Woman's Hospital.

Opposite: Main entrance Woman's Hospital.

Photography: Marie Constantin.

Bradley-Blewster & Associates

Medical Plazas at Our Lady of the Lake Regional Medical Center Baton Rouge, Louisianna

Right: Exterior.

Below right: Fitness center.

Bottom right: Cafe.

Opposite: Atrium lobby.

Photography: W. Carroll Blewster.

Accommodating large and small medical practices was a key objective for the 450, 000-square foot Medical Plaza, in Baton Rouge, Louisiana, designed by Bradley-Blewster & Associates for Our Lady of the Lake Regional Medical Center. The seven-story and ten-story towers and two-story ancillary structure at Medical Plaza are configured accordingly. Thus, small practices are served with the central elevator core providing shallow structural bay depths from all sides of the seven-story tower, while large practices are accommodated by the perimeter elevator core, deeper bays and greater usable floor areas of the ten-story tower. What accounts for the scale of this impressive facility, which also includes a conference center, fitness center, outpatient diagnostic areas, hyperbaric department, retail space, atrium lobby and cafe? Its first and second floors connect to an existing hospital so patients can be transferred here for diagnostic and treatment procedures on the 100-acre campus of the 852-bed Center, Louisiana's largest hospital.

Bradley-Blewster & Associates

Surgical Specialty Centre
Baton Rouge, Louisianna

Focusing on ear, nose, and throat, general surgery, orthopedics, pediatric surgery and urology has proved a successful strategy for Surgical Specialty Centre, a specialized hospital led by physicians in Baton Rouge, Louisiana. The Centre's commitment to its focus was dramatized recently by the completion of a 90,000-square foot hospital and 90,000-square foot medical office building with a shared lobby, designed by Bradley-Blewster & Associates. Although the project spanned a mere 15 months, its facilities are as extensive as those of comparable health care institutions, including eight operating suites, four minor procedure rooms, 12 private pre-op rooms, eight-bed post anesthesia, 12-bed stepdown recovery, 14 private inpatient rooms, physical therapy area and gymnasium, treatment rooms, hydrotherapy, medical durable goods supplier, physician clinics, diagnostic imaging, pharmacy and coffee shop. Designed with patients' convenience in mind, the interior of the Centre offers a healing environment with furnishings comparable to those of a fine hotel, where private inpatient rooms are equipped with such amenities as TV, DVD, VCR, Internet connections, refrigerator, microwave, and access to a book and video library.

Above: Atrium.

Opposite, top left: Entrance.

Opposite, upper left: Conference room.

Opposite, lower left: Inpatient room.

Opposite, bottom left: Lobby.

Photography: Marie Constantin.

Bradley-Blewster & Associates

Lake Surgery Center
Baton Rouge, Louisianna

Today's health care consumers want advanced medical services delivered in a friendly, comfortable and convenient atmosphere, which is just what Our Lady of the Lake Regional Medical Center, in Baton Rouge, Louisiana, offers in the new, 23,385-square foot, one-story Lake Surgery Center, designed by Bradley-Blewster & Associates. Created for patients and families in only nine months, the brick, aluminum and glass-clad Center, encompassing six ORs, pre-op, post-op and discharge waiting for 12 patients, treatment room and waiting room, takes its patient and staff flow through a progressive set of spaces to eliminate traffic crossover. While high-technology equipment is present throughout the facility, the interior design emphasizes warm earth tones, natural lighting, and inviting, comfortable furnishings, continuing the tradition of compassionate care established when Mother de Bethanie Crowley and the Franciscan Missionaries of Our Lady established what is now Louisiana's largest hospital in 1923.

BSA LifeStructures

9365 Counselors Row
Indianapolis, IN 46240
317.819.7878
317.819.7288 (Fax)
www.bsalifestructures.com

BSA LifeStructures

St. Vincent Mercy Hospital
Elwood, Indiana

Blackford Community Hospital
Hartford City, Indiana

Small rural hospitals are getting a new lease on life thanks to the three-pronged cure of architecture, critical access hospital designation and the financial backing of larger healthcare systems. With the support of St. Vincent Health, one of Indiana's largest healthcare systems and a member of Ascension Health, and the design services of BSA LifeStructures, these hospitals were transformed to provide better facilities and additional services that are closer to home. At St. Vincent Mercy Hospital, in Elwood, BSA LifeStructures created a 40,000-square-foot addition and renovation that gave the institution a new patient entry and registration, emergency department, radiology, laboratory and medical specialty clinics. St. Vincent Jennings Hospital, in North Vernon, needed a 61,700-square-foot addition and renovation that enabled it to make the transition to friendly, community-oriented outpatient service without interrupting operations. And St. Vincent Randolph, in Winchester, gave its rural population a much-needed, 62,000-square-foot, 25-bed critical access hospital. For another major Indiana healthcare system, Cardinal

Above: Main entry of St. Vincent Mercy in Elwood.

Above left: Detail of facade.

Above right: Main lobby.

Photography: Dan Francis

Below: Sketch of Blackford Community Hospital.

Illustration: Courtesy of BSA LifeStructures

St. Vincent Jennings Hospital
North Vernon, Indiana

St, Vincent Randolph Hospital
Winchester, Indiana

Health System, BSA LifeStructures recently designed Blackford Community Hospital, in Hartford City, a 45,745-square-foot replacement hospital and 11,295-square-foot medical office building that emphasizes efficiency. Diverse as they are, the new facilities for St. Vincent Health and Cardinal Health System are improving the quality of life for people throughout Indiana.

Above: Lobby and registration of St. Vincent Jennings Hospital.

Left: Spiritual center.

Opposite left: Main entry.

Photography: Steve Richardson

Below left: View from imaging station into lobby area at St. Vincent Hospital.

Below right: Main entry on south facade.

Lower left: Corridor.

Photography: Dan Francis

BSA LifeStructures

Plainfield Medical Center
Plainfield, Indiana

Plainfield, Indiana, a community that's attracting new businesses and residents, has prompted Hendricks Regional Health to take a major step forward by developing the 108,000-square-foot, three-story Plainfield Medical Center, a handsome brick and glass structure designed by BSA LifeStructures. For over 10 years, Hendricks leased space in Plainfield that offered only laboratory and radiology services. Today, the new environment provides immediate care, occupational medicine, laboratory/radiology and physical/occupational therapy, along with physicians focusing on family practice, internal medicine/pediatrics, ophthalmology and dermatology. Trudy B. Tharp, vice president, Hendricks Regional Health, reports, "People in the community are very pleased to have these services close to their homes and businesses. The building itself is beautiful and stands out as one of the most visible buildings coming into Plainfield."

Left: Stair tower.

Below left: Facade.

Below right: Atrium.

Photography: Tony Fredrick/CS Kern, Karl Pfeffer Jr., Greg Murphey

BSA LifeStructures

Landsbaum Center for Health Education
Terre Haute, Indiana

Above: Main entry.
Left: Atrium rotunda.
Below right: Facade.
Photography: Greg Murphey

A shared vision to provide health educational programming has resulted in the new 34,000-square-foot, two-story Landsbaum Center for Health Education in Terre Haute, Indiana—a building that has become a national model for collaboration. Designed by BSA LifeStructures, the facility brings together education programs to train nurses, medical students and family practice residents from Indiana State University School of Nursing, Indiana University School of Medicine and Union Hospital's Midwest Center for Rural Health for careers in rural, underserved communities. The state-of-the-art facility allows them to collaborate and to share facilities and technology, like medical simulators. Within this versatile environment, students and faculty have access to such well-equipped and attractive accommodations as a 150-seat lecture hall, classrooms, conference rooms, public/teaching clinic, student team rooms, offices and circular central lobby. "I love this building. It's incredibly well designed," said Dr. James R. Buechler, director of the Midwest Center for Rural Health and Family Practice Residency Program, Union Hospital. "Usually after you get into a new building , you think of all the things you wish you'd done differently. I can't say that about this building."

BSA LifeStructures

St. Vincent Carmel Hospital Addition
Carmel, Indiana

Above: Labor delivery recovery room in the new maternity services unit.

Left: Entrance.

Below left: Lobby.

Photography: Riccardo Cosciasecca, Scott McDonald/ Hedrich Blessing

A need for more space for additional services recently gave St. Vincent Carmel Hospital, in Carmel, Indiana, an opportunity to transform its image through a 105,000-square-foot, three-story addition, designed by BSA LifeStructures. The new facilities include a lobby and registration area, emergency department, maternity services unit, acute care nursing unit for bariatrics and orthopedics, short stay unit, endoscopy area, dining area and gift shop. The new construction introduces a patient-focused environment with a hotel-like ambiance, particularly in maternity services. According to Michael Chittenden, Vice President and Administrator for St. Vincent Carmel, patients, families and staff all appreciate what he calls "a more hospitable atmosphere and a more conducive healing environment to complement our philosophy of holistic care."

BSA LifeStructures

Ball Memorial Hospital
Emergency Department
Muncie, Indiana

When patients enter an emergency department, their stress levels are typically high. They have health needs to be addressed and are often in physical discomfort. In addition, they usually have to sit next to other ailing patients in a waiting room until they can be treated, which adds to the stress that patients already feel. Ball Memorial Hospital in Muncie, Indiana, addressed those issues with a new kind of emergency department—one without a waiting room. With its architecture and interior design elements, the new 22,300-square-foot emergency department, designed by BSA LifeStructures, is meeting the hospital's goal of creating the best possible experience for its patients. Upon entering the new emergency department, which was relocated to the front of the hospital, each patient is greeted at the reception area and immediately taken to one of 35 private rooms equipped with TVs and telephones as well as the medical equipment most patients need in emergency care. The facility also boasts its own digital radiology room, CT scan room and dedicated elevator to the surgical unit. America's first "no waiting room" ED is off to an inspired start.

Top: Nurses station.

Above: Entrance and concierge area.

Left: Entrance.

Photography: Tony Frederick/ C.S. Kern

55

BSA LifeStructures

Central Indiana Orthopedics
Anderson, Indiana

The long, low, brick-and-fritted glass-clad structure housing Central Indiana Orthopedics appears as an unmistakable yet welcome "billboard," making use of its visibility in the setting adjacent to Interstate 69 in Anderson, Indiana. The 46,000-square foot, one-story facility, designed by BSA Life-Structures, provides comprehensive orthopedic care under one roof through a two-operating room surgery center, outpatient clinic and physical rehabilitation and sports medicine center. Efficient connections between surgery, clinics, imaging and rehabilitation make the building operate smoothly for patients and staff. A patient-friendly environment, featuring attractive and comfortable furnishings, natural light and outdoor views, soft lighting and artwork, takes the hard edge off such high-technology facilities as three digital R/F rooms, EMG room, bone densitometry equipment and fixed site MRI, all part of the Center's diagnostic imaging services. John Hargrave, Director of Marketing for Central Indiana Orthopedics, said patients have provided positive feedback since the facility's opening. "The office is very peaceful and relaxing," he said. "Patients love the natural light through the front windows and skylights. Central Indiana Orthopedics' design and color provide a welcoming feeling."

Right: Clinic reception.

Below left: Main entrance drop-off canopy.

Below right: Exterior seen from I-69.

Photography: Scott McDonald/ Hedrich Blessing, Terry Wieckert, Skyking Aerial Photography

Burt Hill Kosar Rittelmann Associates

400 Morgan Center
Butler, PA 16001
724.285.4761
724.285.6815 (Fax)
www.burthill.com

Burt Hill Kosar Rittlemann Associates

UPMC Shadyside
Posner Tower, 3 East/4 East Inpatient Medical
Pittsburgh, Pennsylvania

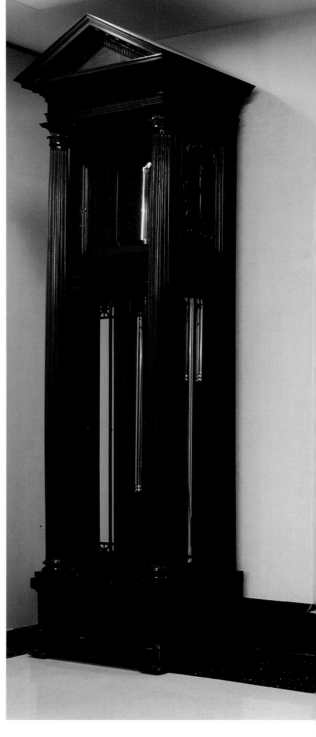

Why have Pittsburgh and the tri-state area looked to the University of Pittsburgh Medical Center Shadyside for health care since 1866? One reason is the 486-bed tertiary care hospital's willingness to make critical physical changes to serve its patient population, as two recent construction projects by Burt Hill Kosar Rittlemann Associates demonstrate. At Posner Tower, a 48,000-square foot renovation and expansion resulted in a new level 1 main entry, new 2nd level state-of-the-art operating rooms that were expanded from 5 to 21 operating rooms. A sterile storage area, and the new level 3 surgical staff and doctor locker rooms, staff lounge, conference room and on-call rooms. At the Inpatient Medical Building, 24,000 square feet on floors 3 East and 4 East, originally designed as office space, were creatively reconfigured for patient care with service spaces between patient rooms and central corridors. Despite structural and mechanical complexities, both projects function smoothly, introducing a stylish, hospitality-style ambiance that staff, patients and families all appreciate.

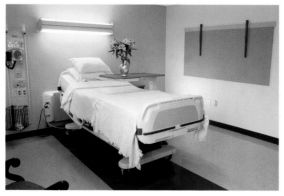

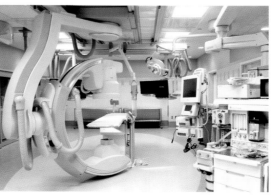

Above: Main entry to Posner Tower.

Left: Operating room.

Far left: Patient room.

Opposite: Patient floor lounge.

Photography: Jeff Swensen.

Burt Hill Kosar Rittlemann Associates
UPMC Cancer Center
John P. Murtha Pavilion
Johnstown, Pennsylvania

Left: Exterior.

Below left: Oncology treatment area.

Below right: Nurses station in oncology.

Bottom right: Reception and main waiting room.

Opposite: Lobby.

Photography: Edward Massery.

Because cancer patients experience considerable stress during treatment, patients and families in Johnstown, Pennsylvania have looked forward to the completion of the new, 18,000-square foot, two-story John P. Murtha Pavilion at the University of Pittsburgh Medical Center's local Cancer Center, designed by Burt Hill Kosar Rittelmann Associates. They have not been disappointed. Patients find their concerns addressed as soon as they arrive at the Pavilion's dramatic entrance and see the dramatic, two-story lobby that directs them to oncology and radiation treatment areas. While oncology patients spend lengthy hours in treatment chairs offset by panoramic views, individual televisions and guest chairs, radiation patients find their isolation relieved by sensitive colors and lighting, and family members are welcomed by an information library, wellness garden and other public areas that recognize their importance to patients.

Burt Hill Kosar Rittlemann Associates

UPMC Lee Regional
Patient Care Facility
Johnstown, Pennsylvania

Visitors to Johnstown, an historic Pennsylvania community dating from 1794 that flourished as a steel making center beginning in the mid-19th century, may not realize at first that this city of some 25,000 residents endured the worst flood in the nation's history. The community has long since recovered from the loss of 2,200 lives and much of its built environment after the South Fork Dam collapsed on May 31, 1889. However, the well-being of Johnstown remains a top priority for institutions like University of Pittsburgh Medical Center Lee Regional, an 80-plus-year-old hospital that recently added a 95,000 -square foot, six-level patient care facility, designed by Burt Hill Kosar Rittelmann Associates. The structure, housing the emergency department, women and children's services, rehabilitation care, and boiler and chiller plant for the entire hospital, has been developed to consolidate women's and children's services, including all obstetrics care, holding nursery and NICU, and to group post-orthopedic surgical patients and rehabilitation patients around similar therapy needs, all within the context of a caring environment that raises operating efficiency, minimizes patient movement, and introduces numerous patient-friendly amenities. Interestingly, the new emergency department is a half-floor above street level, a poignant reminder of Johnstown's location on a flood plain.

Above: Exterior.

Left: Emergency department.

Opposite above: OB floor lounge.

Opposite below: LDR room.

Photography: Jeff Swensen.

Burt Hill Kosar Rittlemann Associates

UPMC Shadyside
Hopwood Health Resource Center Library
Pittsburgh, Pennsylvania

Right: Reading area within book stacks.

Below: Reception/transaction area.

Photography: Edward Massery.

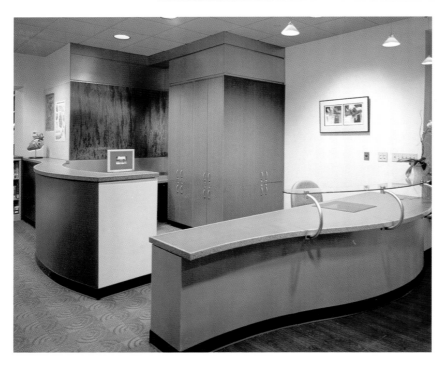

To assist patients and families who want to research information from doctors in greater depth, University of Pittsburgh Medical Center Shadyside recently opened the new, 4,300-square foot Hopwood Health Resource Center Library, designed by Burt Hill Kosar Rittelmann Associates. Hopwood Library, incorporating a reception/transaction area, book stacks and reading areas for 30, represents an inviting oasis for study within the busy, 486-bed hospital. Its special appeal comes from combining the physical appeal of wood furnishings, lively colors and coordinated carpet and textiles with the intimacy of reading areas intermingled with book stacks. Inquisitive readers are happy to learn they can browse among more than 1,200 books, pamphlets, health magazines and newsletters, Internet links to health-related Web sites, videotapes, audiotapes, and even anatomy models.

Cannon Design

2170 Whitehaven Road
Grand Island, NY 14072
716.773.6800
716.773.5909 (Fax)
www.cannondesign.com
chillers@cannondesign.com

Boston
Baltimore
Buffalo
Chicago
Jacksonville
Los Angeles
New York
St. Louis
Vancouver
Washington DC

Cannon Design

Washington University Medical Center/BJH
Center for Advanced Medicine and
Siteman Cancer Center
St. Louis, Missouri

The concept of patient experience, from arrival to wayfinding to final destination, has guided the planning of the impressive Center for Advanced Medicine and Siteman Cancer Center. The recently completed, 744,005 square foot, 14 story flagship facility at Washington University Medical Center in St. Louis consolidates services for 17 multi-disciplinary clinical centers. Because circulation pathways are organized around an interior skylit atrium, patients can easily visualize their destination within the complex building. The design responds to staff needs as well, since a clinic module developed as the planning template for the Center gives physicians wide flexibility in meeting their practice requirements. Departments can, therefore expand or change locations without major renovations. As Dr. Ronald Evens, President of Barnes Jewish Hospital, proclaims, "Cancer patients at the Siteman Cancer Center can be assured of the latest treatments and care, including all the clinical and psychological components, in a patient-friendly environment."

Top left: Lobby.
Top right: Waiting area.
Above right: Exterior w/HOK.
Right: Procedure room.
Opposite: Atrium.
Photography: Tim Hursley.

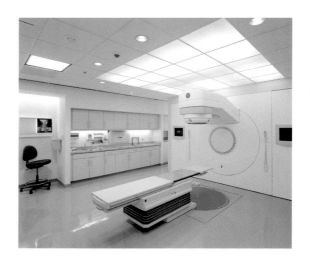

Cannon Design

OSF Saint Francis Medical Center
Center for Health
Peoria, Illinois

It seems only natural for OSF Saint Francis Medical Center to introduce the Peoria community to a new and innovative ambulatory health care service, the Center for Health, since the Medical Center has been a leading health care provider in central Illinois since 1876. The 136,200 square foot Center, designed by Cannon Design, offers almost every service a traditional hospital would provide, with the exception of inpatient beds. Its patient-friendly setting uses a central courtyard to serve as a focal point to organize patient circulation for clear wayfinding and logical access to services. However, the foundation of its spatial concept lies in the dramatic, curving concourse that flanks the array of clinical services and offers patients nearly immediate visibility to every destination when they arrive. Natural light from the concourse spills into the building interior, and the views and access that the concourse offers to the Serenity Garden, a lush, one acre landscape, provide a positive distraction for patients and families alike. When future innovations in health care require change, the concourse and each element of the Center for Health can expand with minimal disruption, key to a building designed to double in size.

Above: Concourse and garden.
Right: Waiting area.
Far right: Exterior.
Photography: G Factor Studio

Cannon Design

North Arundel Hospital
Tate Cancer Center
Glen Burnie, Maryland

Above right: Lobby and reception area.

Right: Exterior at dusk.

Below right: CT simulator.

Bottom right: Linear accelerator treatment area.

Photography: Michael Dersin.

The opening of the new Tate Cancer Center, in Glen Burnie, Maryland, marks an important milestone for North Arundel Hospital. The 60,000 square foot, three story Center, designed by Cannon Design, assembles cancer specialists from the hospital and sub-specialists from University of Maryland Medical System to offer radiation services, medical oncology services, multi-disciplinary clinics, clinical trials and public education. The facility's environment enhances the treatment outcome and emotional outlook of patients, families and staff through such details as a bright and airy, 12 bed infusion area overlooking a terraced healing garden, theatrical lighting above the patient in the linear accelerator treatment area, a family waiting area with access and views to a private landscaped garden, and a multistory circulation space that encourages casual interaction among patients, family, physicians and staff, demonstrating that quality care can be compassionate as well.

Cannon Design

Detroit Medical Center
Lawrence & Idell Weisberg Cancer Center
Farmington Hills, Michigan

A beckoning lodge may not be what cancer patients and families expect at the Lawrence & Idell Weisberg Cancer Center, in Farmington Hills, Michigan, but that's the point of the new,18,100 square foot, one story, stone clad facility, designed by Cannon Design in association with TMP Associates. This joint effort of the Barbara Ann Karmanos Cancer Institute and Detroit Medical Center departs from convention by creating a warm, patient-centered atmosphere at its wooded site. Under the exposed wood trusses and beams of the award-winning building's gable roof, such amenities as a fireplace, home-like waiting room, waterfall, individual changing rooms, kitchenettes, views of nature from treatment areas, Arts and Crafts furniture and artwork bolster the spirits of patients undergoing chemotherapy, radiation oncology and other sophisticated cancer treatments. As Dr. Jeffrey Forman, Director of the Center, says, "Not a week goes by without patients thanking us for creating such a wonderful therapeutic atmosphere."

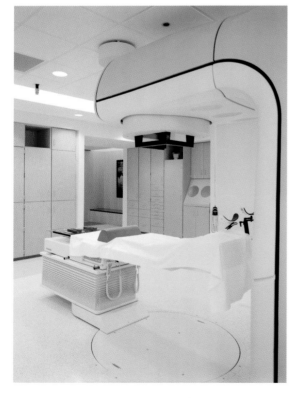

Above left: Waiting room.

Above right: Infusion area.

Left: Linear accelerator.

Right: Art Gallery along public corridor.

Opposite: Exterior.

Photography: Beth Singer, Laszlo Regos.

Cannon Design

Brigham & Women's Hospital
Shapiro Pavilion
Boston, Massachusetts

Patients who want hospital accommodations tailored to personal and business needs provided the motivation for Boston's Brigham and Women's Hospital, a major teaching hospital of Harvard Medical School, to develop its exceptional new, 6,000 square foot Shapiro Pavilion. Offering the services and amenities that characterize an elegant club or hotel, the Pavilion's suites are clustered into six radial, pod-like units that enable staff to properly attend patient needs. Each unit features a bedroom with standard patient bed, European-style private bath, kitchenette and separate office lounge/family area, all appointed in warm wood features, custom cabinetry and other quality furnishings that ensure a residential style ambiance. In honoring the Shapiro Pavilion for design excellence, the Boston Society of Architects stated, "This is without a doubt the best healing environment we had the opportunity to examine." Brigham and Women's notes that the suites are in great demand.

Top: Nurses station/reception.

Above: Patient care unit.

Right: Patient suite.

Photography: Richard Mandelkorn, Farrell Associates.

Caruana & Associates

3633 Long Beach Blvd.
Suite 200
Long Beach, CA 90807
562.595.5666
562.595.5577 (Fax)
www.caruana.com

Caruana & Associates

Long Beach Memorial Medical Center
Emergency Room Remodel
Long Beach, California

Left: Nurses station.

Below: Low acuity area.

Bottom: Examination room.

Opposite: Waiting area.

Photography: Charles LeNoir.

You don't expect personal greetings in emergency rooms. However, since these facilities bring together patient populations with little in common except acute physical and emotional stress, the remodeling of the 35,000-square foot, two-level, 53-bed emergency department at Long Beach Memorial Medical Center, designed by Caruana & Associates, has provided a welcome opportunity to meet patient and staff needs better through spatial reorganization. The ED,one

of the largest west of the Mississippi, offers more than improved efficiency. Created as a unified space at the intersection of four independent structures, it improves circulation by separating walk-in and ambulance entrances, promotes patient-staff interaction by replacing traditional corridors and examination rooms with suites whose individual pods can be opened or closed according to patient load, and introduces technological upgrades such as bedside

computers for patient admission and charting that raise overall performance. Enhanced efficiency is clearly a benefit of such features as treatment spaces with identical layouts and universal equipment that are supervised by centralized nurses stations. But the overall gain for patients and staff comes from interiors whose configurations, forms, colors and finishes offer comfort and privacy where they are so needed.

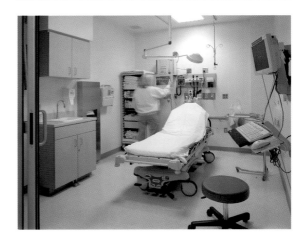

Caruana & Associates

Hoag Memorial Hospital Presbyterian
Kitchen & Cafeteria Upgrade
Newport Beach, California

Could upgrading a kitchen and cafeteria actually improve a health care institution's well-being? Hoag Memorial Hospital Presbyterian, a 409-bed, acute-care medical center in Newport Beach, California, serving the community for nearly 50 years, regards its food service facility as a key social gathering place as well as a critical component in its operations. Thus, when the hospital retained Caruana & Associates to replace a 20,000-square foot kitchen, servery and 238-seat dining room, they insisted that service to patients, staff and visitors continue uninterrupted and in-house. What has emerged, now that the mobile and interim units deployed during the four-phase project are gone, is a elegant and up-to-date design that puts a fresh glow on one of Hoag Memorial's most visible features.

Above: Cashier.
Right: Radial servery.
Opposite above: Entrance.
Photography: Charles LeNoir.

77

Caruana & Associates

Torrance Memorial Medical Center
Family Medicine Center
Manhattan Beach, California

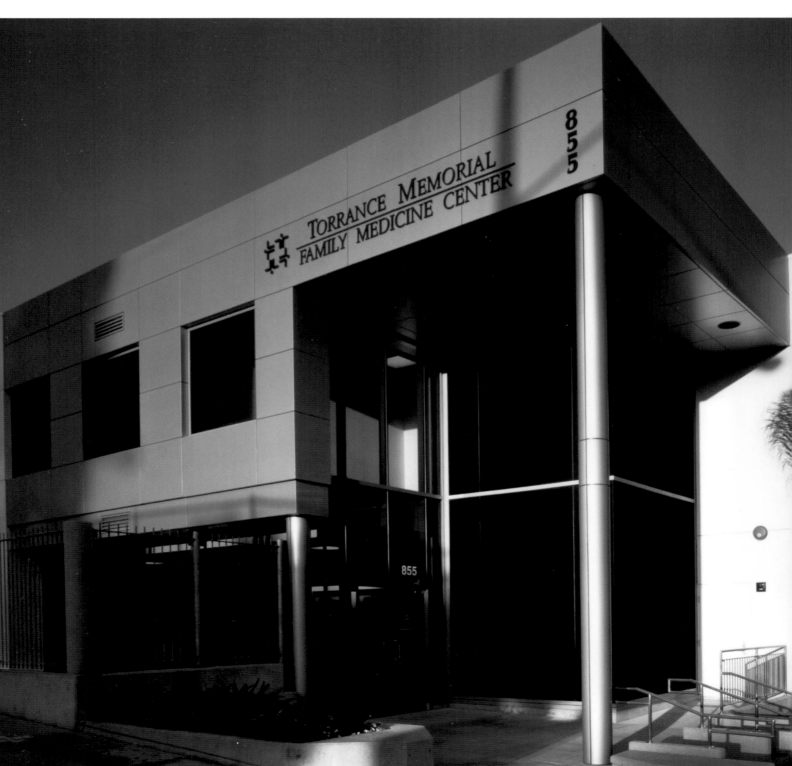

Right: Entry lobby.
Opposite above: Back entrance.
Opposite below: Front entrance.
Photography: Charles LeNoir.

A time-tested way to attract patients to a hospital is to provide superior medical offices for their physicians, a strategy put to good use recently--despite a tight site and height restrictions by Torrance Memorial Medical Center, in Manhattan Beach, California. The institution, was established in 1920 by Jared Torrance, the real estate developer who founded the City of Torrance. The new 40,000 -square foot, three-story Family Medicine Center, designed by Caruana & Associates is located on busy Manhattan Beach Boulevard, to serve as medical office space for private practices and a wellness center for health education. Physicians and patients find the facility easy to use, thanks to multiple access through entries at the front, back and below grade parking level, easy wayfinding along a linear corridor with natural light and views at the ends, full use of the hospital data center through a T1 line, and attractive, contemporary architecture and interior design. Shrewd as the design may be in resolving its site problems with multiple floors and recessed parking, the fact that physicians like being here may be all patients need to know.

Caruana & Associates

Sky Park Imaging Center
PET/CT Scan Room
Torrance, California

Well aware how isolated, confined and disoriented patients feel lying motionless up to 45 minutes for scanning, Sky Park Imaging Center, in Torrance, California, confronts the difficulties directly in its new PET/CT Scan Room, designed by Caruana & Associates. The scanner's bulk, for example, is offset by a 10-foot ceiling back-lit with a photographic image of a tropical sky. In addition, the adjoining control room is angled into the scan room, capped with an elliptical soffit and glazed with a frameless, lead shielded window to bring patients and staff closer, while soft colors and lighting foster a sense of serenity. How effective is the design? Most patients praise it spontaneously.

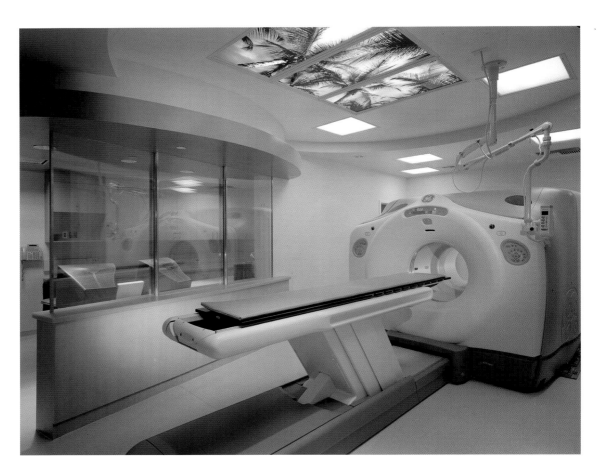

Above: Scan room.

Right: Control room.

Photography: Charles LeNoir.

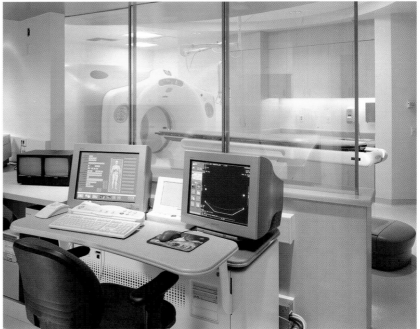

Champlin/Haupt Architects

424 E. Fourth Street
Cincinnati, OH 45202
513.241.4474
513.241.0081 (Fax)
all@charchitects.com
www.charchitects.com

Champlin/Haupt Architects

The Christ Hospital
Special Care Nursery
Cincinnati, Ohio

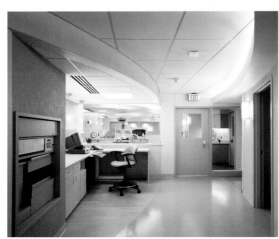

Consistently cited as one of America's best hospitals, Cincinnati's Christ Hospital, a 550-bed, not-for-profit, acute care facility, draws on over a century of service to provide a satisfying experience for expectant mothers and families at its Birthing Center, where mothers occupy hotel-like private birthing suites outfitted with state-of-the-art equipment. A recent addition to the Center, a 10,000-square foot, level II Special Care Nursery, designed by Champlin/Haupt Architects, assures that neonatal intermediate care for up to 15 premature infants meets the Center's standards. In this facility, which includes isolation, co-habitational and transitional infant care stations, breastfeeding room and support areas, medical equipment is discreetly concealed. The project also features walls with neutral tones that don't affect infant skin colors, computerized dimming which acclimatizes infants to night and day, and public family areas and family conference rooms that have Internet service.

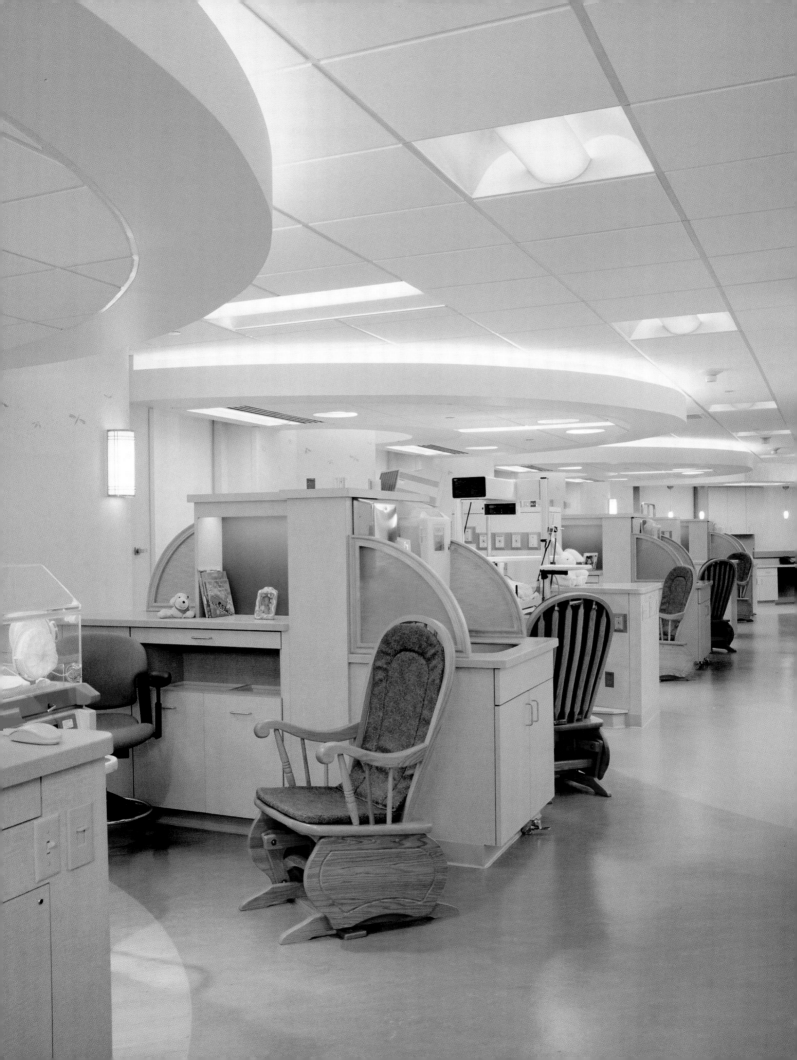

Champlin/Haupt Architects

Mercy Hospital Fairfield
Hopsital Expansion and Heart Center
Fairfield, Ohio

Above: ICU and cardiovascular units.

Below: Nurses station in ICU.

Bottom: Exterior of addition.

Illustrations: Brian Carr.

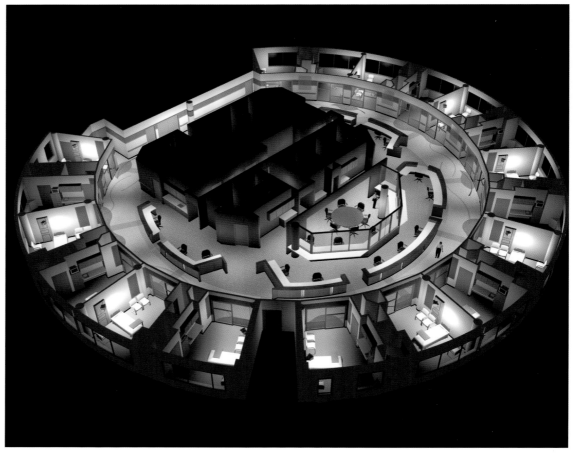

Mercy Hospital Fairfield, serving Fairfield, Ohio, nearby Butler County and the northern Hamilton County suburbs of Forest Park and Greenhills since 1978, won't be the same when a 250,000-square foot, five-story renovation and new construction project, designed by Champlin/Haupt Architects, is completed. The project will nearly double the size of the current building, raise the status of Butler County's only open-heart program to a specialty heart hospital within the hospital, and allow the emergency department and nearly every medical, surgical and diagnostic service area to add patient beds and treatment areas, as well as provide a new entrance, lobby, chapel, gift shop, cafeteria and additional office space for physicians. The radial organization of ICU and cardiovascular patient rooms monitored by central nurse stations will be among its most striking aspects. In addition, there will be a new, patient-centered environment, blending old and new architecture. The project introduces a new central lobby, and provides new access to public areas while maintaining non-public routes for patients and staff with no interruptions to hospital operations during construction. Says Mark Hood, president, "Mercy Hospital Fairfield employees, physicians and volunteers recognize the importance of this once-in-a-career opportunity...."

Champlin/Haupt Architects

Drake Center, Inc
Cincinnati, Ohio

Above: Warm-Water Aquatic Therapy Center.

Left: Lobby.

Below left: Coffee shop.

Below right: Architectural addition.

Photography: Greg Matulionis, Robert Ames Cook (pool).

A Cinderella story with an appropriately happy ending recently concluded when an aging medical complex in Cincinnati, Ohio, once known as the County Hospital emerged as Drake Center, the area's premier facility for physical and medical rehabilitation. At its 42-acre campus west of I-75, the Center has completed a 395,000-square foot renovation and new construction project, designed by Champlin/Haupt Architects, involving the inpatient day hospital, outpatient clinics, physical therapy, aquatic therapy, laboratory, cafeteria, on-site daycare and coffee shop. The award-winning project dramatically revitalizes the campus. Multiple entrances to the main building, for example, give different client cultures easier access and make Drake Center more user-friendly. Furthermore, reorganized horizontal and vertical circulation plans improve wayfinding, and a patient-centered environment featuring natural light, inviting colors, and comfortable furnishings makes patients, visitors and staff feel good. Patients ending acute care stays at other institutions can now turn to Drake Center with renewed hope.

Champlin/Haupt Architects

The Christ Hospital
Reception and Public Space Modernization
Cincinnati, Ohio

Top left: Lobby short-term seating.

Above left: Waiting area.

Above right: Reception/greeting station.

Photography: Dave Brown Photography.

Why do so many people get lost in hospitals? The Christ Hospital, a 100-plus-year-old institution serving Cincinnati, Ohio, with distinction named "One of America's Best Hospitals in 2003" by US News & World Report has confronted the problem of nondescript and disorienting public spaces by modernizing 20,000 square feet of lobby, waiting areas, reception/ greeting stations, public spaces and informal gathering places, with the help of Champlin/Haupt Architects. Now, patients, visitors and staff alike take notice of the formerly small and austere lobby, which has added a short-term seating area, greeting station, plantscaping, as well as visitor-friendly corridors and waiting areas. Good lighting, nature-inspired colors, quality materials such as terrazzo, hardwood veneer wallcoverings and acrylic accent panels, and contemporary furnishings with traditional influences complete the picture.

Champlin/Haupt Architects

St. Elizabeth Medical Center
Emergency Department
Edgewood, Kentucky

Because a warm comforting place is not what patients and families expect or find in a typical hospital's emergency department, St. Elizabeth Medical Center, a nationally recognized health care institution in Edgewood, Kentucky that has served northern Kentucky since 1861, recently decided to improve the experience as well as expand to meet growing patient volume. In fact, its new emergency department, designed by Champlin/Haupt Architects, improves the standard ED significantly. The ED looms large at 30,000 square feet, encompassing a waiting area, 43 treatment spaces, six trauma rooms, decontamination area, staff offices and locker rooms, digital photography room and rape treatment area. Yet it's a more patient-friendly environment than ever, thanks to such features as an easily identifiable canopy and entrance, good wayfinding along curvilinear circulation paths to public waiting areas, waiting areas with low walls for privacy, offices enjoying borrowed daylight through glazed wall panels, and boldly colored, attractive and comfortable furnishings. An ED may never be a warm, comforting place, but to 57,000 patients arriving each year, St. Elizabeth's ED may be the next best thing.

Above left: Entrance lobby.
Above right: Waiting area.
Top right: Canopy.
Photography: Greg Matulionis, Robert Ames Cook (canopy).

Champlin/Haupt Architects

The Christ Hospital School of Nursing Cincinnati, Ohio

Right: Library.

Below: Exterior.

Bottom left: Nursing skills center.

Bottom right: Reception room.

Photography: Greg Matulionis.

The Christ Hospital's respected School of Nursing dates from 1902, nearly as long ago as the 550-bed Cincinnati institution itself. To rejuvenate the School, the Hospital recently developed a new, 54,000-square foot, three-story, brick and limestone-clad building, designed by Champlin/Haupt Architects, with modern classrooms, science laboratory, nursing skills center, and faculty and administration offices for 220 nursing students, faculty and administrators. By intent, such amenities as the lunchroom, break areas, fitness center, computer center and casual study spaces also help recruit students. Yet the new scheme also honors the past, since the beautiful interiors of the School's former home are evoked through salvaged elements such as fireplace surrounds, wood paneling and bookcases, brass lighting fixtures, Rookwood drinking fountains, fine furniture and School art collection and historical archive. Everyday walks along the racetrack corridor system are thus living history tours.

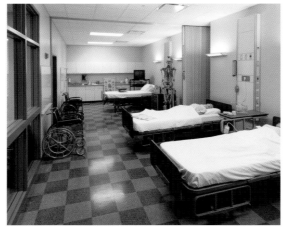

Christner Inc.

7711 Bonhomme Avenue Suite 100
St. Louis, MO 63105
314.725.2927
314.725.2928 (Fax)
www.christnerinc.com

Christner Inc.

Parkland Health Center-Bonne Terre
Bonne Terre, Missouri

Small can be beautiful, as residents of St. Francois County, Missouri have happily discovered. After the 1991 merger of Farmington Community Hospital and Bonne Terre Hospital, located at opposite ends of the county, to form Parkland Health Center, part of BJC HealthCare, a non-profit, integrated health care system, Bonne Terre Hospital was reorganized to provide, 24-hour emergency services and clinic services. The challenge in replacing its existing building with Parkland Health Center-Bonne Terre, a 21,400-square foot, two-story, three-bed facility, designed by Christner Inc., has been to give the new facility a strong public presence despite its small size. The award-winning design features an extra-height entrance, incorporating columns, a sweeping brise soleil and a floor-to-ceiling glass curtain wall enclosing the waiting room, a monumental wall separating emergency from clinical space, and an efficient and flexible interior that can be reconfigured as needed. The new hospital has proved to be a popular alternative to its dated predecessor.

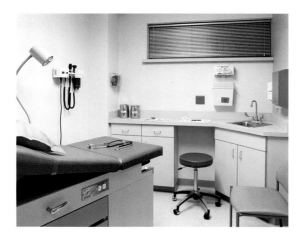

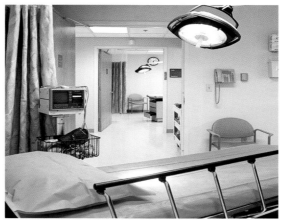

Above: Full front elevation.

Left: Treatment room.

Far left: Examination room.

Opposite top: Registration desk.

Opposite center: Waiting area and gift shop.

Photography: Sam Fentress.

Christner Inc.

David C. Pratt Cancer Center
St. John's Mercy Medical Center
St. Louis, Missouri

With evidence mounting that the active support of families can greatly improve hospital patient outcomes, St. John's Mercy Medical Center, a century-old Catholic institution that is the second largest private hospital in metropolitan St. Louis, has inaugurated a new era of cancer care at the David C. Pratt Cancer Center. The new 94,000-square foot, three-level facility offers a state-of-the-art healing environment for families as well as patients and staff. A complete range of cancer care facilities, such as diagnostic imaging, radiation oncology, infusion therapy, clinical research, physician offices and education resources, operates within an airy and open setting that revolves around a soaring, ovoid-shaped atrium, and is furnished with understated yet upscale materials and furnishings. A landscaped entrance circle allows patients to be dropped off at the front door, and the building is adjacent to a new 1,720-car parking garage convenient for patients and their families.

Top: Infusion area.
Above left: Nurses station.
Above right: Exterior facing I-270.
Right upper: Pediatric oncology.
Right lower: Linear accelerator.
Opposite: Atrium.
Photography: Sam Fentress.

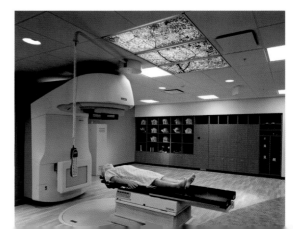

Christner Inc.

Patient Care Wing
SSM Cardinal Glennon Children's Hospital
St. Louis, Missouri

"Our love for kids just keeps on growing" is the credo of SSM Cardinal Glennon Children's Hospital, a not-for-profit St. Louis teaching hospital affiliated with Saint Louis University Schools of Medicine and Nursing and nine other educational institutions, founded in 1956. Its commitment to children from birth to age 18 is impressively reaffirmed in the new, 115,000-square foot, four-story Patient Care Wing, designed by Christner Inc. The two lower floors bring together the hospital's specialty clinics, providing 60 examination rooms and other modern facilities for day patients of some 40+ subspecialty services, such as allergy /asthma, cardiology and orthopedics. The two upper floors contain 48 hospital rooms that facilitate a much-welcomed change-over from semi-private to private rooms throughout the hospital that cares for children.

Top right: Patient room.

Upper right: Exterior.

Upper far right: Registration, clinics floor.

Right: Play room, inpatient floor.

Far right: Nurses station, inpatient floor.

Photography: Sam Fentress.

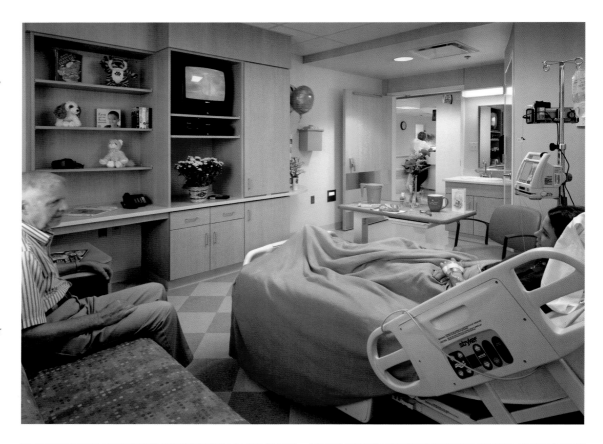

Christner Inc.

Professional Office Building
Missouri Baptist Medical Center
St. Louis, Missouri

Patients and visitors to St. Louis's Missouri Baptist Medical Center might be surprised to learn that this vibrant medical campus, with 489 beds, a thousand medical staff members and 2,300 employees all began with one patient, one doctor and one room in 1884. (In that year, Dr. William Mayfield successfully treated a nearly blind young woman in his home, and the hordes of new patients that followed inspired the community to establish what ultimately became Missouri Baptist Medical Center.) Today, physicians are established tenants on the current campus in west St. Louis County, so the impressive, new, 136,458-square foot, six-floor professional office building, designed by Christner Inc., takes care to fit into the existing architecture, aligning on a couple of levels with the main hospital building to open direct connections. Yet the POB does more than relate to its context. By inserting a cylindrical tower between the two rectangular masses that enclose the bulk of the new space for some 100 physicians, the brick, concrete and limestone building reduces its apparent bulk and brings a fresh, contemporary public face to the hospital, prominently located at a major freeway interchange.

Christner Inc.

Emergency and Ambulatory Services Addition
Lincoln County Medical Center
Troy, Missouri

Upper left: Donor garden.

Center left: Ambulatory surgery.

Lower left: Emergency.

Upper right: Front entrance
with canopy.

Photography: Sam Fentress.

When Lincoln County Medical Center began planning their new expansion and renovation project, in addition to gaining needed space, their priority was to improve patient convenience and to reinforce patient confidence. The resulting project brought together fragmented ambulatory services into a new setting that is conveniently located on the first floor. A new emergency department greatly improved access, comfort and privacy for patients, and a complete renovation and expansion of radiology brought added convenience for outpatients as well as quick access for emergency patients. A soaring front entrance with a generous covered drop-off area enhances the image of this rural hospital as a source of convenient and up-to-date care. Since completion of the facility, the local residents have shown their approval with steadily increasing volume.

Cromwell Architects Engineers, Inc.

101 S. Spring Street
Little Rock, AR 72201
501.372.2900
501.372.0482 (Fax)
www.cromwell.com

Cromwell Architects Engineers

Heart Clinic Arkansas
Little Rock, Arkansas

Right: Main entrance.

Lower right: Stress testing room.

Opposite: Main reception and waiting room.

Photography: Richard Johnson.

In the landscaped "city park" style waiting room, water cascades into a stone-lined pool, welcoming patients to the 46,000 square foot Heart Clinic Arkansas in Little Rock. This design element is one of the many ways the attractive; stone-and-brick structure serves patients and staff in this facility created for Arkansas' largest cardiology group. By assembling three of its five clinics under one roof, the Clinic expands its services and appointment scheduling options for its 24 practicing physicians. The exam areas are planned to maximize doctor efficiency with three closely positioned exam rooms per doctor. Staff circulation avoids patient waiting areas since the practice and support areas of the clinic wrap around central waiting in a U-shape. The plan is organized into east and west clinic wings, with shared treatment areas such as a nuclear camera, echocardiogram, treadmills and laboratories located between the two clinics. Ergonomic seating finished in soothing colors and patterns contribute to the relaxing atmosphere of the park-like setting

Cromwell Architects Engineers

Arkansas Children's Hospital
Pediatric Intensive Care Unit
Little Rock, Arkansas

The replacement of an out-moded pediatric intensive care unit gave Arkansas Children's Hospital, one of America's largest pediatric medical centers serving children from birth to age 21, the opportunity to develop an extraordinary family-focused facility. The 24,100 SF, 26-bed Donald W. Reynolds PICU incorporates efficient space planning and intricate architectural details to provide families and staff with an environment that is aesthetically soothing as well as functional. The 'Four Seasons of Arkansas' theme provides a sense of orientation and makes each patient room special. Not only does this meticu-lously planned environment employ state-of-the-art equipment, it also offers staff improved patient access and supervision. Private rooms, some with panoramic views of the state capitol out spacious windows, provide parents with daybeds and private toilets. To quote Dr. Sunny Anand, chief of pediatric

Above: Corridor and nursing station.

Opposite upper left: Entrance.

Opposite middle left: Private rooms and charting alcove.

Opposite middle right: Concierge desk.

Opposite lower left: Semi-private observation room.

Photography: Tim Hursley.

critical care medicine for Arkansas Children's, "Visitors and family members have reported greater comfort and have found the environment and interior design calming and soothing, perhaps during the most stressful period of their lives. The new design of the new PICU has resulted in improved patient care, improved therapeutic outcomes and increased staff performance and efficiency."

Cromwell Architects Engineers

Jackson T. Stephens Spine and
Neurosciences Institute
University of Arkansas for Medical Sciences
Little Rock, Arkansas

Above: Elevator lobby.

Upper right: Waiting room.

Middle right: Custom designed swimming pool with underwater track.

Lower right: Reception area.

Opposite: Exterior of tower.

Photography: Tim Hursley.

The Jackson T. Stephens Spine and Neurosciences Institute overlooks the University of Arkansas for Medical Sciences campus in Little Rock, Arkansas. This award winning facility stands 12-stories tall and contains 214,000 SF of office and clinic space as well as a comprehensive rehabilitation facility in the basement, research and teaching laboratories on the upper floors and a 350-seat auditorium on the 12th floor. The four columns at the corners contain mechanical and electrical systems — the 'spine' of the building. Contemporary interiors that display concern for patient comfort are exhibited through curvilinear architectural detailing using stone, wood, and a soothing palette of khaki, purple and green along with the extensive use of indirect lighting.

Cromwell Architects Engineers   Jonesboro Ambulatory Surgery Center
Jonesboro, Arkansas

There's a self-effacing dignity to the 28,500-square foot, one-story structure in brick and pre-cast concrete, designed by Cromwell Architects Engineers, that houses Jonesboro Ambulatory Surgery Center, in Jonesboro, Arkansas. Yet belies its ability to simultaneously create efficient space for medical procedures and sensitively address patients' needs. The Center's facilities, including six operating rooms, four endoscopic procedure rooms, pre-op and recovery areas, supported by staff locker rooms, sterile processing, waiting areas, conference room, physicians' offices, consultation rooms and business office, incorporate such features as a one-way patient flow so pre-op and post-op patients do not cross paths, flexible swing beds for morning pre-op use and afternoon post-op use, separate pediatric recovery area where parents can comfort their children, endoscopy treatment area near pre-op and post-op beds to aid quick patient turnover, spacious equipment storage areas, and abundant daylight even in internal rooms. With facilities like the Center, ambulatory surgery is taking its rightful place alongside inpatient surgery.

Devenney Group

1500 E. Bethany Home Road
Suite 200
Phoenix, AZ 85014
602.943.8950
602.943.7645 (Fax)
www.devenneygroup.com

Devenney Group

Virginia G. Piper Cancer Center
Scottsdale Healthcare
Scottsdale, Arizona

Left: Exterior.

Below: Waiting room.

Opposite: Entrance and lobby.

Photography: A.F. Payne Photographic, Inc.

Insights from cancer patients help explain why the new Virginia G. Piper Cancer Center, in Scottsdale, Arizona, successfully combines the academic strengths of Arizona Cancer Center in clinical and laboratory-based programs with the patient-focused community hospital services of Scottsdale Healthcare. In fact, the willingness of cancer patients to share insights on diagnosis, treatment and recovery with the building team is reflected throughout the 104,000-square foot, four-story Piper Center, designed by Devenney Group. Thus, the Center offers radiation therapy, infusion chemotherapy, bone marrow transplant therapy, treatment for lymph edema, and supportive therapies using music and art, journaling, stress management, meditation and massage within a healing environment featuring natural light, home-light furnishings and such amenities as a reference library, a family support room, conference and meeting spaces, a boutique for prosthetics, wigs and apparel, and even a demonstration kitchen where patients learn to meet specific dietary needs.

Devenney Group

The Peaks at Flagstaff
Flagstaff, Arizona

Left: Landscaped exterior.

Below: Lounge.

Opposite: Entrance lobby.

Photography: Craig Passey, DGL (exterior), Kitchell Inc. (interior).

Tourists, photographers and film producers know Flagstaff, Arizona, population 57,700, for its spectacular scenery, which includes such attractions as the Grand Canyon and nearby Wupatki and Walnut Canyon National Monuments. That's why nature figures so prominently in the siting and views at The Peaks at Flagstaff, a new, 120,000-square foot, 161-bed intergenerational senior living community, designed by Devenney Group. However, there's much more than scenery at this appealing facility, which actively engages its residents as contributors to its educational and cultural institutions. The post-and-beam architecture of The Peaks combines traditional elements of a thriving downtown, including decentralized dining, small galleries, shopping, library, wellness center and classrooms, with familiar aspects of a residential neighborhood, such as family room-style lounges, terraces, outdoor dining, exposed pine trusses and generous outdoor views. Here, residents enjoy quality health care in a social setting where they can simultaneously age and grow.

Devenney Group

Flagstaff Medical Center
Flagstaff, Arizona

Since 1936, Flagstaff Medical Center, a not-for-profit member of Northern Arizona Healthcare, has evolved from a small rural facility to one of Arizona's most successful hospitals, operating a major urban campus in Flagstaff. The 242-bed Center has grown along with the community it serves, and it's still growing as it approaches its seventh decade. The implementation of a five-phase master plan that will substantially transform the Center, with both planning and design by Devenney Group, began in 1984 and will continue for several more years. Ongoing evaluation of the Center's 20-year-old, four-story hospital building, surrounded by old homes converted to medical uses, has identified the need for more land, expanded inpatient and outpatient facilities, a gradual replacement of

outmoded buildings, and altogether new structures to be added to the campus. As a flourishing work in progress, the Center can point to such recent and current projects as a new women's center, outpatient diagnostics addition, ambulatory surgery center, four-story patient tower, 400-car parking structure, bio-med department and second phase, three-story OR tower, all designed by Devenney Group. And there's more to come, including a 26 bed med/surg TI and a remodeling of the existing cancer center, both in design, reaffirming the foresight of Dr. Charles Sechrist, founder of Flagstaff Hospital, the cornerstone of Flagstaff Medical Center.

Right: West Tower rendering.

Illustration: Devenney Group Architects.

Devenney Group

Current and Recent Healthcare Projects

Top: Scottsdale Oncology, Scottsdale, Arizona. Photography: Richard Abrams.

Above left: John C. Lincoln Hospital, Phoenix, Arizona.

Above right: Arizona Heart Institute, Phoenix, Arizona.

Left: Lutheran Heart Hospital, Mesa, Arizona.

Photography: Hunt Photography

Illustration: Courtesy of Devenney Group.

Earl Swensson Associates, Inc.

2100 West End Avenue
Suite 1200
Nashville, TN 37203
615.329.9445
615.329.0046 (Fax)
www.esarch.com
info@esarch.com

Earl Swensson Associates, Inc.

Monroe Carell, Jr. Children's Hospital at Vanderbilt
Vanderbilt University Medical Center
Nashville, Tennessee

Though middle-age Americans might question whether life begins again at 30, Vanderbilt Children's Hospital, in Nashville, Tennessee, has no doubts. Having outgrown its space in the adult hospital at Vanderbilt University Medical Center, VCH recently moved into the impressive new, 616,785-square foot, eight-story, 206-inpatient bed Monroe Carell, Jr. Children's Hospital at Vanderbilt, designed by Earl Swensson Associates. The Hospital's inspiring, family-centered environment encourages family participation through accommodations in individual patient rooms and such facilities as family sleep areas, family lounges with kitchens, laundry rooms and business centers, quiet rooms, and a "Main Street" on the main level (second floor) featuring a resource center, pharmacy, conference center/board room, chapel and performance area.
A "ribbons of hope and rivers of healing," theme enlivens the building inside and out in such ways as the swooping steel ribbons on Main Street's ceiling.

Above left: Front entrance.

Top right: Isolation patient room.

Middle right: Main street.

Left: NICU patient room.

Right: Performance stage.

Opposite: Grand stair on 1st floor.

Photography: Scott McDonald and Craig Dugan/Hedrich Blessing. Exterior photo from Neil Brake

Earl Swensson Associates, Inc. Parrish Medical Center
Titusville, Florida

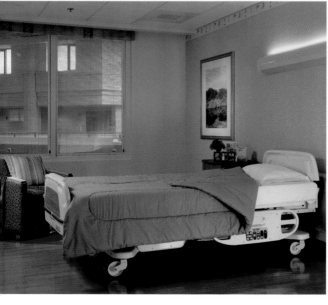

Even if Parrish Medical Center, in Titusville, Florida, were not the designated primary emergency medical receiving facility for Kennedy Space Center shuttle crews and ground support personnel, it would merit attention. An affiliate of the H. Lee Moffitt Cancer Center and Research Institute at the University of South Florida in Tampa, and the Florida Hospital cardiac program in Orlando, Parrish now has a 346,000-square foot, five-floor, 210-bed replacement hospital, designed by Earl Swensson Associates, offering an outstanding healing experience for patients and families. Not only are its atrium and patient tower scaled to pedestrian size by its architecture of curving forms, its interior design's relaxing colors, subtle lighting, and attractive furnishings complement such spaces as the soothing, landscaped lobby, efficient nurse control centers and versatile private patient rooms. This is what George Mikitarian, president of Parrish, hails as a "new world of capabilities for patient care and community pride."

Above: Lobby information desk.

Far left: Patient room.

Left: MRI suite.

Opposite: Lobby.

Photography: Scott McDonald/Hedrich Blessing.

Earl Swensson Associates, Inc.

The Villages Regional Hospital
The Villages, Florida

A preview of aging's impact on America is being enacted at The Villages Regional Hospital, a new, 106,000-square foot, two-story, 60-bed adult acute-care facility in The Villages, Florida, designed by Earl Swensson Associates. Though this uncommonly attractive facility was planned for future expansion, it's already growing now. Fortunately, the design allows costly-to-move clinical services, such as ER, surgery and imaging, to expand in place without halting operations. Efficiency is critical as well, so registration is centrally located to serve general admissions and emergency, decentralized nursing stations eliminate trips to a central station, and patient areas are arrayed in wings with satellite nurse support centers. Last but not least is the patient-friendly environment, embracing both the architecture, reflecting the community's Spanish Colonial architecture, and the interior design, featuring a main lobby that suggests a charming village square.

Above left: Exterior courtyard.

Left: Patient room.

Far left: Admission and wait area.

Opposite: Main lobby.

Photography: Scott McDonald/Hedrich Blessing.

Earl Swensson Associates, Inc.

River Region Medical Center
Vicksburg, Mississippi

Two hospitals merging in Vicksburg, Mississippi have created the largest single hospital ever constructed in the Magnolia State, River Region Medical Center, a 227-bed acute care hospital with a level II 27-bed, state-of-the-art emergency room. Sizable as the 391,196-square foot, six-story structure is, Earl Swensson Associates has designed it to be cost-effectively assimilated into the life of the Civil War town, while bringing a higher level of women's healthcare to the region through Mississippi's first digital mammography and eight LDR suites in The Childbirth Center. Careful planning has been rewarded in numerous ways. The sloping site, for example, will let the Center expand vertically and horizontally.

The building's circular entry draws patients and families inside the two-story lobby, whose columns, fountains, stairway and plantings hark back to the region's Southern traditions while creating some of its own.

Left: Lobby.
Below left: Operating room.
Below center: Nurses station.
Below right: Entrance.
Photography: Bob Shimer/Hedrich Blessing.

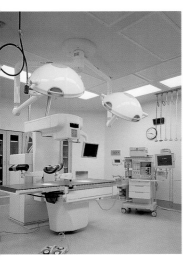

EwingCole

Federal Reserve Bank Building
100 North 6th Street
Philadelphia, PA 19106
215.923.2020
215.351.5346 (Fax)
www.ewingcole.com

EwingCole

Memorial Sloan-Kettering
Ambulatory Cancer Care Center
Commack, New York

City and suburban living still differ in 21st-century America. Witness the public's fascination with urban lifestyles, fashion and music. So, New York's Memorial Sloan-Kettering Cancer Center, a leader in cancer detection, diagnosis and treatment for over a century, took care in translating its urban outpatient cancer program into a suburban setting for its new Ambulatory Cancer Care Center in Commack, New York. This handsome, 50,000-square foot, two-story building, designed by EwingCole for radiation oncology, medical oncology,

diagnostic imaging, surgical oncology, patient education, library and conference area, delivers a quality of care and patient experience that satisfy both "worried well" and very ill cancer patients living 50 miles from Manhattan. Daylight, for example, seems everywhere. The building's linear form permits such window-friendly spaces as examination rooms, consultation rooms and waiting areas to occupy the perimeter, while interior circulation paths typically end in windows, and the center enjoys a skylight. What makes patients so comfortable is the way

their visits are layered into color-coded and specially illuminated public, intimate and treatment zones, depending on their medical condition. Wherever they are, patients find interiors shaped by organic forms and natural colors, textures and materials, such as the first-floor lobby's 12-foot-long aquarium, which encourage them to see themselves in a new, healing light.

Above: Exterior.

Left: First-floor library.

Lower left: Second-floor reception.

Opposite: Medical oncology.

Photography: Jeffrey Totaro.

EwingCole

Morgan Stanley Children's Hospital of NewYork-Presbyterian
New York, New York

Clockwise from upper left:
Entry lobby, neonatal intensive care unit, wait and play room, pediatric intensive care patient room.

Right: New tower and existing construction.

Photography: Peter Paige (interiors), David Lamb/courtesy of Davis Brody Bond.

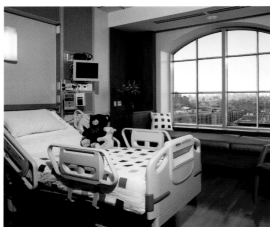

No children's hospital can duplicate home for sick children. However, New York's impressive, new, 265,000-square foot, 10-story, 191-bed Morgan Stanley Children's Hospital at NewYork-Presbyterian Hospital comes close. By connecting two existing buildings with a new patient tower, the design by EwingCole with Davis Brody Bond creates "super floors" that streamline functional spaces and circulation, consolidate medical expertise and minimize patient transfers. Besides giving medical personnel advanced technology and integrated work areas, classrooms and conference areas to facilitate teamwork, the new Hospital warmly welcomes families into the healing process. Such amenities as "family alcoves" for work and sleep in patient rooms, a PICU family lounge and nourishment station, a NICU "Launch Pad" where parents can sleep and prepare to take baby home, and special places like a Child Life Center, a playroom where children learn coping mechanisms, a Winter Garden theater for live entertainment, and a classroom staffed by public school teachers create new possibilities for families in pediatric care. To quote Dr. Herbert Pardes, president of NewYork-Presbyterian, "We now have the physical plant to match the expert clinical care and cutting-edge research that we do here every day."

EwingCole

Cancer Prevention Pavilion
Fox Chase Cancer Center
Philadelphia, Pennsylvania

Preventing cancer is experimental in nature, and the new, 120,000-square foot, four-story Cancer Prevention Pavilion at Philadelphia's Fox Chase Cancer Center, designed by EwingCole, is admittedly experimental. But linking research to patient care lets the Pavilion create an intriguing environment where laboratory scientists can integrate their work with clinical trials and risk assessment programs. The flexible design serves Fox Chase, designated as one of America's first comprehensive cancer centers in 1974 by the National Cancer Institute, in various ways. As a research facility, it capitalizes on flex lab design to minimize wall rebuilding and major structural and mechanical alterations. The outpatient environment, by contrast, is less clinical and institutional in a residential-style design that facilitates wellness and early intervention along with patient care. In addition, the Pavilion acts as a bridge between other facilities on the Fox Chase campus.

Right: Entrance lobby.

Below left: Clinical floor waiting room.

Below right: MRI.

Opposite: Exterior.

Photography: Jeffrey Totaro.

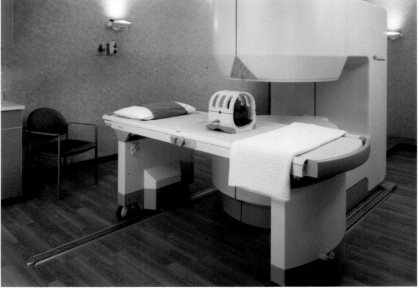

EwingCole

Ambulatory Health Care Center
McGuire Air Force Base
Wrightstown, New Jersey

What could be better for the United States Air Force at McGuire Air Force Base, in Wrightstown, New Jersey, than a new Ambulatory Health Care Center that enhances the quality of life for military personnel and their families? The Center enables the 305th Medical Wing to provide the highest level of outpatient medical care, including the care of flightline pilots. The Center compares favorably to private sector facilities in aesthetics while meeting base and military design standards and guidelines thanks to a flexible, state-of-the-art, and undeniably attractive design by EwingCole. In fact, the new 160,000-square foot Center, encompassing family practice, pediatrics, gynecology, ophthalmology, optometry, emergency medicine, ENT /audiology, flight medicine, mental health, ambulatory surgery, radiology, physical / occupational therapy and robotic pharmacy, impresses civilians as much as military personnel and their families. It's easy to see why. One of the nation's largest military outpatient facilities, the Center comprises two efficient and accessible clinical zones organized around a two-story circulation spine or "Mall," a monumental, barrel-vaulted space that is highlighted by a grand stairway leading to a central rotunda illuminated by skylights, circulation bridges, built-in seating and departmental reception kiosks. "When you think of a military-type building, you think of a cut-and-dry building," Wrightstown mayor Tom Harper has commented. "You don't think of a building like this."

Above: The Mall.

Left: Same day surgery staff work area.

Photography: Jeffrey Totaro.

FKP Architects, Inc.

8 Greenway Plaza
Suite 300
Houston, TX
77046-0899
713.621.2100
713.621.2178 (Fax)

3535 Travis
Suite 260
Dallas, TX
75204-1403
214.750.9900
214.750.9115 (Fax)

www.fkp.com

FKP Architects, Inc

Texas Children's Hospital
Clinical Care Center
Houston, Texas

It started with a three-story, 106-bed pediatric hospital dedicated on May 15, 1953. Today, 737-bed Texas Children's Hospital is America's largest freestanding pediatric hospital and is ranked by Child magazine and U.S. News & World Report among the nation's top five children's hospitals. An affiliate of Baylor College of Medicine and a critical component of Houston's renowned Texas Medical Center, Texas Children's faced radical changes in the post-1990s health care market. In 1995, Texas Children's began to rethink its patient care

delivery, retool its business approach and launched a major facility development program. The hospital's recently completed, award-winning building program has created 1.26 million square feet of new construction encompassing an outpatient Clinical Care Center, an inpatient bed and diagnostic /treatment tower addition and 350,000 square feet of renovated space in a research building plus various diagnostic/treatment and support areas. The new 818,000-square foot, 17-story Clinical Care Center, designed by FKP Architects

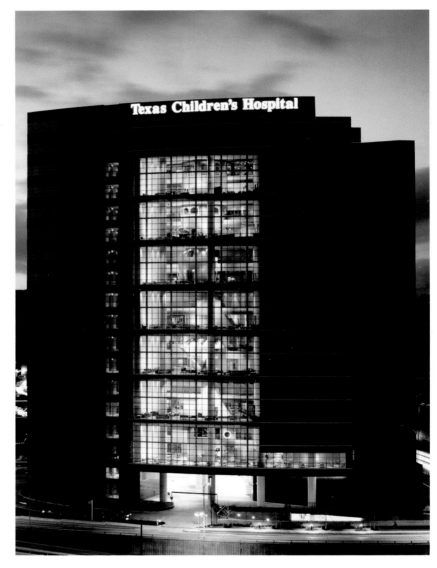

as the hospital's central outpatient facility, clearly demonstrates how good design can provide flexibility, create a family-friendly atmosphere, improve overall efficiency and reinforce the Hospital's Integrated Delivery System. The Center houses a complex environment, incorporating 10 floors of pediatric sub-specialty clinics and physicians' offices, the Texas Children's Cancer Center, an eight-operating room ambulatory surgery suite, outpatient laboratory, imaging and

other clinical services. Designed to reduce stress and calm fears, the facility conveys a non-threatening, intimate feeling to patients and families. Clinic floors are organized around two-story waiting rooms where boldly colored, oversized geometric shapes assist in wayfinding, function as central check-in areas and provide play spaces. Clinics with similar functions and services are grouped together with physician offices one floor above or below the clinic floors, allowing care-

Above: Exterior.

Left: Food court.

Opposite: Waiting room with balloon-shaped play form.

Photography: Craig Dugan/Hedrich Blessing.

givers and staff to move quickly between them. To further maximize the use of space, examination rooms are clustered in modules of 10-12, where physicians can "timeshare" space by using the same room at different time periods. Central medical record storage and common check-in areas create additional efficiencies. Frequently used outpatient services such as the pharmacy, laboratory, blood donor center, conference center and food court are easily accessible to patients and staff alike. In fact, a combination of warmth, effectiveness and flexibility permeates the entire Center. Throughout this innovative family and child-friendly environment, a new vision of health care design has emerged. The curving and orthogonal forms, bright colors against white surfaces, casual contemporary furnishings and details like glass doors at entry portals that let children look before entering, create a space that redefines pediatric health care delivery.

Above: Cone-shaped play form in waiting room.

Right: Gazebo.

FKP Architects, Inc

Texas Children's Hospital
Feigin Research Center
Houston, Texas

Left: Exterior.

Bottom: Laboratory.

Below: Conference center lobby.

Photography: Hester + Hardaway Photographers.

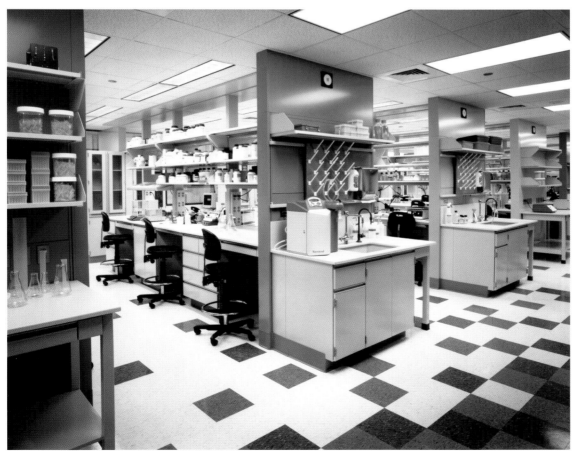

Thanks to the 151,000 square foot renovation of the existing 12-story Feigin Center Building, research programs were recently accorded a marvelous opportunity to grow at Texas Children's Hospital in Houston, Texas. FKP Architects converted the mixed-use facility to a dedicated research building, which included infrastructure upgrades and a new exterior mechanical chase. An interesting consequence has been the transition from the "territorial" to the "universal" laboratory, a facility whose generic footprint offers maximum flexibility to handle fluctuating assignments in its large, open spaces. The design incorporates a movable laboratory wall system and a flexible casework system that users can reconfigure as needed. Interactive spaces promote communication and collaboration among users. Color is introduced to visually organize the labs, such as bright yellow swoops in the floor, which point to exit paths and safety equipment. These playful colors help create a humanizing environment where none is usually found.

FKP Architects, Inc

Texas Children's Hospital
West Tower Expansion
Houston, Texas

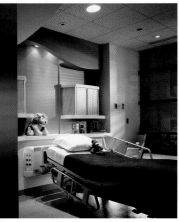

Above right: Nursing team station and "front porch".

Top left: West tower expansion at foreground.

Above left: Patient room.

Left: Elevator lobby and reception area.

Opposite: Heart Center lobby.

Photography: Craig Dugan & Scott McDonald / Hedrich Blessing.

Caring for some of the world's sickest children, such as those battling cancer, having heart defects repaired or undergoing liver transplants, Houston's prestigious Texas Children's Hospital recently created a new facility offering children and families the best possible experience. The resulting West Tower Expansion, encompassing 485,000 square feet of new construction designed by FKP Architects, has placed a 15-story addition atop the hospital's West Tower. Much more than a facelift, the project replaced the small 40-year old,

inpatient bed units with comfortable 330-square foot private rooms. The new rooms give parents space for overnight stays, add numerous family amenities, and position bedside nursing pods directly outside bedrooms. In addition, the construction has enabled the four-level Texas Children's Heart Center to consolidate previously scattered services into an integrated facility, created the 140-bed Texas Children's Newborn Clinic, and introduced the popular family service floor—a getaway place for patients and families featuring a

delicatessen, beauty salon, library, business center, pre-teen and teen rooms, and Radio Lollipop, the in-house children's radio station.

FKP Architects, Inc

Texas Children's Hospital
Abercrombie West Tower Renovation
Houston, Texas

An institution as large and complex as Texas Children's Hospital is continuously involved in ongoing construction projects. Consider FKP Architects' participation in an 182,900 square foot renovation and expansion in the Abercrombie and West Tower Buildings. While the spaces differ in form and function – 140 bed Newborn Intensive Care Center, Ronald McDonald Family Sleep Center, emergency center/rapid treatment center, emergency clinic/ambulatory treatment center, gift shop, chapel and support areas, they all help achieve a state-of-the-art environment that is flexible and family-friendly. Mark Wallace, CEO of Texas Children's sums up FKP Architects' overall contribution by saying, "I must tell you, in spite of how optimistic I was, the space, the buildings, how well it functions, how attractive it is… It's really exceeded my expectations."

Above: Neonatal Intensive Care Unit.

Right: NICU Team station.

Far right: Waiting & Registration.

Photography: Hester & Hardaway Photographers.

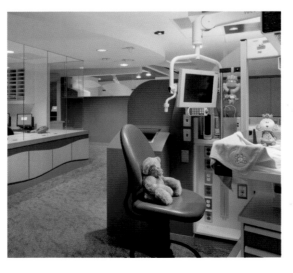

Francis Cauffman Foley Hoffmann Architects, Ltd.

2120 Arch Street
Philadelphia, PA 19103
215-568-8250
215-568-2639 (Fax)
www.fcfh-did.com

Francis Cauffman Foley Hoffmann Architects, Ltd.

Lankenau Hospital
Wynnewood, Pennsylvania

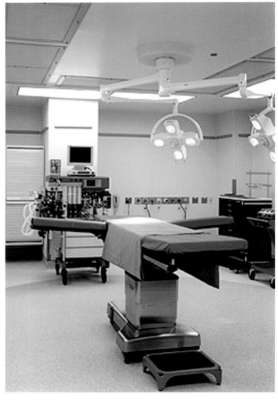

Years of remodeling can have detrimental consquences for hospitals. For this reason, Lankenau Hospital, in Wynnewood, Pennsylvania, an acute-care hospital founded in 1860, recently asked Francis Cauffman Foley Hoffmann Architects to develop a strategic operations plan to chart a new path. As a result, the firm's effective expansion projects, part of a 310,000-square foot master plan implementation, are having an immediate impact on operations. The new Emergency Department, for example, occupies a larger and more advanced facility that can handle up to 45,000 cases a year. Two 30-bed Rosengarten acute care units have been dramatically transformed into a state-of-the-art, patient-centered, 32,600-square foot environment. And the redesigned main lobby and main corridor now form a clear, sunny connection between hospital and medical office buildings, telling doctors and patients that Lankenau is ready to grow.

Above left: Emergency department entry and canopy.

Top right: Waiting room.

Upper right: Ambulatory surgery operating room.

Lower right: Patient room.

Bottom right: Emergency room nurses' station.

Opposite: Main lobby.

Photography: Don Pearse.

Francis Cauffman Foley Hoffmann Architects, Ltd.

The Heart and Cancer Center at Albert Einstein Medical Center
Philadelphia, Pennsylvania

As a respected teaching hospital serving the Philadelphia community, Albert Einstein Medical Center takes a long-term view of its facilities. Accordingly, the recent consolidation of out patient services in an 80,000-square foot space and the construction of a new, 36,000-square foot Heart and Cancer Center, both designed by Francis Cauffman Foley Hoffmann Architects, represent but one phase of a master plan involving 326,000 square feet of space that lets Einstein respond to the changing needs of physicians and patients. Indeed, the project has produced an advanced Heart Center with four catheterization laboratories and one electrophysiology laboratory with digital recording and archiving, and a state-of-the-art Cancer Center with a chemotherapy suite alongside patient examination rooms and resource center. Equally important, the project has reduced operating costs and updated the utility plant — attracting more physicians and patients to Einstein.

Left: Lobby.
Below: Canopy and entrance.
Opposite: Catheterization laboratory.
Photography: Don Pearse.

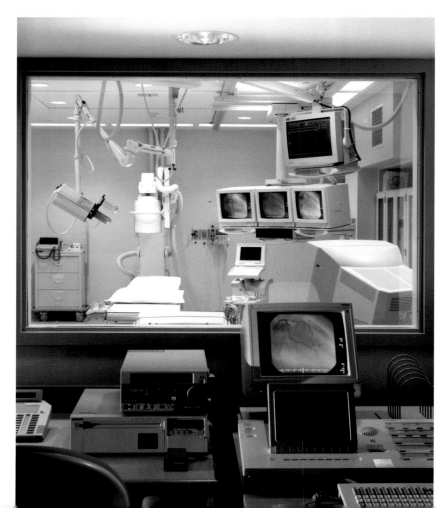

140

Francis Cauffman Foley Hoffmann Architects, Ltd.

The Heart Hospital at Geisinger
Wyoming Valley Medical Center
Wilkes-Barre, Pennsylvania

Above left: Cardiac rehabilitation.
Above right: Patient hallway.
Right: Main lobby.
Lower right: Exterior.
Photography: Don Pearse.

When people in northeastern Pennsylvania look to Geisinger Wyoming Valley Medical Center, in Wilkes-Barre, for medical services, cardiovascular patients can expect outstanding care from the new, freestanding, 50,000 square foot, three-story Heart Hospital, designed by Francis Cauffman Foley Hoffmann Architects. The Hospital provides complete cardiovascular services, including a cardiology clinic and cardiac rehabilitation facility on level I, an in/out-patient, non-invasive diag-nostic area with vascular echo/EKG and stress testing laboratories on level II, and a 10-bed inpatient step down unit and cardiac catherization laboratory on level III. Its organization is driven by horizontal connections to the existing Medical Center supporting the cardiovascular program, highlighted by direct circulation links on level II. Yet the handsome Modernist glass-and-brick structure has a presence of its own that must please the two million residents of the Wyoming Valley region, who once traveled from as far away as Maryland for treatment.

Francis Cauffman Foley Hoffmann Architects, Ltd.

Critical Care Building
Our Lady of Lourdes Medical Center
Camden, New Jersey

Above left: Patient room.

Left: Third floor waiting area.

Below: Street perspective.

Photography: Francis Cauffman Foly Hoffmann Architects, Ltd.

Nearly 50 years after the Franciscan Sisters of Allegany, New York, founded the teaching hospital in Camden, New Jersey now known as Our Lady of Lourdes Medical Center, the strength of their commitment is manifested in such facilities as the new, 147,000-square foot, seven-story Critical Care Building, designed by Francis Cauffman Foley Hoffmann Architects.

This latest addition to the existing campus houses a 32-bed medical/surgical unit, two 21-bed critical care units, two new operating rooms, two new catherization/ electrophysiology laboratories, new emergency department for 50,000 visits/year, new 6-bed CVU, 15-bed PACU and ASU with three procedural rooms, new 15,000-square foot School of Nursing, and

renovated and expanded surgery suite. Commenting on its modern, effective and patient-friendly environment, Kim Barnes, administrator of planning and business development for Lourdes Health System, says, "We are thrilled with the creative solutions Francis Cauffman came up with for seemingly insurmountable problems."

Francis Cauffman Foley Hoffmann Architects, Ltd.

DuPont at Jefferson Pediatrics
Thomas Jefferson University Hospital
Philadelphia, Pennsylvania

A toy train theme takes children on a symbolic journey to duPont at Jefferson Pediatrics in Philadelphia's Thomas Jefferson University Hospital. This new, 32,000-square foot pediatric facility, designed by Francis Cauffman Foley Hoffmann Architects, exemplifies the affiliation of Thomas Jefferson University Hospital, founded in 1825, with duPont Hospital for Children that operates a regional system of pediatric care. The facility, which encompasses examination space for pediatric generalists and specialists, rehabilitation and oncology suites, physicians' offices and a suite for the Department of Pediatrics, is a modular scheme developed in just 16 weeks that nevertheless provides both a highly functional environment and a reassuring sense of place for children and families. Using such basic materials as drywall, vinyl tile, carpet, aluminum awnings and rails, wood doors and trim, and bright, playful graphics, duPont leads children and families down a "streetscape" of activities that is as easy and fun to follow as a toy train.

FreemanWhite, Inc.

8001 Arrowridge Blvd.
Charlotte NC 28273
704.523.2230
704.523.2235
www.freemanwhite.com

FreemanWhite, Inc.

The Health Park at WakeMed
Raleigh, North Carolina

Top right: Therapy pool.

Above left: Exterior of The Health Park addition.

Above right: Atrium boat and dock.

Right: Pediatric rehabilitation.

Opposite: Elevator tower in atrium.

Photography: Tim Buchman Photography.

Patients willingly waited for treatment at 68-bed WakeMed Rehabilitation Hospital in Raleigh, North Carolina because its care has been first-rate and comprehensive, despite such shortcomings as insufficient internal circulation, lack of space for rehabilitation activities and equipment, and limited resources for helping patients "relearn" basic life skills. All this changed in 2000, when the hospital began developing The Health Park at WakeMed, designed by FreemanWhite. The centerpiece of the dynamic, 42,000-square foot, award-winning space, which includes treatment, exercise and educational facilities, dining room and pediatric rehabilitation, is a sunny "town center" atrium. Here patients receive therapy through familiar settings and activities at the General Store, Coffee Shop, Bank, ATM, Exercise Area, Therapy Pool and Therapy Gym, where they safely practice coping with everyday life even having a full-size automobile for loading groceries and seating. Ironically, WakeMed Rehab is busier than ever, and its waiting period has grown nearly ten-fold.

FreemanWhite, Inc.

Outpatient Diagnostic & Treatment Pavilion
Union Regional Medical Center
Monroe, North Carolina

Determined to stop relinquishing patient care to counterparts in the nearby city of Charlotte, Union Regional Medical Center, the primary health care provider for Union County, North Carolina, recently retained FreemanWhite to transform its small-town inpatient hospital into a modern facility through renovation and expansion. The new esprit at Union Regional, a member of Carolinas HealthCare System, is most visible in the new, 85,000-square foot, two-story Outpatient Diagnostic & Treatment Pavilion. It doesn't hurt that the Pavilion, providing advanced outpatient services in cardiology, oncology, cardiopulmonology, medical imaging, surgery and rehabilitation, is highly visible on a main highway. Once patients and visitors enter, the handsome, contemporary interior of curved ceilings and walkways, natural light, warm earth tones and comfortable furnishings highlighted by a spectacular spiral staircase raises their expectations higher. Increased patient volumes, enhanced outpatient satisfaction and better professional recruitment prompt hospital CEO John Roberts to declare, "We definitely consider the design of the facility an aesthetic asset."

Above: Entry canopy.

Left: Porte cochere.

Opposite: Two-story entry lobby.

Photography: Tim Buchman Photography.

FreemanWhite, Inc.

Cuthbertson Village at Aldersgate
Charlotte, North Carolina

The new master plan by FreemanWhite for Aldersgate, a 56-year-old, 225-acre retirement community developed in Charlotte, North Carolina by Methodist Home, Inc., reinvents the campus to satisfy today's more active seniors. An intriguing consequence of the plan is Cuthbertson Village, a 34,000-square foot assisted living home for residents in the earlier stages of Alzheimer's and other dementias. Envisioned as three 15-resident neighborhoods, with private living units clustered around communal living rooms, dining rooms, kitchens, laundries, den/studies and back porches, Cuthbertson Village offers a holistic, self-contained and stimulating environment where residents can interact with families, staff and the larger community. Its outdoor courtyards and central Town Square with a general store, cinema, pet shop, cafe and garden shop surrounding a central garden with walking path, goldfish pond, stage and aviary are so captivating that staff have reported family members commenting that they wouldn't mind living there themselves.

Top: Courtyard.

Upper left: Resident spa.

Far upper left: Town square.

Left: Dining room.

Far left: Kitchen.

Opposite: Storefront in Town Square.

Photography: Tim Buchman Photography.

FreemanWhite, Inc.

LifeDiagnostics Imaging
Hennepin Faculty Associates
Minneapolis, Minnesota

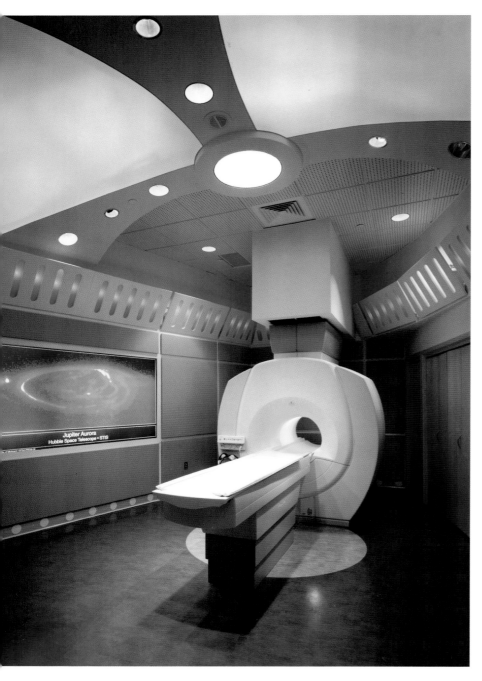

Any patient subjected to an MRI or magnetic resonance imaging knows why a visit to a diagnostic imaging facility can be discomforting or even unsettling. This fact of medical life makes the new, 3,375-square foot Life Diagnostics Imaging office, in Minneapolis particularly impressive. Hennepin Faculty Associates, the independent, nonprofit corporation of more than 250 physicians and dentists who provide professional services at Hennepin County Medical Center, asked FreemanWhite to design an imaging facility to communicate that state-of-the-art services are being provided, lighten the more intimidating side of medical imaging with a distracting, ultramodern setting, make patients in surrounding downtown offices feel comfortable, and generate good word-of-mouth patient referrals. The design achieves its mission by creating a vivid environment that celebrates the capabilities of contemporary science and technology through sleek, futuristic imagery a timely reminder that if you can't beat 'em, join 'em.

Above left: MRI room.

Above right: Staff support area.

Photography: Joel Koyama Photography.

Guenther 5 Architects

3 West 18th Street
New York, NY 10011
212.941.9911
212.941.1422 (Fax)
www.g5arch.com

Guenther 5 Architects

Patrick H. Dollard Discovery Health Center
Harris, New York

Why shouldn't the new Patrick H. Dollard Discovery Health Center, in Harris, New York, be a "green" and "healthy" building, featuring architecture that performs as a high-efficiency energy envelope linked to geothermal heat pumps, and interiors that have no-wax flooring, reduced use of PVC plastics, and no lead or other PBTs to improve indoor air quality and minimize asthma trigger sources? After all, the award-winning, 28,000-square foot, two-story steel and wood structure, designed by Guenther 5 Architects, is a family diagnostic, rehabilitation, research, training and wellness center, created for The Center for Discovery to help families and professionals support individuals with severe disabilities. And healthy doesn't mean dull. Visitors soon find that the clear circulation, abundant daylight, bright colors, cheerful furnishings (often based on renewable materials), and quality lighting (equipped with photocell sensors), produce a joyous, user-friendly environment they can happily return to.

Above left: Exterior.

Above right: Upper level balcony.

Below left: Main entrance.

Opposite: Interior atrium.

Photography: David Allee.

Guenther 5 Architects

Beth Israel Medical Center
New York, New York

Above left: Continuum reception and waiting room.

Above right: Continuum corridor and classrooms.

Left: Renfield resource center.

Opposite: Renfield meditation /reflection space.

Photography: Peter Mauss/Esto (Continuum), Dub Rogers (Renfield).

Great health care institutions such as New York's Beth Israel Medical Center, a 1,368-bed, full-service tertiary teaching hospital founded on Manhattan's Lower East Side before the turn of the 20th century, may never finish organizing their physical plant as they respond to advances in medical technology and changes in health care practice. Two recent projects at Beth Israel, the 12,000-square foot Continuum Center for Health & Healing, and the 4,000-square foot Renfield Center for Beatrice Nurses, both designed by Guenther 5 Architects, demonstrate the broad, evolving concerns of this world-class hospital. At the Continuum Center, an ambulatory facility for integrative medicine that encompasses primary care medicine, OB/GYN, acupuncture, massage and chiropractic therapies, an award-winning, non-traditional design introduces an entry sequence and flow pattern to "slow down" arriving patients, and surrounds them with an environment of healthy building materials and furnishings. For the Renfield Center, a resource, training and contemplative facility named in memory of former Beth Israel trustee and benefactor Beatrice Renfield, a spirited, unconventional and residential-style space for classrooms, private carrels, conference/ training facilities, a meditation /reflection space and nursing education staff offices has been constructed of natural and healthy materials to encourage nurses to foster growth in nursing and create opportunities for research and personal renewal. Modest in scope as these microcosms are, they offer a tantalizing glimpse into the rich diversity at Beth Israel and similar institutions around the world.

Guenther 5 Architects

New York-Presbyterian Medical Center
New York, New York

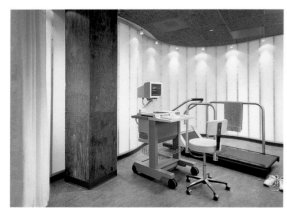

Above top: Berrie reception.

Above right: Irving Dermatology

Above: Berrie exercise room.

Below right: Irving reception.

Bottom right: Irving testing room.

Photography: Peter Mauss/ Esto (Irving), Paul Warchol (Berrie)

Design can make a difference even at sprawling, 2,395-bed New York Presbyterian Hospital, whose Columbia Presbyterian Medical Center and New York Weill Cornell Medical Center are the respective teaching hospitals for Columbia University College of Physicians & Surgeons and Weill Medical College of Cornell University. Consider the 14,000-square foot Herbert Irving Center for Dermatology and Skin Cancer, and the 14,000-square foot Naomi Berrie Diabetes Center, both renovated by Guenther 5 Architects. The Irving Center's H-shaped floor, plagued by confusing circulation and ambiguous identity, was transformed with a wayfinding system letting daylight deep inside plus a dramatic new interior of glass, slate and wood. Integrating the Berrie Center's high-volume clinical practice and research laboratory meant rigorously differentiating clinical and research activities, converting the waiting area into an innovative place to learn, converse, eat, work and relax, and opened up other clinical areas through extensive glazing.

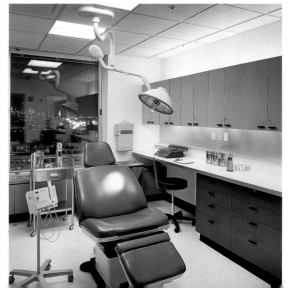

Guenther 5 Architects

Mt. Sinai Medical Center
Lauder Center for Maternity Care
New York, New York

Left: Patient room.

Below: Reception area/nurses' station.

Photography: Paul Warchol.

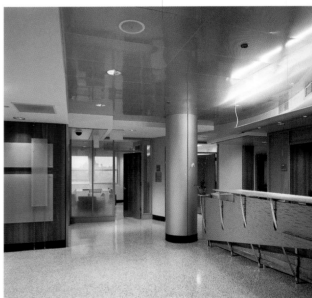

If given the choice between stark, institutional patient rooms and stylish, hotel-like alternatives, expectant mothers know what they want. Their preference provides the departure point for the new, 11,920-square foot, Jo Carole & Ronald S. Lauder Center for Maternity Care at New York's Mt. Sinai Medical Center, designed by Guenther 5 Architects in collaboration with Larsen Shein Ginsberg Snyder. In a subtle and sophisticated environment encompassing patient rooms, newborn nursery, family room, snack area, reception area/nurses' station, staff conference room, nurses' lounge/kitchen and isolation room, a new sensibility is displayed in fresh, contemporary colors, forms and furnishings. New mothers enter motherhood with much on their minds, but their sunny patient rooms at the Lauder Center featuring cherry paneled headwalls, glass tiled baths, individual refrigerators, no-wax floors, handsome textiles and crisp, modern furniture are a joy to experience.

H+L Architecture

1621 18th Street
Suite 110
Denver, CO 80202
303.295.1792
303.292.6437 (Fax)

219 E. Colorado Avenue
Colorado Springs, CO 80903
719.578.9317
719.578.9317 (Fax)
www.hlarch.com

H+L Architecture

Anschutz Outpatient Pavilion
University of Colorado Hospital
Aurora, Colorado

For University of Colorado Hospital, ranked as one of America's best by U.S. News & World Report, the creation of the new, 476,000-square foot, eight-level Anschutz Outpatient Pavilion in Aurora has particular significance as the Hospital's first building on its new, 217-acre campus, the old Fitzsimons Army Medical Center. Numerous features have shaped the Pavilion's award-winning form, designed by H+L Architecture in joint venture with HDR Inc., such as its 24-month fast-track schedule for design and construction, wayfinding based on public perimeter circulation and staff interior circulation, and creative and flexible architecture to accommodate state-of-the-art equipment and staff. However, the building's uniqueness lies in its modular concept, which lets related medical clinics be grouped as adjacent practice cluster modules to share staff, support services and treatment areas. This is one reason why Dennis Brimhall, president of the Hospital, has declared, "...we have achieved our vision."

Above: Pavilion entrance.

Left: Staff corridor.

Below: Exterior.

Opposite: Main waiting area.

Photography: James Berchert, Ron Johnson.

H+L Architecture

Anschutz Inpatient Pavilion
University of Colorado Hospital
Aurora, Colorado

Set the bar high enough to make a hospital stretch, and the results can be astonishing. Among the goals for the newly opened, 482,700-square foot, 12-story, 100-bed Anschutz Inpatient Pavilion at University of Colorado Hospital in Aurora, designed by H+L Architecture, in joint venture with HDR, Inc., have been a leading-edge, patient-focused environment, sustainable design, and the creation of a "flagship" for the Hospital's new Fitzsimons campus. The reaction from visiting donors and board members has been "Wow," for such reasons as patient rooms with family sleeping accommodations, bedside voice and data connections, decentralized caregiver stations and on-demand food service via Web-linked, wireless keyboard-controlled televisions, a "green" environment of environmentally friendly building materials, durable and VOC-free furnishings, advanced energy and lighting systems, abundant daylighting, and a hotel-inspired interior design based on the elements of earth, metal, water, wood and fire. Wow, indeed.

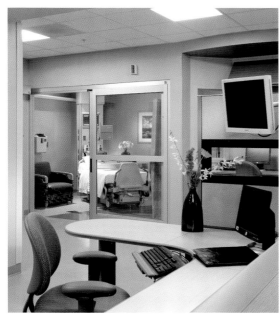

Left: Patient room.
Below: Entrance lobby.
Opposite above: Exterior.
Opposite below: VIP suite.
Photography: James Berchert.

H+L Architecture

South Wing Expansion
Exempla Lutheran Medical Center
Wheat Ridge, Colorado

Above: Heart Center reception.
Right: ICU nurses station.
Opposite: ICU patient room.
Photography: James Berchert.

Two outstanding facilities form the core of the recent, award-winning, 85,000-square foot expansion of the South Wing of Exempla Lutheran Medical Center in Wheat Ridge, Colorado, designed by H+L Architecture. In an agreement with General Electric, a new, third-floor Heart Center consolidates new catheter and EP laboratories, pre/post procedure area, nuclear and echo imaging, EKG, stress testing, cardiac rehabilitation and cardiology support services into a Center of Excellence. It is a "show site" and world-class test site for advanced GE equipment and software that also provides patient-friendly, home-like interiors, natural and indirect light and scenic views. On the fourth floor, a new, three-suite, 18-bed ICU serves patients and families through such features as increased room sizes for patient, family and staff zones, decentralized work pods that place caregivers closer to patients, family waiting areas including separate rooms for family groupings, and public spaces offering families kitchens, children's play areas, A/V equipment and pleasing furnishings including wood floors handsome enough for home.

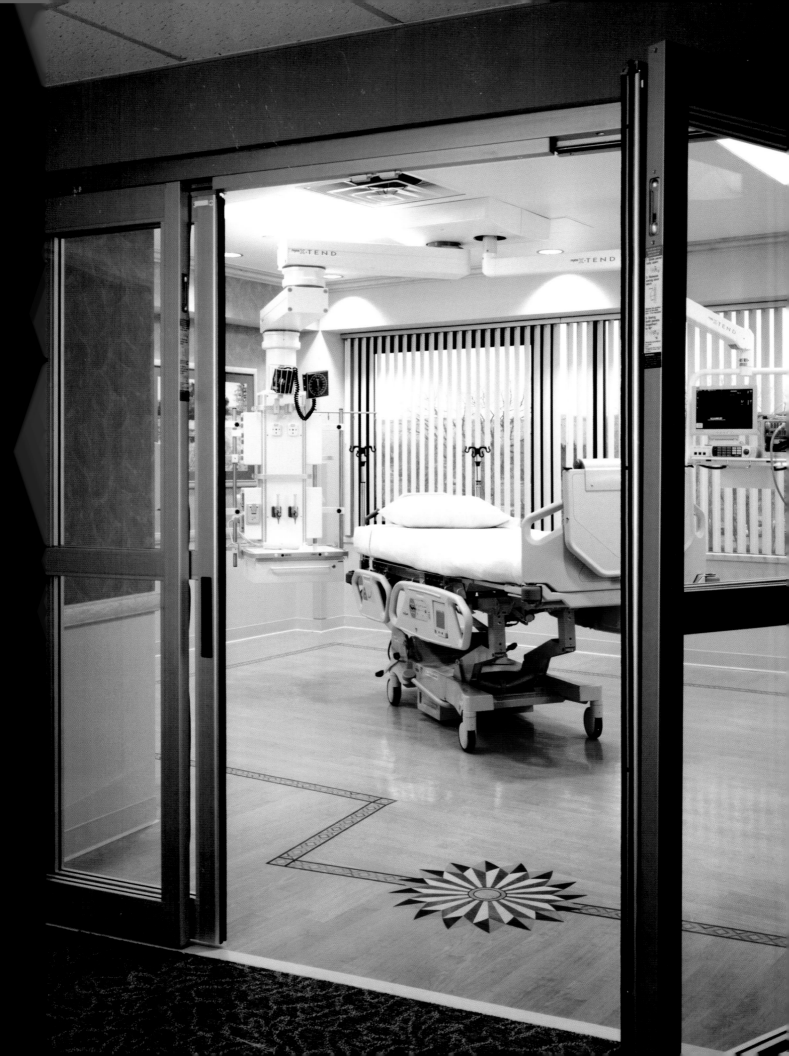

H+L Architecture

The Baby Place
Exempla Saint Joseph Hospital
Denver, Colorado

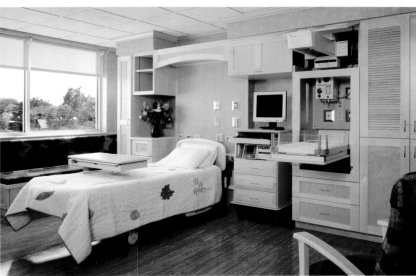

Top left: LDR corridor.

Top right: LDR room.

Above left: Reception.

Above right: Family waiting room.

Photography: James Berchert.

Leadership is demanding, which explains why Exempla Saint Joseph Hospital, recording the highest birth rate among Denver's hospitals, has acted decisively to create a new labor and delivery department to compete with new hospitals and maintain its mission of "Best in Nation" &, "High Tech with High Touch". The Baby Place at E. Atwill Gilman Center for Maternal Child Health is a 26,220-square foot unit with 14 LDRs, two ORs, and a unique LDR and OR swingroom, designed by H+L Architecture, provides a comfortable, Colorado mountain hospitality -like atmosphere for mothers during labor and childbirth, combining technology with a family-focused environment. Thus, each LDR room offers such features as a private bathroom with shower/ whirlpool tub, headwall unit in custom wood fine cabinetry, and full-length sleeping benches with storage underneath. In fact, all of these features are also attracting doctors and staff, the storks who deliver the babies as well as the mothers they serve.

HGA

Minneapolis, Minnesota
612.758.4000

Rochester, Minnesota
507.281.8600

Milwaukee, Wisconsin
414.278.8200

Sacramento, California
916.787.5100

Sanfrancisco, California
415.962.2592

Los Angelas, California
310.553.6888

www.hga.com

HGA

St. Luke's Community Medical Center at The Woodlands
The Woodlands, Texas

In a strategic reach to better serve Houston's burgeoning population base, St. Luke's Episcopal Health System has created a new Community Medical Campus at The Woodlands, a 2,800-acre planned community. The 42-acre, village-like, user-friendly campus opened in 2003. It serves the local Woodlands population of more than 30,000 residents, as well as residents of surrounding areas. Designed by HGA, the 300,000-square foot first phase comprises a central hospital flanked by an 84-bed patient care unit, a Medical Office Building (MOB) and open space for a future patient care tower to nearly triple the bed count, plus three more MOBs and a parking structure. What residents are happily noticing is that the Campus' "Hill Country" design, blending hospitality and convenience with state-of-the-art care, extends a Texas-size welcome.

Above: Patient care unit and garden.

Left: Patient room.

Far left: Terrace with chapel.

Right: Main entrance lobby.

Photography: Aker/Zvonkovic.

HGA

CentraCare Health Plaza
Saint Cloud, Minnesota

Above left: Woodlands entrance and tower.

Above right: Short stay room.

Below Left: Woodlands lobby piano and art.

Right: Imaging center.

Opposite: Prairie entry and lobby.

Photography: Don F. Wong.

Central Minnesota is one of the fastest growing regions in the state. Saint Cloud Hospital had been trying to keep pace, but the existing hospital site was severely landlocked. A new ambulatory care campus was the long-term solution. An interesting aspect of the new campus is the relationship between the building and its natural context. The peaceful campus borders the Sauk River and features a rich variety of native woodlands and restored prairie grasses and flowers. Those three themes river, woodlands and prairie provide inspirtion for the Health Plaza's three atria, as well as the interior design and wayfinding. Natural

materials, references to geographical terrain, art and open spaces help create an environment that encourages patients to discover the essence of their well being, allowing nature to play a role in the healing process.

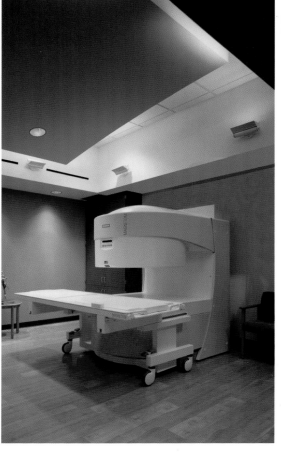

HGA

The M.I.N.D. Institute
University of California-Davis Medical Center
Sacramento, California

Left: Main entrance.

Above: Reception courtyard.

Bottom: Great room.

Right: Entrance lobby.

Photography: Richard Barnes.

Colorful art adorns the walls of the University of California Davis Medical Center's new facilities in Sacramento for the M.I.N.D. (Medical Investigation of Neurodevelopmental Disorders) Institute. The Institute and its new facilities are dedicated to helping children and adults with autism and other neurological developmental disorders. The award-winning new facilities designed by HGA are a reflection of the Institute's commitment to its research to find causes, treatments and cures for those disorders. The project's 8-acre campus setting includes a 72,338-square foot building for the outpatient clinic, food services and resource center/library, and a 27,270-square foot building for the research laboratory and offices for research faculty and staff. (A 31,979-square-foot clinical research facility, designed by HGA, will be added later.) Sophisticated as the new facilities are, they provide children with handsome, residential-style interiors where comfortable furnishings in warm beige and brown tones create a peaceful, home-like setting.

HGA

Oneida Community Health Center
Oneida, Wisconsin

Above: Clerestory at spine.
Left: Entrance.
Below: Clinic waiting.
Photography: Jess Smith.

Decades of declining population left the Oneida Nation of Wisconsin unprepared for rapid population growth as its economy revived in the 1990s. Realizing that its existing 23,000-square foot clinic built in the 1970s could no longer accommodate its expanding and diversifying health care needs, the Tribe invited HGA to design the new 68,000-square foot Oneida Community Health Center to offer comprehensive outpatient medical services plus dental and vision care to Tribal members living in or near the Tribal community. A full-time staff of physicians, nurses and other healthcare professionals work within the striking linear structure of stone, timber and glass whose brightly illuminated circulation spine serves as a symbolic beacon to the community. Designed for flexibility, the Center features a large dividable conference room available for patient education and community outreach, and is conveniently situated for additions that seem increasingly likely in the coming years.

HDR

8404 Indian Hills Drive
Omaha, NE 68114
800.496.6354
402.399-1282 (Fax)
www.hdrinc.com

HDR

Faith Regional Health Services
Norfolk, Nebraska

Above left: Exterior with porte cochere.

Above right: Upper level lounge.

Right: Entrance.

Opposite: Main lobby.

Photography: Tom Kessler.

Because a hospital is only as good as its physicians, nurses and support staff, many hospitals develop quality medical office space to attract the best physicians and their patients. For this reason, Faith Regional Health Services, a regional health system in Norfolk, Nebraska serving over 100,000 people residing within a 75-mile radius, recently retained HDR, to design the new, 70,000-square foot, two-story Medical Offices North. As a freestanding structure, the medical office building provides room for medical offices, surgery center, laboratory and shell space within a sophisticated environment designed for easy wayfinding, abundant daylight and direct access to the nearby hospital building on the West campus of Faith Regional Hospital, a 166-bed acute care facility. Interestingly, the new facility, featuring a spacious, light-filled, two-story atrium and clerestories on the north and south facades, has been so well received that the hospital is investigating the possibility of creating a more appealing entrance on a par with its new neighbor.

The Forum at Carle
Carle Foundation
Urbana, Illinois

Above left: Exterior elevation.

Top right: Auditorium.

Above right: Lobby.

Photography: Tom Kessler.

Teaching comes naturally at 295-bed Carle Foundation Hospital, in Urbana, Illinois, as the primary teaching hospital for the University of Illinois College of Medicine at Urbana Champaign. However, just as health care facilities age, so did the Hospital's previous education center. The new, 42,000-square foot, two-story educational facility,

The Forum at Carle, designed by HDR, introduces a timely, efficient and dignified "signature" building that harmonizes with campus architecture. From its graceful interior, comprising an upper level lobby and 250-seat auditorium and lower level classrooms and office space, to its handsome exterior of brick, concrete and glass, excavated to expose the

lower level to daylight, honor an adjacent park's 35-foot height limit, and plant a healing garden, the new structure is fully prepared to nurture inquiring minds.

Metropolitan Hospital
Grand Rapids, Michigan

Above: Exterior on Village Green.

Below Right: Public service area.

Bottom Right: Main lobby.

Illustrations: HDR

Welcome to Metro Health Village, a 170-acre campus in Grand Rapids, Michigan, planned and designed by HDR, that will soon welcome Metropolitan Health Corporation's new, 465,000-square foot, seven-story, 208-bed Metropolitan Hospital. With medical campuses that resemble residential communities gaining public approval, Metro Health's replacement hospital for the half-century-old institution will become the focal point of the Village as well as a patient-friendly, LEED-certified environment that separates public access areas from inpatient and staff areas for easy wayfinding. Just as the Village is conveniently centered around a Village Green, with the Hospital and specialty retail shops and medical services at opposite ends, the Hospital's departments are linked by access spines leading to "onstage and offstage" areas. Yes, there's even a Village ice cream parlor.

HDR

Children's Hospital
Omaha, Nebraska

You don't regard change lightly when you're Children's Hospital of Omaha, Nebraska, a 142-bed, non-profit organization caring for children since 1948 that offers the only pediatric specialty health care center in the Cornhusker State. When it was time to plan a replacement hospital for the family-centered regional provider, dedicated to cost-effective, quality health care services and advocacy for children from infants through adolescents, Children's Hospital challenged HDR, to develop the 275,000-square foot, 10-story pediatric hospital to function as a world-class health care facility focused on family comfort as well as the care of patients. The result is an award-winning environment that truly resembles "a place where

other children had been before." Evidence of the exceptional care and inspired design that have been incorporated in this brick-and-glass sheathed, cast-in-place concrete structure is visible outside as well as inside. The building's height, for example, has been reduced to a five-story profile through sensitive placement on the sloping, 4.4-acre site beside an existing medical office building, enabling patients to use multiple entry points at different floor levels, and reducing the building's perceived mass. (The MOB has been reskinned to match the Children's Hospital.) Indoors, the hospital has been configured to reduce traffic between departments, allow nurses to see all rooms from nursing stations, address

Above: Dodge Street elevation.
Right: Cafeteria.
Lower right: Auditorium.
Opposite: Atrium.
Photography: Jeffrey Jacobs.

children's concerns, and enable families to participate in their children's care. Although it is unquestionably a large and complex space, accommodating such functions as medical/surgical beds, radiology, emergency, ambulatory procedures, surgery, pediatric intensive care, cafeteria, gift shop and parking garage, it still manages to be easily navigable, caring and even playful to the children and families it serves. The air of assurance is sensed immediately in the public areas, where whimsical "creatures" can be spotted on ceilings, walls and floors, representing artwork created by patients and area school children, against a backdrop of color, water, daylight and indirect lighting. Yet it is decidedly present in patient rooms as well. Each single-occupancy patient room is furnished with a sleep-bed for overnight stays by parents or grandparents, a desk with Internet access, private refrigerator, television and VCR and a private full bath. Utilization studies show that patient satisfaction is rising like children's laughter at Children's Hospital.

Top left: Medical/surgical floor nursing station.

Above left: Pediatric intensive care unit.

Above right: Playroom.

Helman Hurley Charvat Peacock/Architects, Inc.

2601 Westhall Lane
Suite 222
Maitland, FL 32751
407.875.2722
407.475.0811 (Fax)
www.hhcp.com
hfd@hhcp.com

Helman Hurley Charvat Peacock/Architects, Inc.

East Georgia Regional Medical Center
Statesboro, Georgia

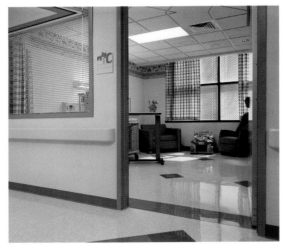

Above left: Pediatric Patient room.

Above right: Main entrance.

Left: Covered drop-off.

Below: LDR room.

Opposite: Women's Pavilion lobby.

Photography: Raymond Martinot.

Statesboro, Georgia is both a rural town and university town one hour west of Savannah. Supported by a diverse economic base, the county seat of Bulloch County recently gained new sophistication with the opening of the new, 233,000-square foot, four-story, 150-bed East Georgia Regional Medical Center, a replacement hospital and adjacent, freestanding Women's Pavilion, both designed by Helman Hurley Charvat Peacock/Architects. The state-of-the-art hospital overcomes a tight site and budget with an effective, comfortable and well organized design anchored by a "main street" spine corridor. It's a considerable improvement over its predecessor, offering such features as the co-located clinical diagnostic services laboratory, radiology suite and cardio-pulmonary functions, offering maximum support to the ED as well as convenience for inpatients and outpatients. Next door, the Women's Pavilion meets women's specific health care needs while being connected directly to the hospital's imaging and surgery suites via an enclosed corridor.

Helman Hurley Charvat Peacock/Architects Inc.

Orlando Regional South Seminole Hospital
Emergency Department Addition
Longwood, Florida

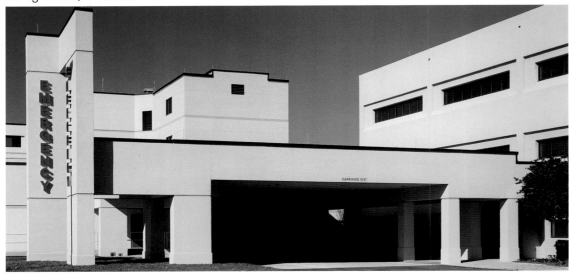

Spatial relationships among people, equipment and other resources are critical in hospitals, and the recent 35,750-square foot addition and 11,630-square foot renovation of the emergency and surgery departments at Orlando Regional South Seminole Hospital, in Long-wood, Florida, convincingly illustrates what good design can accomplish. The project, designed by Helman Hurley Charvat Peacock/Architects, encompasses a 30-bed ED, two "smart" operating room suites, pre-op, recovery and outpatient areas, specialty rooms for trauma and cardiac care, and rooms for patients with gynecological, orthopedic, pediatric and psychiatric conditions. The design's benefits, based on carefully arranged spatial relationships

among the various activities plus clear, efficient circulation, have been dramatic: a supportive, stress-reducing atmosphere and maximized staff efficiency. Stephen Glazier, executive director of the hospital, notes, "Since its opening, the medical staff leadership has repeatedly commented on the design efficiency of the facility and the staff's increased ability to care for patients in a warm, comforting environment."

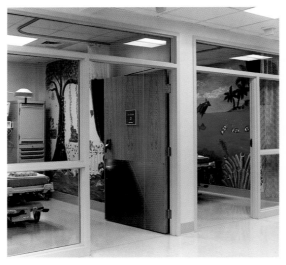

Above: ED entrance.

Upper right: ED specialty rooms.

Lower right: "Smart" operating room.

Far right: Nurse Station.

Photography: Raymond Martinot.

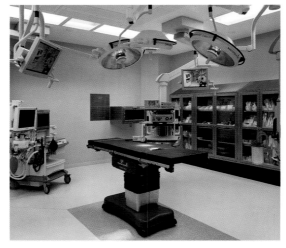

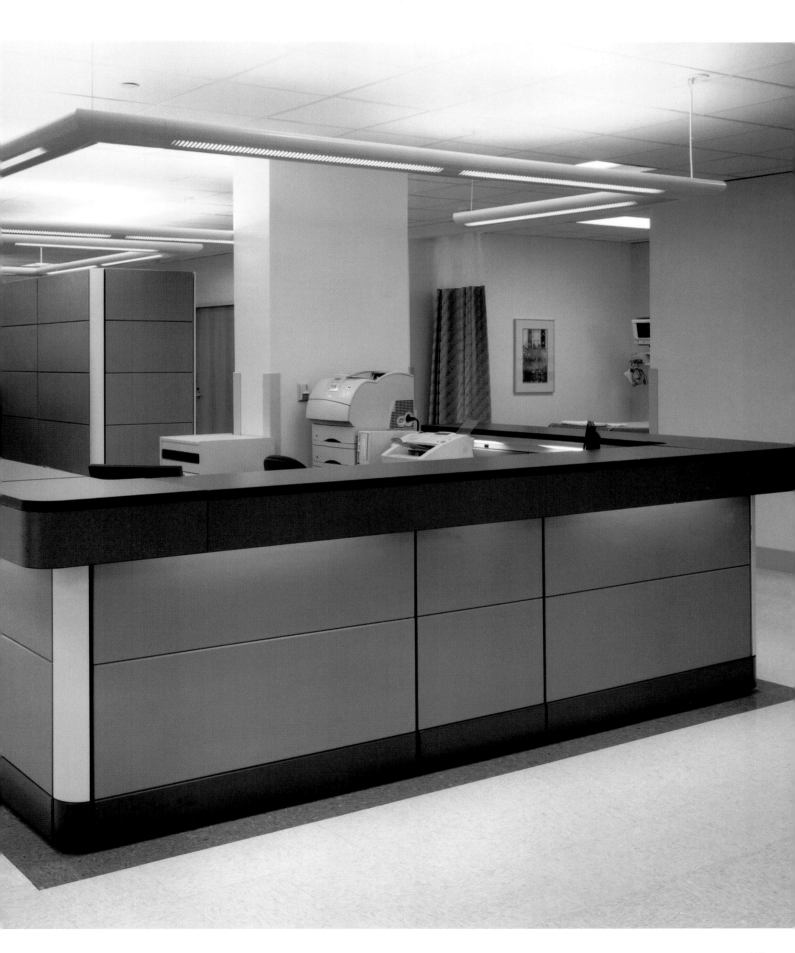

Helman Hurley Charvat Peacock/Architects, Inc.

Medical Center of Southeastern Oklahoma
Women's Center
Durant, Oklahoma

Operating 120 acute-care beds, the Medical Center of Southeastern Oklahoma, in Durant, has been recognized nationally with HCIA-Sachs, Inc.'s "100 Top Hospitals" award for six consecutive years. Now, the hospital has bettered itself with the recent addition of a 20,000-square foot Women's Center, designed by Helman Hurley Charvat Peacock/Architects.

Not only does the relocated Women's Center accommodate an expanded case load with its 20 post-partum beds, five LDRs, one C-section room, two recovery beds, a 10-station nursery, various support spaces, improved access to imaging and direct access to the OR suite, it enhances the comfort of women and families. Within the Center's new, dedicated entry is a

women-friendly environment of wood floors, enclosed headwalls, ceiling fans and home-like furnishings that entire families can appreciate.

Top: New entry.
Below right: Waiting room.
Right: Nurses station.
Far right: LDR.
Opposite: Nursery.
Photography: Raymond Martinot.

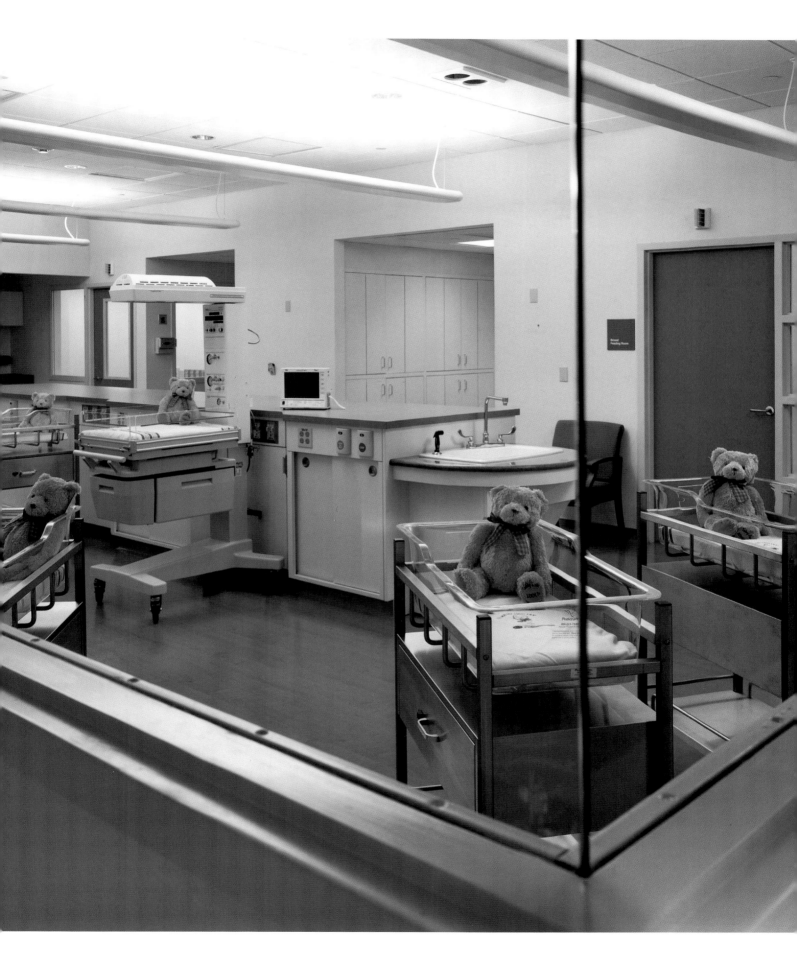

Helman Hurley Charvat Peacock/Architects, Inc.

Biloxi Regional Medical Center
Medical Office Building/Parking Garage
Biloxi, Mississippi

Since medical campuses are seldom built at once, Biloxi Regional Medical Center, a 153-bed, acute care, private hospital in the Vieux Marché district of Biloxi, Mississippi, maintains numerous projects in different stages of development. The recently completed 56,000-square foot, three-story medical office building and attached, 430-car, four-story parking garage, designed by Helman Hurley Charvat Peacock/ Architects, presented a number of challenges that are not unusual in extended development programs. Not only would the buildings occupy a tight site, they had to resemble the existing, brick-clad hospital across the street even though the pre-cast concrete garage would use little brick for budgetary reasons and the MOB needed to be user-friendly. Accordingly, the garage includes brick bands and brick endwalls, and the MOB offers interiors that patients can easily navigate and physicians can custom tailor.

Above left: MOB entrance.

Left: MOB lobby.

Far left: Parking garage.

Photography: Raymond Martinot.

HKS Inc.

1919 McKinney Avenue
Dallas
Texas 75201
214.969.5599
214.969.3397 (Fax)
www.hksinc.com

HKS Inc.

St. Rose Dominican Hospital
Siena Campus
Henderson, Nevada

High above Las Vegas, a radiant new medical center assumes the classic form of a Catholic Spanish colonial mission to practice the latest medical techniques in compassionate service to humanity: St. Rose Dominican Hospital's Siena Campus, a 350,500-square foot, 140-bed facility in Henderson, Nevada, designed by HKS Inc. St. Rose Dominican has served Nevadans since 1947. The new Siena Campus provides such inpatient services as transitional, critical and intermediate care, LDRP and pediatric care, and such outpatient services as same-day surgery, rehabilitation, heart center and cancer center, in a patient-centered environment with a healing garden and rose-covered gazebo at its center. In addition, the Hospital features a circular chapel, easy wayfinding, decentralized diagnostic, therapeutic, administrative and clinical services that can often be delivered bedside, and interiors that are modern, comfortable and assuring in ways no colonial mission could quite equal.

Upper right: Main entrance.

Right: Nurses station.

Far right: Patient room.

Opposite: Bell tower.

Photography: Exterior: Tom Fox Interior: Ed Lasse

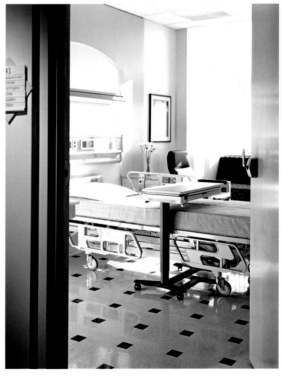

Louise Obici Memorial Hospital
Suffolk, Virginia

Why don't hospitals age gracefully? Upgrading building systems, installing new equipment and configuring new spaces out of old ones can cost almost as much as new construction. For this reason, Louise Obici Memorial Hospital, a gift to the people of Suffolk, Virginia, by Amedeo Obici, the founder of Planter's Peanuts, in memory of his wife, Louise, concluded 49 years of service by yielding to a replacement hospital in 2000. The splendid new, 365,000-square foot, three-story, 150-bed hospital, designed by HKS

Inc., is a versatile, patient-centered facility that is fully equipped for such services as cardiology, radiation therapy, oncology/ hematology, behavioral medicine, emergency, intensive care and women's center. Reflecting today's health care philosophy, it embodies flexibility for growth with minimal disruption to ongoing services, and a healing environment that uses natural light, warm colors, human scale and ample public spaces highlighted by an inviting, landscaped atrium to assure patients and families.

William Giermak, president of Obici Health Systems, comments, "It's a remarkable place that most people wouldn't expect to find in Suffolk, Virginia."

Above left: Floor pattern in atrium. Photographer: Brad Sindle

Above right: Entrance.

Left: Bed tower.

Opposite: Atrium

Photography: Brad Sindle.

HKS Inc.

McKay-Dee Hospital Center
Ogden, Utah

Right: Mountain View Cafe.
Below: Entrance.
Bottom right: Entry lobby.
Opposite: Exterior vista.
Photography: Ed LaCasse

Over 90 years after the Thomas D. Dee Memorial Hospital was founded in Ogden, Utah, by the Dee family in 1910, the newest building to be called the McKay-Dee Hospital Center is thriving as a not-for-profit, acute care, facility serving Weber and North Davis Counties. The 705,000-square foot, five-story Center, designed by HKS Inc., offers a broad array of services, including nationally recognized programs in heart, rehabilitation and newborn intensive care. A four-story atrium running the length of the building forms the heart of a healing environment characterized by abundant daylight, panoramic views, comfortable waiting spaces, ample gathering areas, hotel-like patient rooms, and such service amenities as a family-oriented resource center, excellent food service, user-friendly registration and positive distractions. Attentive service, notes Julie Huntley, vice president of patient care for McKay-Dee, even has readmitted patients "making requests for certain rooms based on their favorite view."

HKS Inc.

University of North Carolina Hospitals
Children's Hospital and Women's
Hospital Chapel Hill, North Carolina

Above: Therapy area, Children's Hospital.

Left: Entry lobby, Women's Hospital.

Below left: Stairway, Women's Hospital.

Photography: Ed LaCasse

Two new worlds have emerged within a 440,000-square foot addition to the University of North Carolina Hospitals in Chapel Hill, namely 136-bed North Carolina Children's Hospital and 54-bed North Carolina Women's Hospital, designed by HKS as two interlinking buildings and a pedestrian concourse. The Children's Hospital takes its inspiration from a child's standpoint, offering a rainbow of colors, interesting displays, and bright, active therapy areas to surround its PICU, intermediate cardiac center and newborn critical care center in a playful environment. Similarly, the Women's Hospital helps women throughout their lives, addressing such issues as ambulatory services, maternal-fetal medicine, gynecology and infertility in a warm, colorful and timeless setting that features flexible clinics, birthing center, inpatient oncology, Women's Resource Center and two protected outdoor gardens. For the Southeast, an essential health care institution is now more valuable than ever.

HMC Architects

3270 Inland Empire BIVD.
Ontario, CA 91764
909.980.8058
909.980.8558 (Fax)

HMC Architects

Kaiser Downey Medical Center
Downey, California

Top: New and existing facilities.

Above left: Spine.

Above right: Patio and sunken garden.

Left: Parking.

Illustration: Klyde Wilson.

With a population of 110,600 in an area of 12.5 square miles, and 3.6 million people living within its metropolitan area, the City of Downey attracts one of the highest concentrations of medical professionals and health care facilities in California, including over 200 medical businesses. The region's importance is reflected in the handsome new Kaiser Downey Medical Center, a one million-square foot facility comprising one seven-story, 352-bed hospital and two medical office buildings, designed by HMC Architects. The Medical Center joins forces with an adjacent existing Kaiser primary care facility to offer comprehensive health care services and share security, parking, dining, and administrative functions. The complex is unified through a central spine, a concourse connecting existing clinics and the new plaza, parking structure and gardens before arriving at the entry to the new Medical Center. All public services, such as pharmacies, imaging, gift shop and cafeteria, will be found here, making the spine, main entrance, outdoor patios and sunken garden a truly welcome place for patients, families and staff.

HMC Architects

Washoe Medical Center at South Meadows Diagnostic and Treatment Pavilion Reno, Nevada

The first acute care community hospital built in Reno, Nevada, in over 20 years, Washoe Medical Center at South Meadows satisfies growing demand for health care services with a new 51,000-square foot Diagnostic and Treatment Pavilion, an addition to a former assisted living and rehabilitation hospital that has been converted to acute care beds, both designed by HMC Architects, and a new 66,000-square foot medical office building. As a result, the pavilion and bed unit include such key facilities as the emergency department, imaging suite, operating rooms, laboratory services, acute care and ICU beds, medical records, pharmacy, and support services in a high-technology space with a home-like atmosphere. Patients and families feel welcome in an environment that separates public spaces from patient care areas, infuses interiors with daylight and views, and successfully uses wood-like laminates, fabrics and other residential -style furnishings to soften the impact of modern medicine.

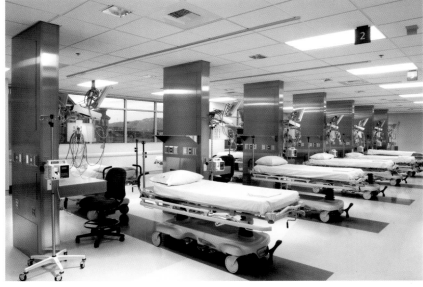

Above: Pavilion facade.

Far left: Atrium.

Above left: Registration.

Middle left: Observation area.

lower left: Waiting room.

Photography: Vance Fox.

205

HMC Architects.

Kaiser West Los Angeles Medical Center
Los Angeles, California

A vigorous game of musical chairs ensues whenever a hospital relocates its operations within an existing building or between existing and new ones, and Kaiser Permanente's West Los Angeles Medical Center, located in a densely developed Los Angeles neighborhood, knows this firsthand. To comply with SB1953 and FEMA, Kaiser West Los Angeles Medical Center is relocating departments in its existing center tower to a new west tower while they are delicensed to serve only outpatient functions, and the existing south tower is remodeled for a new acute care hospital. The project, encompassing 472,795 square feet of renovation and 189,577 square feet for a new west tower, plus a new parking structure, new outpatient pharmacy and central plant addition, is proceeding smoothly thanks to extensive planning and coordinated communication. Among its numerous benefits will be a new entrance to the hospital campus, combining a gift shop and waiting area, soothing, family-friendly environments throughout the interiors, enhanced, color-coded wayfinding, and a glass walkway connecting the existing and new towers that will cast a glow on the neighborhood at night.

HMC Architects

Cedars-Sinai Medical Center
Outpatient Care Unit
Los Angeles, California

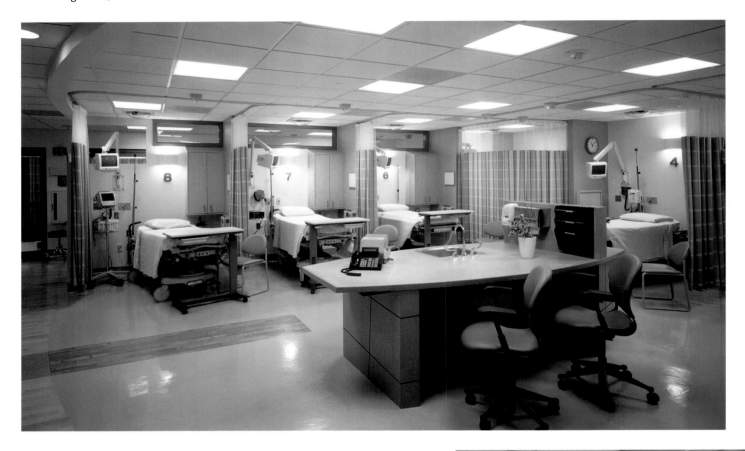

Cedars-Sinai Medical Center has focused on providing the finest health care in Los Angeles since its founding in 1902. Thus, every project, like the conversion of an existing administrative area into a 6,893-square foot, full-service outpatient care unit, designed by HMC Architects has been carefully evaluated to ensure a state-of-the-art environment that will respond to patients' physical and emotional needs. Designed on a fast track schedule, the design meets standard institutional requirements for mechanical, electrical and plumbing systems, medical gases and building materials. Yet the resulting environment transcends these requirements to project a residential-style image of privacy and comfort. A skillful blend of scale, color, texture and materials, partitions of varying height, and the incorporation of clerestory windows where direct daylight is unavailable, provides patients with the satisfaction of knowing their care is first-rate

without relinquishing their connection to the outside world.

Above: Observation beds.
Right: Nursing station.
Photography: Ryan Beck.

Hellmuth, Obata + Kassabaum, P.C.

Atlanta
Berlin
Chicago
Dallas
Greenville
Hong kong
Houston
Kansas City
London
Los Angelas

Mexico City
New York
Orlando
San Fransico
Shanghai
St. Louis
Tampa
Tokyo
Warsaw
Washington DC

Hellmuth, Obata + Kassabaum, P.C.

Center for Advanced Medicine
Washington University Medical Center
St. Louis, Missouri

Acclaimed as the "jewel in the crown" of Washington University Medical Center, a 230-acre complex in St. Louis comprising Washington University School of Medicine, Barnes-Jewish Hospital, St. Louis Children's Hospital, Barnard Hospital, Siteman Cancer Center and the Central Institute for the Deaf, the new, 670,000-square foot, 14-story Center for Advanced Medicine, designed by Hellmuth, Obata + Kassabaum, is a patient-centered ambulatory care facility that physicians, patients, families, educators and students praise for innovation and convenience. This award-winning joint project of Barnes-Jewish Hospital and Washington University School of Medicine offers cancer care, surgery and women's services as well as ambulatory care on large, open floors grouped around an interior atrium. What health care professionals appreciate about the design is its accommodation of changing operations through such provisions as elevators and mechanical shafts located on the periphery for easier space planning, standardized room sizes that simplify room assignments, and clinical modules with interconnecting corridors that form flexible physicians' practice suites and multi-use spaces within suites where physicians practicing alone or in large groups can function equally well. For their part, patients and families cite easy wayfinding, cheerful colors, good lighting, such quality materials as stone, wood and frosted glass, and comfortable furnishings as reasons why their experiences at the Center are so satisfying. "My experiences and treatments," one patient recently observed, "have really blown apart my old opinion that the larger the building, the colder the basic foundation. I feel warmth here!"

Above left: Entrance.
Left: View of atrium from elevator lobby.
Far left: Waiting area.
Opposite: Elevator bank.
Photography: Timothy Hursley.

Hellmuth, Obata + Kassabaum, P.C.

Modernization and Expansion
Rockefeller University Hospital and Nurses Residence
New York, New York

Above: Microbiology research laboratory.

Opposite: Individual laboratory bench.

Photography: Bob Zucker.

Patients at New York's Rockefeller University Hospital differ from patients elsewhere in one important way: They are chosen by Hospital physicians because they have an illness or condition being studied, or they are healthy volunteers needed for study, and they receive treatment without charge. Yet the Hospital, founded in 1910 and respected for biomedical research, needs renewal much like other health care facilities. A recent, 40,000-square foot, seven-story modernization and

expansion of the Hospital and Nurses Residence, designed by Hellmuth, Obata + Kassabaum, has created modern post-graduate microbiology research laboratories and inpatient and outpatient clinical facilities in a 1904 building that remained occupied during construction. Modern as the setting is, it's comfortable enough for the inpatient/outpatient facility's head nurse to declare she's "in love with her new space."

Hellmuth, Obata + Kassabaum, P.C.

University Health Network-Toronto General Hospital Clinical Services Building Toronto, Ontario, Canada

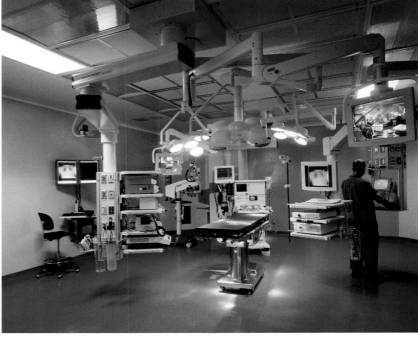

A leading role in health care comes naturally to Toronto General Hospital, in Toronto, Ontario, Canada, a member of the University Health Network. The Hospital has provided advanced acute care patient services to greater Toronto ever since it began operating as York Hospital in 1829, and is proud to claim such firsts as the development and first clinical use of insulin to treat diabetes, the world's first successful single lung transplant, and the first external heart pacemaker used in open heart resuscitation. The recent opening of the 437,000-square foot, 12-story, 224-bed Clinical Services Building, designed by Hellmuth, Obata and Kassabaum, represents a major milestone in UHN's Project 2003 redevelopment and renewal plan, establishing an extraordinary environment for patient care in cardiology, vascular surgery, neurosurgery, orthopedic surgery and solid organ transplantation. In addressing the condition of the existing physical plant and master plan, consolidating clinical services in optimal locations, eliminating clinical service duplication, removing excess outpatient and support space, creating new accommodations for surgery, imaging, oncology and high-acuity beds, and

Top left: Exterior of Patient Court.

Top : Operating room.

Above: Patient room facing Patient Court.

Opposite: Original Thomas Bell building.

Hellmuth, Obata + Kassabaum, P.C.

introducing centers of respite for patients, families and staff, the glass, limestone and brick-clad structure demonstrates how well a patient-focused environment complements state-of-the-art medical technology and practice. For example, 22 sophisticated operating rooms in the CSB serve the advanced surgery performed at UHN, the entire building is wired for high-speed Internet access, and an installed PACS system sends images and test results wherever physicians' computers need them. Simultaneously, every occupant of the CSB enjoys the support of an exceptional architecture that features a luminous, transparent lobby, the McEwen Atrium, at street level as a front door for the community, and a lush indoor garden, the Patient Court, on the fourth floor for patients to explore as well as a sensitive interior design of soothing colors, natural lighting and comfortable furnishings that include a rich variety of spaces where patients and families can gather together, and staff members can sense the importance of their contributions to patient care, medical research and health care education.

Above: Entrance to McEwen Atrium.

Left: McEwen Atrium.

Photography: David Whittaker.

216

Jonathan Bailey Associates

1701 N. Market Street, Suite 400
Dallas, Texas 75202
469.227.3900
469.227.3901 (Fax)
www.jonathanbailey.com

Jonathan Bailey Associates

Health Central
Ocoee, Florida

Above: Evening view of addition.

Left: Wave-like canopy leading to entrance.

Opposite: Entrance porte cochere and atrium.

Photography: Charles Davis Smith, AIA.

Life in central Florida has resembled a theme park ride since Walt Disney World arrived over 30 years ago. A recent example of the region's dynamics can be observed in Ocoee, a city of some 23,000 residents just minutes from Walt Disney World Resorts and downtown Orlando. Health Central, a 171-bed acute-care hospital developed on an 85-acre site by the West Orange Healthcare District, has completed an award-winning renovation and expansion of its "medical mall" concept, designed by Jonathan Bailey Associates. Ocoee was founded in the 1850s and remained a small bedroom community of Orlando until its population surged in the 1990s. The latest expansion of Health Central, which opened its doors in 1993, accommodates change and enhances flexibility in health care delivery systems while introducing a new, public oriented venue, highlighted by a sunny, central atrium, so community events can be staged without disturbing hospital operations. Among the facilities in this

Right: Nursing station.
Below: Operating room.
Opposite: Atrium interior.

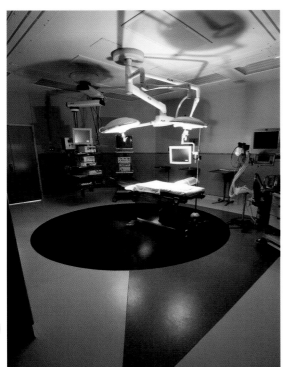

ambitious ambitious project are surgery, radiology, emergency, diagnostic cardiology, express care, labor delivery recovery unit, medical office building, nuclear medicine, laboratory, medical records, dietary, receiving and distribution, and admissions/patient business. To achieve the hospital's goals, the design minimizes public and staff circulation and incorporates flexible elements in areas of constantly changing acuteness, configures new pediatric and OB nursing units to lessen circulation and improve nursing efficiency. The design introduces a case cart system in central sterile processing to improve operational efficiency and maintain a sterile environment for surgical supplies. It also upgrades the patient care unit and patient rooms with improved circulation, higher ceilings and large windows, and promotes a healing environment with daylight, good wayfinding, modern furnishings and colorful, stimulating interiors. Richard Irwin, Jr., president of Health Central, isn't alone in saying, "I am so proud of our design and so is our community!"

Jonathan Bailey Associates

Hexham General Hospital
Hexham, Northumberland,
United Kingdom

How do you bring fresh, new ideas in health care to a proud, venerable community? On a sloping site in the historic abbey town of Hexham in Northumberland, United Kingdom, Hexham General Hospital has met this challenge by opening a handsome, 159,300-square foot, three-level, 98-bed hospital, designed by Jonathan Bailey Associates, to provide state-of-the-art health care while respectfully acknowledging the landscape and vernacular surrounding it. Constrained to a "brownfield" site adjacent to the existing hospital infrastructure, Hexham General makes the most of its resources. Its extremely efficient footprint separates inpatient and outpatient flows to avoid congestion and preserve privacy, replaces the traditional hospital corridor and wards with three fan-shaped nursing units positioned close to surgery and elevator core, and opens separate garden and ground level entrances for service and public/staff access. Patients and families are gratified that its patient-centered interiors offer such amenities as the centralized atrium, which eases the transition from outdoors to indoors, public/patient corridors that incorporate accent colors, natural textures and dramatic lighting to promote wayfinding, and public and patient rooms appointed in comfortable, contemporary furnishings, live plantings and artwork. Reflecting public praise for the new building, the Northumbria Healthcare NHS Trust calls it "one of the country's finest new hospitals."

Above: Exterior.

Opposite above: Atrium.

Opposite below left: Nurse station.

Photography: Paul Bock.

Jonathan Bailey Associates

Children's Cancer Hospital
Cairo, Egypt

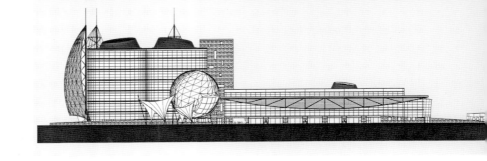

Above: Elevation showing "cloverleaf" nursing unit at left.

Left: Scale model.

Below: Entry lobby.

Photography: Paul Bardagjy.

Whereas about 1 percent of children in America get cancer, the incidence in Egypt is about 6.4 percent, making cancer the number one killer of Egyptian children. To aid the children, the Association of Friends of the National Cancer Institute is now completing The Childrens Cancer Hospital, a 327,369 -square foot, 6-story, 150-bed hospital in Cairo. Designed by Jonathan Bailey Associates, this new hospital will estab-lish the first full-service teaching facility for pediatric oncology in the Middle East. Not only will the facility follow a U.S. health care model while enabling local practices to be implemented, iit will offer many thoughtful features. Examples include a "cloverleaf" nursing unit with three sub-nursing stations and central nursing to monitor all patient rooms (which are equipped to become ICU beds), diagnostic and therapeutic areas located within play areas to ease the discomfort of chemotherapy and other treatments, large waiting areas for families accompanying patients, patient rooms equipped with telephone, Internet and Nintendo access, and a prayer room. Interior design uses bright colors, custom animal and plant-shaped furniture, and other playful furnishings designed for "positive distraction." All this is intended to give new hope to children in the Middle East and North Africa.

Kaplan McLaughlin Diaz

222 Vallejo Street
San Francisco, CA 94111
1.800.822.5191
415.394.7158 (Fax)
www.kmd-arch.com

Kaplan McLaughlin Diaz

Duke University Children's Health Center
Durham, North Carolina

Top: Water fountain scaled for adults and children.

Above left: Atrium balcony.

Above right: Exterior.

Right: Nurses station.

Opposite: Grand Atrium and Family Center.

Photography: Jeff Goldberg/Esto, Larry Hawley.

Children can spot the outdoor play area before entering Duke University's new, 125,000-square foot, five-story Children's Health Center, designed by Kaplan McLaughlin Diaz. Indeed, who could resist such temptations as an interactive water garden, story-telling area, and K's Court, a miniature basketball court named for legendary Duke men's basketball coach Mike Krzyzewski? Such perceptive details typify this joyous, award-winning design, which creates a children's hospital by uniting existing but scattered inpatient, outpatient and diagnostic services for children in a single, recognizable location. Two concepts that drive the facility, encouraging discovery for children and creating flexible modular examination clusters for medical school programs, have resulted in a versatile space centered around a five-story Grand Atrium and Family Center that serves as main entry point and general waiting area. Child-scaled vignettes even make wayfinding through the 128-bed hospital as rewarding as watching the Blue Devils play.

Kaplan McLaughlin Diaz

Harrison Silverdale Healthcare Campus
Silverdale, Washington

An hour's ferry ride southwest of Seattle, the 230,000 residents of Kitsap County, Washington occupy a rugged land settled by self-sufficient loggers and millworkers, but their loyalty to Harrison Hospital dates back to the deadly influenza epidemic of 1918. Today, Harrison is one of the region's busiest medical centers, and the support of mother/baby care, outpatient surgery, rehabilitation services, and urgent care at Harrison Silverdale has been entrusted to a new, 82,000-square foot Women's and Children's Surgery Center and 41,000-square foot Hospital Office Building, both designed by Kaplan McLaughlin Diaz. The 44-bed Center, which includes a birthing facility, medical/surgical neonatal unit, and gynecology/emergency/surgical center with a rehabilitation clinic, is the first phase of a future 250-bed hospital. The hospital's three specialties form a T shape on a sloping site, giving each specialty a separate entry and framing sweeping views of the pine forest, Olympic Mountains, and Puget Sound. Its attractive yet functional interiors, designed to increase operating efficiency 16 percent, resemble a lodge, echoing Kitsap's cultural heritage. The director of facilities happily observes, "From the first day, our community has embraced this facility."

Top: ER entry.
Above right: LDRP room.
Right: Exterior.
Opposite: Birthing Center lobby.
Photography: Lara Swimmer.

Kaplan McLaughlin Diaz

Sutter Maternity and Surgery Center
Santa Cruz, California

Keeping up with a young and diverse population of 50,000 in Santa Cruz, a city halfway between San Francisco and Monterey, has produced a remarkable new facility for perinatal and medical/surgical services, Sutter Maternity and Surgery Center. The award-winning, 63,306-square foot, two-story hospital, designed by Kaplan McLaughlin Diaz, features a birthing center with 12 LDRP rooms, C-section surgical suite, five operating rooms, 18 post-surgical recovery inpatient rooms and a medical office for the Santa Cruz Medical Clinic. Its exceptional environment, combining hotel ambiance with hospital safety and security, began as a quest for an alternative to an existing, religious-sponsored institution that teamed the Clinic, a multi-specialty medical group, with Sutter Health, a not-for-profit, non-religious northern California health care system. Patient and staff input from the two organizations revealed the region's desire for efficient professional care in a home-like, "patient-friendly" setting. The resulting construction, placing physicians' offices and the surgical suite on the first floor, and medical/surgical rooms and LDRP suites on the second floor, anchored by a luminous, two-story high rotunda, was surely a factor when Sutter Santa Cruz recently received the highest patient satisfaction results ever recorded by Parkside Associates, a national patient satisfaction firm.

Above: Exterior.

Right: LDRP room.

Far right: Patient lounge.

Opposite: Waiting room.

Photography: Erich Ansel Koyama Architecture Photography, Whittaker Photography.

Kaplan McLaughlin Diaz

Little Company of Mary Hospital
Hannon Tower
Torrance, California

Continuity and change make odd bedfellows, but the new Hannon Tower, a 22,500-square foot renovation and 123,000-square foot, five-story tower at the campus of Little Company of Mary Hospital in Torrance, California, designed by Kaplan McLaughlin Diaz, shows how felicitous the pairing can be. The project, encompassing lobby/waiting areas, emergency, pharmacy, critical care, labor/delivery and two medical/surgical units, is among the first facilities to have acuity adaptable rooms. Because all toilets are on the exterior wall, corridor partitions can be changed to sliding glass doors to convert beds to high acuity or intensive care at minimal cost. Even so, the design fosters a humanistic environment, in keeping with the four-decade-old campus, extending a warm welcome from the Catholic health ministry of the Little Company of Mary Sisters.

Above: Exterior.

Left: Healing garden.

Far left: Patient room.

Lower left: Nurses station.

Far lower left: Lobby.

Photography: Jeff Goldberg/Esto, Larry Hawley.

Karlsberger Companies

99 E. Main Street
Columbus, OH 43215
614.461.9500
614.461.6324 (Fax)
www.karlsberger.com

Karlsberger Companies

Batchelor Children's Research Institute
University of Miami School of Medicine
Miami, Florida

One of a handful of facilities of its kind, Batchelor Children's Research Institute is a new, 148,000-square foot, nine-story structure consolidating clinical and research components of the prestigious Department of Pediatrics at University of Miami School of Medicine, in Miami, Florida. The award-winning facility, designed by Karlsberger, anchors a newly created quadrangle of research and patient facilities with its distinct blend of Mediterranean Revival and Art Deco architecture, and a graceful, two-story entry pavilion, which extends the lobby. Inside, clinical space is housed on the two lower floors, while research facilities occupy the floors above, encouraging collaboration and communication among scientists in the quest for cures to childhood diseases.

Above: Exterior.
Below left: Lobby and clinic areas.
Right: Pavilion.
Photography: Robert Benson.

Karlsberger Companies

The Children's Hospital of Philadelphia
Philadelphia, Pennsylvania

Images left from top to bottom: Gift shop, new south tower expansion, decentralized charting area, Connelly Resource Center for families.

Photography: Robert Benson, Brad Feinknopf and Gary Knight & Associates.

Ranked as the best children's hospital in the U.S., The Children's Hospital of Philadelphia is driven by its quest to remain on the cutting edge of patient care and reseach; to meet its aggressive demand in growth; and to support its leadership in the implemention of family-centered care. Karlsberger has served Children's Hospital for some 15 years, designing its initial major renovation program, which was completed in 1998. Today, Karlsberger is working with KPF, the architect-of-record, on the South Tower expansion, which will greatly expand its healing environment, defined by color, daylight and movement, while attracting the best staff possible.

Karlsberger Companies

Phoenix Children's Hospital
Phoenix, Arizona

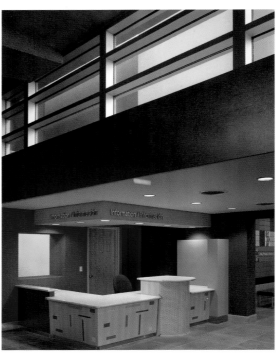

Above left clockwise from upper left: Light tower at entry and reception.

Opposite: Concourse.

Top right: Main entrance.

Right: Universal PICU room.

Photography: Gary Knight & Associates.

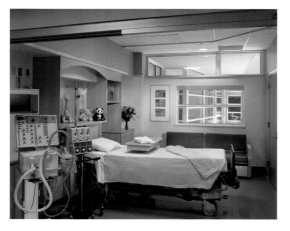

Phoenix Children's Hospital has been remarkably transformed from a hospital within Good Samaritan Hospital to a freestanding institution in its own right. Besides having to add staff, equipment and leadership once shared with Good Samaritan, it needed to develop a new building on a tight schedule and budget. The award-winning facility, created by Karlsberger in association with Stein-Cox Group, designed a new, 307-bed Phoenix Children's Hospital out of a shuttered 1960s adult acute care institution, combining 351,987 square feet of renovation with 38,040 square feet of new construction. Existing random additions, anonymous interiors and poor wayfinding have yielded to a design that features an attractive, central concourse connecting such amenities as waiting areas, family resource center, conference/consult areas and dining, the rich colors and textures of the Southwest, creative daylighting, vibrant public and children's play spaces, and ICUs and inpatient rooms where healing can calmly progress.

Karlsberger Companies

St. Vincent Children's Hospital
Indianapolis, Indiana

It started as a one-floor renovation within an existing building of St. Vincent Hospitals and Health Services in Indianapolis. Now, following comprehensive studies by St. Vincent and Karlsberger, a new, 128,000-square foot, four-story addition is welcoming pediatric patients, families and staff to St. Vincent Children's Hospital. The "children's hospital within a hospital," providing 40 private medical/ surgical beds, 15-bed PICU, 17-bed pediatric ED, outpatient clinic for cancer and blood disease care, family accommodations, playroom, resource center and lobby, is as child-focused as it is technically advanced and cost-effective. The exterior defines the Hospital as a place for children with its bold, playful forms, while the interior is bright, colorful and accommodating.

A healing environment, the three-story lobby helps families orient themselves and patient rooms offer zones for nursing care, family space and private toilet /shower rooms so families know they're welcome.

Top right: Meditation room.
Above: Main entrance.
Above left: Atrium.
Photography: Brad Feinknopf.

Larsen Shein Ginsberg Snyder, LLP

170 Varick Street
New York, NY 10013
212.803.0300
212.803.0370 (Fax)
www.lsgsarchitects.com
email@lsgsarchitects.com

Larsen Shein Ginsberg Snyder, LLP   Dyson Center for Cancer Care
Vassar Brothers Medical Center
Poughkeepsie, New York

Top: Exterior.

Above right: Lounge.

Left: Atrium entrance.

Opposite: Chemotherapy area.

Photography: Chuck Choi.

Creating an oncology facility, where cancer patients receive chemotherapy or radiation treatment, is a formidable challenge. The 42,000-square foot Dyson Center for Cancer Care at Vassar Brothers Medical Center, in Poughkeepsie, New York, serving Hudson Valley residents was designed by Larsen Shein Ginsberg Snyder in association with Perkins Eastman Architects. The project includes 36,000 square feet of new space in a three-story ambulatory oncology pavilion adjacent to the existing hospital, and 6,000 square feet of renovated space, housing two linear accelerators and a simulator. Outside views, natural lighting, comfortable, contemporary furnishings, and an efficient layout where patients with the highest acuity travel the shortest distance help explain why Susan L. Davis, president of Vassar Brothers Medical Center, said, "Every day, as new patients come to receive their treatments, they comment on the comforting and relaxing environment, full of natural light and soft finishes."

Larsen Shein Ginsberg Snyder, LLP   Lauder Center for Maternity Care
Mount Sinai Medical Center
New York, New York

Hospitals are enthusiastically enhancing the birthing experience. At New York's Mount Sinai Medical Center, the new Lauder Center for Maternity Care, designed by Larsen Shein Ginsberg Snyder with Guenther 5 Architects as consultants, minimizes the post-partum floors institutional appearance while maintaining its state-of-the-art capability. In the first of three phases, the design for an 11,920 square foot floor established an ambience between patient rooms, corridors and the nursery area by opening a tightly configured, single corridor space to allow daylight to penetrate from Central Park across Fifth Avenue. In the patient rooms, medical gas and other clinical items were concealed behind a hardwood-paneled head-wall, and a translucent window with curtains was installed between the bedroom and adjoining toilet. The hospitality inspired furnishings evokes a spa-like setting nurturing mothers and infants alike.

Above: Reception.

Opposite Top: Patient room.

Far left: Bathroom in patient's room.

Left: Nursery.

Photography: Paul Warchol.

Larsen Shein Ginsberg Snyder, LLP

Ambulatory Surgery, PACU
Long Island Jewish Medical Center
New Hyde Park, New York

Right: Waiting and play area.
Lower right: PACU.
Bottom right: Recovery space.
Far right: Ambulatory surgery reception.

Photography: Andrea Brizzi.

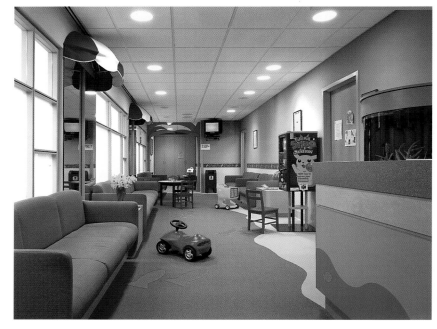

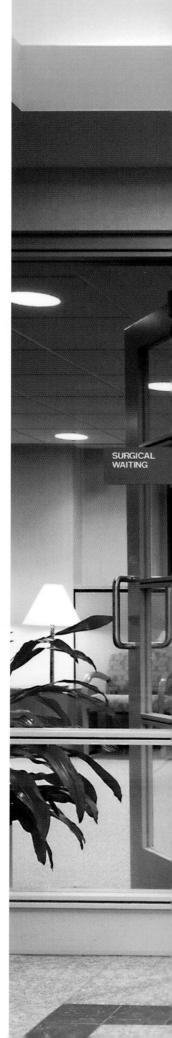

How do you renovate active hospital space without interruption? With care and vision, judging from the successful modernization of 26,000 square feet for the ambulatory surgery and pediatric acute care units at the Long Island Jewish Medical Center, in New Hyde Park, New York, designed by Larsen Shein Ginsberg Snyder. Renovation of the adult area, including the 24-bay ambulatory pre-op and inpatient holding spaces, 19-bay PACU, nurses station, family waiting areas, reception, registration, dressing rooms, on-call rooms, and examination and procedure rooms, cut a 70-foot wide by 295-foot long swath through the first floor necessitating a host of other facility enhancements. The pediatric area contained an 8-bay phase 2 recovery space and a 9-bay PACU, a nurses station, waiting and play area. Yet operations never ceased, thanks to close coordination of pedestrian traffic, the phased remodeling of departments and precise monitoring of off-hour tie-ins. Paul Hochenberg, vice president for administration at Long Island Jewish Medical Center, upon walking through the space, commented, that the result was "a world class space."

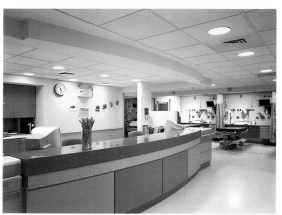

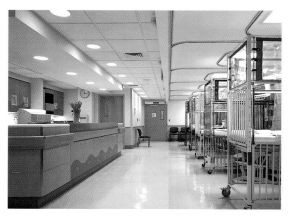

Larsen Shein Ginsberg Snyder, LLP

Major Modernization
St. Francis Hospital
Roslyn, New York

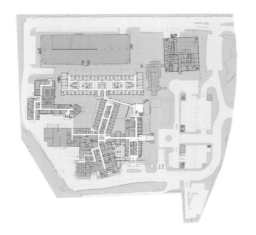

One of America's leading heart hospitals, with the Northeast's highest cardiac caseload, has developed a major modernization plan for its 15-acre suburban campus. Having operated their 279-bed hospital in overcrowded conditions for 10 years, Larsen Shein Ginsberg Snyder was asked to prepare a master plan and design solution for campus-wide improvements. The project adds 155,000 sf of new hospital space, including 200 intensive and acute care beds, 14 operating rooms, 3 cath labs and expanded recovery, support services, non-invasive cardiology and imaging departments. The project renovates 65,000 sf of existing space, adds a 350 car underground garage, modifies the site circulation and upgrades the central plant. The project right-sizes current deficiencies and encourages a patient-focused care environment with bedside services, enhanced staff to patient visualization and improved working environments, while also providing public conveniences such as dedicated parking and easy access to inpatient and outpatient lobbies and services.

Top: Campus site first floor plan.

Above: New patient/visitor drop-off area.

Right: Detail of outpatient lobby addition.

Illustrations: Courtesy of Larsen Shein Ginsberg Snyder.

Marshall Erdman & Associates

5117 University Avenue
P.O. Box 5249
Madison, WI 53705
608.238.0211
608.238.5604 (Fax)
www.erdman.com

Marshall Erdman & Associates

The Health & Wellness Center by Doylestown Hospital
Warrington, Pennsylvania

Patients aren't the only people succumbing to the calming and delightful environment at the Health & Wellness Center by Doylestown Hospital, in Warrington, Pennsylvania, a new, 127,500-square foot, three-story ambulatory clinical space and wellness center, designed by Marshall Erdman & Associates. That's fine with the 40 physicians and staff members operating the five-OR ambulatory surgery center, women's health, diagnostic imaging, orthopedics and sports medicine centers, as well as the wellness center featuring lap pool, whirlpool and therapy pool, day spa, cafe, healing garden and 100-seat auditorium with break-out rooms. The Center's goals of a patient-centered environment, easy wayfinding, convenience for patients and increased market share, are addressed through traditional architecture, *Feng Shui* design elements, hospitality-style interiors, generous daylight and views, and clear spatial organization around a richly landscaped atrium with a two-story waterfall and koi pond. Reporting on the community's response, Robert Bauer, vice president of finance for Doylestown Hospital, says, "Ancillary use has totally surpassed our expectations."

Above left: Atrium.

Above right: Lap pool, whirlpool and therapy pool.

Left: Health Design Center.

Opposite: Exterior.

Photography: Mike Rebholz Photography.

Marshall Erdman & Associates

The Busse Center for Specialty Medicine
Northwest Community Hospital
Arlington Heights, Illinois

Increasingly, medical centers agree: A patient focus is key to today's health care market. Yet paying attention to doctors and other staff members is equally important, as illustrated by 500-bed Northwest Community Hospital's new, 185,000-square foot, eight-story William J. and Marian H. Busse Center for Specialty Medicine and attached 920-car parking structure, in Arlington Heights, Illinois. The attractive design from Marshall Erdman & Associates provides needed expansion space on floors one and two for the Hospital's outpatient services, including cardiology and diagnostics, ultrasound suite, breast center, endoscopy center and laboratory services. Floors three to eight, however, are devoted to medical offices where affiliated physicians can offer a host of services, including pediatrics, OB/GYN, neurology, plastic surgery and urology, in suites adjacent to the hospital. The project's dual nature allows Northwest Community to create centers of excellence through expanded outpatient services and affiliated physicians, establish an upscale, patient-centered environment, operate a readily understood and HIPAA-compliant registration area, and seamlessly integrate new and old construction with clearly identified inpatient and outpatient entrances bringing out the best in both patients and physicians.

Above: Stairs to women's health center.

Opposite: Monumental stairs.

Right: Exterior

Below Right: Recovery

Photography: Mike Rebholz Photography

Marshall Erdman & Associates

Cleveland Clinic Florida
Naples, Florida

Above: Exterior.

Opposite above: Main lobby.

Opposite below left: Inpatient room.

Opposite below right: Inpatient room.

Photography: Mike Rebholz Photography.

The coming of the prestigious Cleveland Clinic to Florida in 1988, bringing world-class medical diagnosis and treatment to an affluent and sophisticated population in Fort Lauderdale, was so enthusiastically received that Cleveland Clinic Florida has expanded to Naples. Here, the Clinic's new, 195,000-square foot, 70-bed inpatient hospital and 184,000-square foot, multi-specialty clinic, both four-story structures designed by Marshall Erdman & Associates, are connected by a two-story surgical and diagnostic spine, and by a common approach to their interiors. As a result of Marshall Erdman's patented *Healing Hospitality*® design technique, hospital and clinic maintain a continuous, patient-centered environment where patient rooms have "family zones" for family members, bathrooms are detailed to reduce the risk of injuries, and hospitality-style interiors calm and reassure patients and families drawn here from around the world.

Marshall Erdman & Associates

Institute for Orthopaedics and Neurosurgery
Bend, Oregon

By the time the 129,000-square foot, three-story structure is ready, the Institute for Orthopaedics and Neurosurgery, in Bend, Oregon, intends to be the premier regional facility of its kind in central Oregon. Its claim will rest primarily on its personnel, of course, who will have access to such facilities as four ORs, two procedure rooms, 64 examination rooms, diagnostic imaging, physical therapy and rehabilitation, sports medicine, orthotics and prosthetics, registration, waiting areas, offices and a cafe. Yet its spatial organization will play a vital, supporting role, providing designated entries for core clinical operations, affiliated but independent health care providers, and surgery and diagnostic components, and the introduction of 16 clinical pods, each comprising four examination rooms, one procedure room, and workspaces for the physician and medical assistant. And its visual environment will embrace the central Oregon vernacular with a comfortable, attractive and patient-centered setting of wood, stone, glass and water features much like the natural surroundings outside its windows.

Top: Front elevation.

Above: Registration.

Right: Aerial view of circular drive.

Illustrations: Marshall Erdman & Associates.

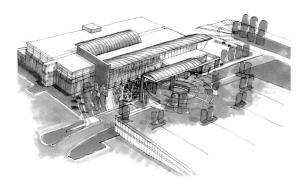

Matthei & Colin Associates

332 S. Michigan Avenue, Suite 614
Chicago, IL 60604
312.939.4002
312.939.8164 (Fax)
www.mca-architecture.com

Matthei & Colin Associates

Edward Heart Hospital
Naperville, Illinois

A quiet revolution in heart care is taking place just 1/2 mile south of downtown Naperville, Illinois at Edward Heart Hospital, part of the Edward Hospital campus of Edward Hospital & Health Services, a not-for-profit, regional health care provider based in Naperville that serves the western suburbs of Chicago. Patients, families and friends may suspect that the new, 153,565-square foot, five-story, 71-bed facility, designed by Matthei & Colin Associates, is not a typical hospital as soon as they enter the building, because a waterfall, koi pond and healing garden are located just outside the lobby, some patient rooms display outdoor balconies, and the lobby is furnished with a fireplace, spiral staircase, cherry wood millwork and abundant natural light. Delightful as these amenities are, they represent just one facet of many in a program establishing Edward as a dedicated "hospital within a hospital" for the delivery of cardiovascular services that de-institutionalizes the patient experience and provides a more holistic, positive patient outcome. "Opening Edward Heart Hospital is a big step toward realizing our dream of bringing focused, world-class heart care to the western suburbs," says Pamela Meyer Davis, president and CEO of Edward Hospital & Health Services. "We want to be the regional provider of choice for cardiovascular services. We will redefine

everything from paperwork to patient rooms to deliver truly people-friendly heart care. We have a tremendous cardiovascular program at Edward that now has a facility worthy of its growing stature." The strategy involves such key tactics as implementing a relationship-based model of care to enhance communications between patients/families and their caregivers, providing patient-centric amenities enhancing both the physical facilities and operations, improving physician access

to electronic medical records, clinical technologies and resources and clearly delineating outpatient services and parking for visitors. It's a tall order, to be sure. But Edward which comprises a 15-bed CCU, two 28-bed, private room inpatient units, plus three ORs, four catheter laboratories and such support facilities as MRI, CT scanners, nuclear medicine, outpatient clinics, rehabilitation and physicians' offices is up to the task. A key feature is that each inpatient unit is

tended by several decentralized nursing stations with adjacent lounges where family members can meet the nursing staff to discuss the patient's well-being and follow-up care at home, removing clinical conversation from the patient room and preventing possible disruption of care. It's not the only way the patient's family is encouraged to participate in patient care. Such patient room features as the discreetly hidden equipment, natural lighting, and handsome interior

appointments that include cherry wood paneling, sconce lighting, and convertible banquette, which unfolds for overnight stays, appeal as much to family as to the patient. Outside the patient room, family rooms on each floor allow family members to sit quietly, watch TV, share experiences, and prepare food in the kitchen facilities, patient floor lounges host special events such as concerts by professional musicians, and supplementary amenities like the healing garden help increase the patient's sense of autonomy and intellectual stimulation. "We believe that your surroundings can affect the healing process," Davis declares. "The more you feel like you're at home, the more comfortable you are and the faster you may heal." Seldom is this concept expressed more eloquently than at Edward Heart Hospital, which recently received 1st place in the Healthcare Environment Awards from Contract Magazine and the Center for Health Design.

Mitchell Associates

One Avenue of the Arts
Wilmington, DE 19801
302.594.9400
302.594.9420 (Fax)
www.mitchellai.com

Mitchell Associates

Children's Medical Center of Dallas
Dallas, Texas

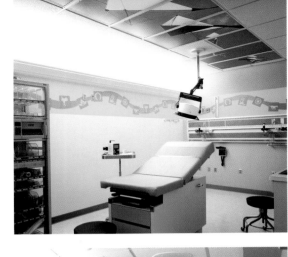

Upper right: Examination room.

Right: Corridor.

Lower right: Employee recognition display

Bottom right: Patient room.

Opposite: Artwork at nurses' station.

Photography: Scott Williams.

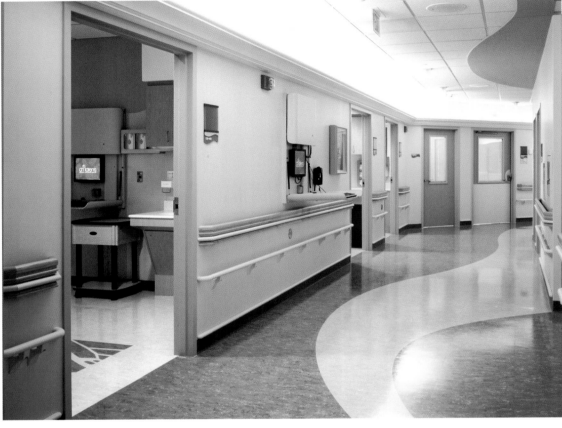

The only health care facility in Dallas dealing exclusively with a variety of diseases and disorders among children from birth to age 18, Children's Medical Center of Dallas is a respected institution that's expanding simply to keep up with the rapidly growing pediatric population of north Texas. A recent, 159,630-square foot, six-floor renovation and addition, designed by Mitchell Associates, is an exceptional contribution to this ongoing effort. In 88 acute care rooms, 44 critical care rooms and support spaces, children, families and staff occupy a warm, friendly and "child-right" environment that addresses children's needs while promoting effective infection control. Private rooms, for example, are configured to ensure a child/family-focused experience,"Texas icons" serve as wayfinding, artwork and decorative symbols, and fiber optic ceiling treatments help to soften the institutional setting details that help keep the nearly 90-year-old referral hospital as youthful as its patients.

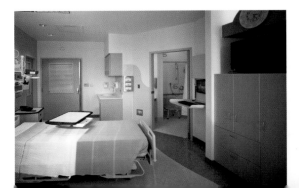

Mitchell Associates

Louise Obici Memorial Hospital
Suffolk, Virginia

Above left: Admitting area.

Above right: Nurses' station.

Top right: Chapel.

Right: History display.

Opposite: Atrium.

Photography: Barry Halkin Photography.

Residents of greater Suffolk, Virginia who entrust their health to Louise Obici Memorial Hospital are the beneficiaries of a generous fellow citizen, Amedeo Obici, founder of Planter's Peanuts. Not only did the Obici Charitable Trust, established to memorialize Obici's wife Louise, finance the original hospital that opened in 1951, it continues its support through the recent completion of the award-winning, 365,000-square foot, three-story, 130-bed replacement hospital, designed by Mitchell Associates. The new structure, organized around a three-story atrium and entrance rotunda with patient wings that extend gracefully from family center waiting areas, sustains a hotel-like environment incorporating the Planetree concept of patient-centered care. Bill Giermak, CEO of Obici Health System, proudly reports, "People comment that the facility looks more like a hotel or shopping mall."

Mitchell Associates

Upper Chesapeake Medical Center
Bel Air, Maryland

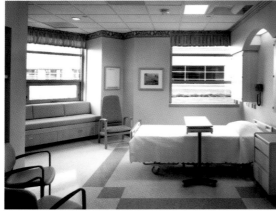

Top: Nurses' station.

Center: Cafeteria.

Above: Patient room.

Right: Three-story atrium.

Photography: Barry Halkin Photography.

Hospital patients often require more than medical attention, so Upper Chesapeake Medical Center's new, 280,000-square foot, two-story, 120-bed replacement hospital in Bel Air, Maryland, has developed a physical setting that also supports their emotional well-being. In fact, Harford County's leading acute care hospital offers an exceptional environment, designed by Mitchell Associates, with such amenities as special areas in patient rooms where family members can stay overnight, carpeted public areas with indirect lighting, soothing colors and warm wood finishes, a HealthLink Community Resource Center giving patients and families health information and Internet connections, and private consultation areas for physicians and family members to discuss patients' care. Commenting on the new facilities, Lyle Sheldon, president of Upper Chesapeake Health, calls the new hospital "a jewel for the community we serve."

Mitchell Associates

Duke University Medical Center and Duke Children's Hospital & Health Center
Durham, North Carolina

"We wish to thank...." Like, Duke Children's Hospital, a respected provider of comprehensive medical and surgical services for infants, children, and adolescents in Durham, North Carolina, publicly acknowledges the benefactors whose generosity is often critical to its success. In a recent example, donors helped finance and operate Duke's new,125,000 -square foot, five-story Children's Health Center, part of Duke University Medical Center. Accordingly, Duke retained Mitchell Associates to create indoor and outdoor donor recognition displays that would complement the new facility's architecture. Requirements for the displays were more demanding than a casual onlooker might realize: to express permanence yet remain flexible to accommodate regular changes, recognize employee contributions with interactive wall displays that children and visitors could change, and supplement the interior wayfinding system. The results are enlivening the environment in ways children of all ages can appreciate.

Top: The Welcome Center sign combines donor recognition and wayfinding.

Above: Transparent panels bearing donor names overlay photographs of campus architecture.

Right: Wall designates Children's Play Area and donor.

Far right: Interchangeable wall graphics.

Photography: Chris Hildreth/Duke University Photography.

272

Moon Mayoras Architects, Inc.

655 "G" Street, Suite A
San Diego, CA 92101
619.235.9780
619.235.9773 (Fax)
www.moonmayoras.com

Moon Mayoras Architects, Inc.

Three Rivers Community Hospital and Health Center
Grants Pass, Oregon

A new source of pride for Grants Pass, Oregon, the gateway to the Rogue River, a world-famous fishing and rafting waterway, has nothing and everything to do with the scenic north end of the Rogue Valley. The development of Three Rivers Community Hospital and Health Center, a 196,000-square foot, three-story, 98-bed facility designed by Moon Mayoras Architects, Inc. for Asante Health System, enlisted broad community support to merge two aging hospitals to form a modern and more effective one. One obvious product of the new hospital's economical, braced-frame construction, which constitutes a hospital,

two medical office buildings, cancer center and central power plant, is a 300-foot long, 30-foot wide, two-story lobby offering dramatic views of the surrounding mountains. Indeed, nature is present throughout the therapeutic environment at Three Rivers, which uses the convergence of three rivers in Grants Pass as a metaphor for its floors. The first floor evokes the Rogue River, a mighty, active river used by many people, in its public areas, administration and support services, the second floor reflects the Illinois River, a smaller yet spirited river, in its family birthing, surgery, critical care, and areas of respite, while the third floor emulates the Applegate River, a quiet river, in its patient care units. Noting the widespread popularity of Three Rivers, Paul Janke, hospital administrator, predicts, "This new hospital will make Grants Pass a much more livable and desirable place to be."

Above: Main entrance.
Opposite upper right: Lobby.
Opposite lower left: Braced frame in lobby.
Opposite lower right: Birthing room.
Photography: Lanphier Associates.

Moon Mayoras Architects, Inc.

Chandler Regional Hospital
Chandler, Arizona

Chandler Regional Hospital has enjoyed a well-earned reputation for maintaining quality care in the region surrounding Chandler, Arizona since it opened in 1961, even in the face of continuous population growth across the East Valley. The recent, 50,480-square foot project provides 28 new medical beds and 28 new surgical beds. Designed by Moon Mayoras Architects, Inc. this project typifies its pragmatic yet family centered approach to facility management. Since each irregularly shaped existing floor plate could not be readily converted into a single patient care unit, the

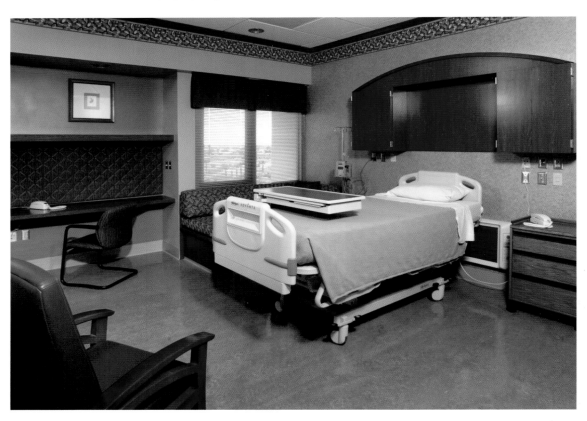

design solution establishes three separate nurse stations, so each floor can be flexibly used as one, two or three distinct units. This decentralized arrangement, furnished with calming and tasteful interiors, such as patient rooms with family desk areas, custom millwork, built-in furniture, wall sconces and warm, natural colors, not only compensates for the irregular floors, it affords patients the personalized care they've come to expect at Chandler Regional Hopsital.

Top: Patient room.

Above left: Fourth floor family waiting area.

Above right: Nurse station.

Photography: Denny Collins/DC Photography.

Moon Mayoras Architects, Inc.

Grossmont Spring Valley Family Health Center
Spring Valley, California

Top: Main entrance.

Above: Small "houses" for internal play.

Photography: M. Christina Mayoras.

Families without health insurance in metropolitan San Diego have depended on the Family Health Centers of San Diego for nearly three decades. This federally funded network, comprised of numerous primary care clinics throughout the County of San Diego, mobile medical units and other sites providing ancillary services, recently retained Moon Mayoras Architects, Inc. to design its 8,000-square foot, one-story Grossmont Spring Valley Family Health Center in Spring Valley, with the goal of creating a visual presence in the community, as well as a more efficient and appealing environment for patients and staff. The results have worked wonders for the Center, which includes 12 examination rooms, a procedure room, laboratory/specimen drawing area, outpatient registration and offices/support space. The new exterior is playful and responsive to its site, and the new interior offers efficient staff flow, bright and cheerful furnishings, an interior garden, and a water element in the waiting room that provides a sense of comfort to everyone who experiences it.

Moon Mayoras Architects, Inc.

Lucy Curci Cancer Center
Eisenhower Medical Center
Rancho Mirage, California

As the only not-for-profit hospital serving the desert resort communities of California's Coachella Valley, Eisenhower Medical Center has provided high quality, compassionate care for 30 years to residents and visitors through a full range of state-of-the-art diagnostic, treatment and emergency facilities. The 100-acre medical complex, a cherished, local landmark inaugurated by comedian Bob Hope and his wife Dolores and named in honor of President Dwight D. Eisenhower, who lived part time in the Coachella Valley during retirement, operates such impressive facilities as the 261-bed Eisenhower Memorial Hospital, Annenberg Center for Health Sciences, Barbara Sinatra Children's Center, Betty Ford Center, and Charles and Kay Hanson Birthing Center. The recent renovation and expansion of the former Heart Institute of the Desert to become the new, 80,565-square foot, two-story Lucy Curci Cancer Center, designed by Moon Mayoras Architects Inc., enhances Eisenhower's cancer care by combining all comprehensive outpatient cancer services at one convenient, fully integrated location. The facilty is named in honor of Coachella Valley real estate developer John Curci's late wife Lucy. The facility houses an outpatient imaging center, radiation oncology, infusion therapy center, breast center and central plant within an existing, pre-cast concrete exterior that could not be substantially altered. The interior, by contrast, has been noticeably transformed into a patient-friendly environment through the use of warm and inviting colors and finishes, natural and indirect lighting, lush indoor plantings, comfortable, ergonomic furniture and such focal points as the

Above: Reception area.

Right: Waiting room.

Opposite: Main lobby and water wall.

Photography: Steve McClelland Photography, Vic Hernandez.

views of the Center's healing garden through its windows and the majestic, indoor water wall whose visual and audible presence has proved to be soothing to both patients and staff. Thus, patients in need of such services as radiation therapy, stereotactic radiotherapy to the brain, high dose rate radiation therapy, 3-D conformal radiation therapy, chemotherapy, immunotherapy, gene therapy, autologous bone marrow transplant, anti-angiogenesis drugs, monoclonal antibodies, genetic testing, or clinical trials can now immerse themselves in an optimal setting that helps them cope with the stress and discomfort of cancer treatment.

NBBJ

111 S. Jackson Street
Seattle, WA 98104
206.223.5555

www.nbbj.com
health@nbbj.com

Beijing
Columbus
London
Los Angeles
New York
San Francisco
Seattle

NBBJ

Swedish Medical Center, Cancer Institute
Seattle, Washington

Early cancer detection, advances in cancer treatment and innovative methods of caring for cancer patients are raising cancer survival rates nationwide, prompting the Swedish Medical Center to continue setting Seattle's highest standards for cancer care by upgrading its oncology facilities. The challenge confronting the Swedish Cancer Institute, which opened in 1932 as the first cancer care center west of the Mississippi, has been to create the "beautiful garden" sought by doctors, staff and patients on a tight downtown site bounded by an existing 14-story medical pavilion, parking lot, and one-story, drive-up bank. The Institute's handsome new, 92,055-square foot, structure, designed by NBBJ, is the product of close consultations between the architect and numerous user groups and patients. Here, patients find not only leading cancer specialists, comprehensive treatment, and state-of-the-art facilities, but also the "urban oasis" everyone wants.

Top: Entrance.
Above left: Infusion area.
Opposite: Outdoor garden.
Photography: Assassi Productions (top), Dominic Arizona Bonucelli (bottom).

NBBJ

Southcentral Foundation
Primary Care Center II
Anchorage, Alaska

When the Southcentral Foundation developed downtown Anchorage's Primary Care Center in the mid-1990s, planners knew patient volume at the adjacent Alaska Native Medical Center would cause the PCC to rapidly outgrow its own space. In just four years ANMC saw patient volume reach 350,000 visits — 250,000 more than its intended capacity. This surge in demand, caused by population growth and the trend among Alaska Natives to move from rural villages to Anchorage, encouraged the Foundation to build its new, 60,000-square foot addition, designed by NBBJ, to the PCC's existing 40,000-square foot facility. Phase II of the PCC represents a fascinating, transformational environment where traditional Native Alaskan healing combines with Western medical care. As the PCC's main gathering place, the entrance lobby linking the PCC's two clinic buildings uses the curvilinear geometry of two sweeping arcs of structural timber to define a space endowed with daylight, open views and carefully chosen Native artwork. This welcoming gesture is carried throughout the PCC, which now includes a patient resource center and Internet cafe along with needed additional room for such ongoing programs as family medicine, pediatrics, women's health and Native healing practices, embracing patients arriving from as close as nearby neighborhoods and as far as remote villages.

Top: Entrance.

Upper left: Patient resource center.

Left: View from entrance lobby.

Opposite: Entrance lobby and reception desk.

Photography: Assassi Productions

NBBJ

Promedica Bay Park Community Hospital
Toledo, Ohio

Above left: Entrance.

Top right: Nurse stations.

Above right: View of patient room.

Photography: Brad Feinknopf (left), Paul Wardnol (right top/bottom).

More than a health care treatment center, the new, 294,777-square foot, Bay Park Community Hospital, in Toledo, Ohio, designed by NBBJ, is also a community destination where people gather for educational programs, community events and recreational activities. Consequently, the idea of making connections is expressed in the meandering outdoor pathways, dubbed the "braid," that link adjacent neighborhoods to the hospital, as well as the central interior circulation spine. Yet Bay Park is very much concerned with supporting patients, families and staff. Such elements as generous windows in patient rooms, lobby and family waiting areas at the ends of corridors, a fireplace and lounge seating in the main lobby, patient rooms with space for families and personal storage, and an attractive cafeteria and coffee bar are among the ways the hospital creates a healing environment. This is making friends among both patients and health care professionals including 10,000 residents who visited on opening day.

NBBJ

Promedica Toledo Hospital
Emergency Pavilion
Toledo, Ohio

Managing 75,000 annual visits, Toledo Hospital's emergency department, a Level One trauma center, was handling one-third more patients than it was designed for. However, alleviating the ED went beyond augmenting its capacity. To accommodate new technology and care giver practices, enhance flexibility and increase patient and family satisfaction, the hospital asked NBBJ to design a new, 56,000-square foot, building adjacent to the existing hospital. The new ED provides 52 new examination rooms and a radiology suite, improves parking and incorporates "non-specialized" rooms to anticipate future changes in medical technology and practice. Patients and families appreciate the changes and the calming atmosphere of pleasing materials, colors and forms that surrounds them once they arrive in the sunlit, two-story main waiting room.

Top right: Examination rooms.

Above left: Entrance.

Above right: Main waiting room.

Photography: Brad Feinknopf

287

NBBJ

United States Navy, Naval Hospital Bremerton
Clinic Addition and Renovation
Bremerton, Washington

The Naval Hospital in Bremerton, Washington is praised for demonstrating how health care can be delivered throughout the armed forces, and the new, 220,450-square foot Clinic Addition and Renovation, designed by NBBJ, aptly displays the Hospital's philosophy. Commenting on the project's advanced medical technology and healing environment, Rear Admiral Donald Arthur recently said, "I have toured this facility and am in awe."

Left: Waiting room.
Below left: Resource center.
Below right: Cafe.
Photography: Assassi Productions.

Odell Associates Inc.

525 North Tyron Street
Charlotte, NC 28202
704.414.1000
704.414.1111 (Fax)
www.odell.com

Odell Associates Inc.

The Johns Hopkins Hospital
Comprehensive Cancer Center
Baltimore, Maryland

Right: Hospital campus.

Below right: Post-operative area.

Bottom: Exterior.

Opposite: Atrium.

Photography: Tim Buchman.

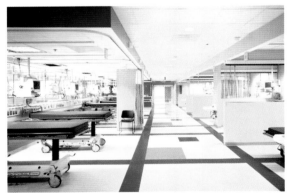

While the stately exterior of the new Harry and Jeanette Weinberg Building, part of the Sidney Kimmel Comprehensive Cancer Center at Baltimore's legendary Johns Hopkins Hospital, honors campus architectural tradition by using brick and precast concrete, the lively interior of the 400,000-square foot, five-story structure, designed by Odell Associates, honors another Johns Hopkins tradition by embodying the most progressive concepts available in cancer treatment design. Facilities for five linear accelerators, outpatient and inpatient chemotherapy, oncology outpatient programs, 140 inpatient beds, 16 operating rooms, 20 surgical intensive /intermediate care beds, and such support services as blood bank, radiology and central sterilization reflect timely suggestions from key user groups. Consequently, there are departmental adjacencies based on efficient flows of people and materials, medical services separated by level, spatial identities reinforced by design themes and visual cues. Standard building materials are chosen for value, maintenance and durability, while interior design that promotes wayfinding and healing. Two landscaped, three-story atriums include reception and family waiting rooms that extend an unexpectedly sunny welcome.

Odell Associates Inc.

Shriners Hospital for Children
Boston, Massachusetts

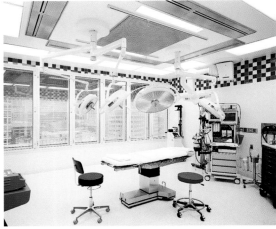

Top right: Operating room.
Above left: Exterior.
Above right: Entrance lobby.
Opposite: Completed hospital.
Photography: Tim Buchman.

Tumultuous technological advances and procedural changes have made replacement hospitals commonplace in recent years. But few are likely to confront what Boston's respected Shriners Hospital for Children faced. Not only would a new, 200,000 square foot, 8-story, 30-bed pediatric burn hospital, designed by Odell Associates, have to fit a tight urban site, but it would also be constructed above the existing facility, which would remain fully operational until its replacement was ready. Three key design determinants were land and relocation costs, as well as Shriners' desire to maintain its below street-level link to Massachusetts General Hospital. A phased construction schedule was developed to perform this exacting operation, starting when a platform of steel trusses was erected above the existing building. Once construction above the truss level was completed, ongoing hospital functions relocated to the new upper levels, the existing building was demolished, and the new lower levels were built. More importantly for children and families, the new Shriners provides a colorful, patient-friendly and modern environment where children's acute burns, "healed" burns, severe scarring of limbs and scarring and deformity of the face can be treated.

Odell Associates Inc.

Sentara Careplex Hospital
Hampton, Virginia

Growing demand for health care services in Virginia's Hampton Roads community has seen the replacement of an aging outpatient ambulatory surgical center in Hampton expand into Sentara Healthcare's new, full-service Sentara Careplex Hospital, a 330,000-square foot, five-story, 196-inpatient bed facility, designed by Odell Associates. The award-winning facility, which includes an emergency room, operating rooms, inpatient private bedrooms, ICU, CCU, PACU, LDR, radiology imaging services, EP and catheter laboratories, conference center, cafeteria and supporting services, is characterized by the use of efficient, large nursing units on inpatient floors, and the development of a healing environment based on an aquatic theme, reflecting local geography and culture. Its patient-centered focus is evident when patients and families enter the main lobby to find public functions and outpatient services conveniently organized along a pedestrian mall, and proceed to the warm, spa-like inpatient areas housed in two masses flanking a garden courtyard.

Above: Exterior.
Left: Nursing station.
Below left: Entrance.
Opposite: Main lobby.
Photography: Photo Reflections.

Odell Associates Inc.

Bon Secours St. Francis Medical Center
Midlothian, Virginia

A health care institution with a discernible tie between indoors and outdoors will dramatically distinguish the new, 225,000-square foot, five-story, 130-inpatient bed Bon Secours St. Francis Medical Center, in Midlothian, Virginia. The presence of a healing garden and labyrinth at the replacement hospital designed by Odell Associates, along with a chapel in the lobby atrium, is a natural extension of the image of St. Francis. Not only is this consistent with the hospital's membership in the Bon Secours Health System, a Catholic health care ministry headquartered in Marriottsville, Maryland, that operates health care facilities in nine states. It's also a practical response to a wooded, rolling terrain that the Center wants to develop with minimal disruption, which will result in multiple entry points at three distinct levels, public spaces with direct outdoor access, and architecture with a traditional feel.

Top: Interior

Above left: Corridor

Above right: Exterior

Illustration: Courtesy of Odell Associates.

OWP/P

111 West Washington Street
Suite 2100
IL, 60602
312.332.9600
312.332.9601 (Fax)
www.owpp.com

OWP/P

Sherman Hospital Ambulatory Care Center
Elgin, Illinois

A plea in the newspapers of Elgin, Illinois over a century ago "Women of Elgin, young and old, rich and poor, married and single, come let us reason together, and lend a hand in the world's great work" resulted in establishing a local hospital as the first priority for the fledgling Elgin Woman's Club. Club members set to work building public support for their cause, and Sherman Hospital opened on July 7, 1888, in a two-story house donated by local drug store owner Henry Sherman. Today, Sherman Hospital has grown to 353 beds, one of the largest medical facilities in the northwest suburbs of Chicago. It remains no less determined than its founders as it upgrades its services through a new 80,000-square foot, two-story Ambulatory Care Center and 30,000-square foot Medical Office Building, designed by OWP/P. The addition completes the reorganization of Sherman Hospital by bringing together such outpatient services as an outpatient chemotherapy unit, pre-procedure and recovery, patient registration and gift shop on the first floor, a new cardiology unit

Top: Garden.

Above left: Entrance.

Opposite: New entry.

Photography: Chris Barrett/ Hedrich-Blessing.

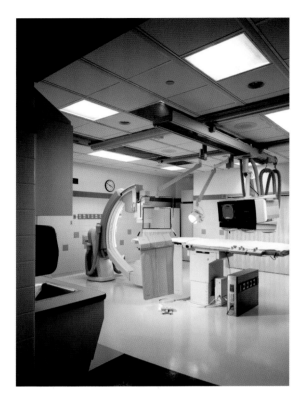

with three catheterization and two EP laboratories on the second floor, and a 200-seat conference room on the lower level. Not only are the ACC and MOB conveniently connected at the first and second floors, enabling patients to undergo all outpatient services, from office visits through testing, under one roof; they are also linked to two existing buildings to define a new courtyard. The addition alters the campus landscape in more subtle ways as well. Patients and visitors invariably sense a fresh, patient-focused approach to good wayfinding, natural light, views to nature, and architecture that reduces anxiety and builds confidence as soon as they encounter the Hospital's new entrance, which projects a strong sense of place. As patients leave the reception desk in the skylit atrium or adjoining waiting room, the scale is reduced, privacy is increased, and the design of the public and clinical spaces they encounter combines colors, forms and furnishings to sustain a world of perma-nence and security around them. The administrative director of clinical services happily confirms, "The design is extremely patient-focused and it makes it easy for our patients to access services."

Above: Cardiology suite.

Right: Waiting area.

Opposite: Connection to existing hospital.

OWP/P

Northwestern Community Hospital
Replacement Cafeteria
Arlington Heights, Illinois

Right: Entrance to cafeteria.

Bottom: Exterior of cafeteria.

Photography: Craig Dubin at Hedrich-Blessing.

Staff recruitment and retention problems recently turned the replacement of a tired, existing cafeteria at Northwestern Community Hospital, a respected, 500-bed hospital in Arlington Heights, Illinois, into a critical symbolic gesture to the staff. Although the new space, a former surgical suite at the juncture of four different building expansions, was far from ideal, the centrally located, 15,750-square foot, 340-seat cafeteria designed by OWP/P succeeds by turning liabilities into assets. The lack of windows, disparate floor levels, oddly placed columns and low ceilings are all factored into the new, elegant, restaurant-like environment. Multi-level ceiling planes, a 168-foot x 28-foot skylight, and relatively open spaces that include a servery, two rotundas with water features, and three dining areas that can be used for special events during normal food service, are imaginatively interpreted with understated color, lighting, form, texture and furnishings that make the new cafeteria a favorite place for bridal showers and monthly doctors' dinners.

OWP/P

Lutheran General Hospital
Surgery Expansion
Park Ridge, Illinois

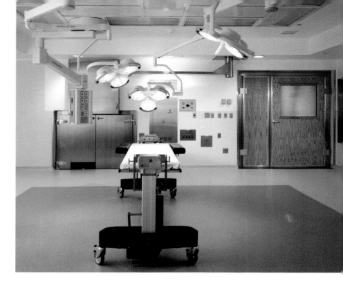

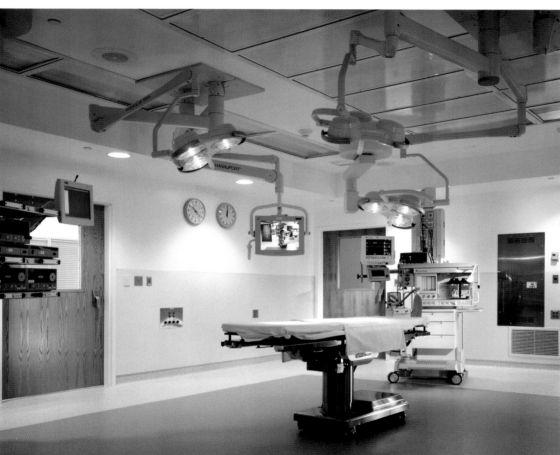

Above: View of OR-1 OR and equipment room.

Left: OR-1 OR with building systems controls.

Below: Pediatric acute care unit.

Photography: Chris Barrett/Hedrich Blessing (surgery suite), Jon Miller /Hedrich Blessing (PACU).

To become a leader in minimally invasive surgery for pediatric patients, Lutheran General Hospital, in Park Ridge, Illinois, recently worked with OWP/P to convert former office space into a 3,550-square foot pediatric acute care unit and a 5,570-square foot surgical suite serving children and adults. The facility's key elements are an OR-1 fully integrated operating room, which incorporates significant amounts of high-technology equipment, conduit and wiring to conduct endoscopic or minimally invasive surgery, and an intraoperative MRI, a fully shielded room designed to take MRIs right before and immediately after neurosurgery. Despite the complexities of threading new technology into old infrastructure, the results are clean, organized and optimal for infection control.

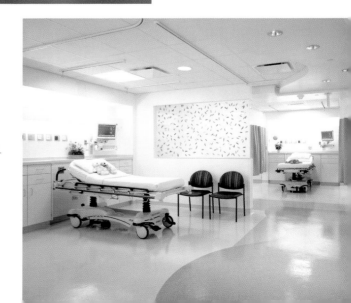

OWP/P

Banner Good Samaritan Medical Center
Emergency Generator Plant, Chiller Plant
Phoenix, Arizona

Right: Interior of chiller plant.
Below: Rooftop condensers.
Photography: OWP/P.

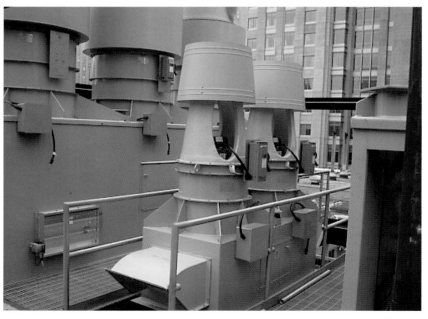

Recent additions and renovations at Banner Good Samaritan Medical Center in Phoenix, Arizona, totaling 305,000 square feet of space for ambulatory care, imaging, cardiology, inpatient tower and neonatal ICU expansion, prompted a thorough evaluation of the Center's facility infrastructure with OWP/P. The goals established in the review--enhanced access to emergency power, new electrical service, new chilled water plant and additional upgrades have been met by an award-winning project creating a new emergency generator plant, featuring two 1000 KW paralleled natural gas generators for chiller back-up and peak shaving, and a new chiller plant, incorporating five 1000-ton chillers in a conversion from constant flow to primary-secondary variable flow.

Perkins Eastman

115 Fifth Avenue
New York, NY 10003
212.353.7200
212.353.7676 (Fax)
www.perkinseastman.com

Charlotte
Chicago
Pittsburgh
San Francisco
Stamford
Toronto

Perkins Eastman

The Cardiac and Vascular Institute at New York University Medical Center New York, New York

Despite formidable programmatic challenges, a splendid, new central gateway to the diagnostic, treatment and support services at New York University Medical Center's respected Cardiac and Vascular Institute is now a reality with the completion of the 12,000-square foot Jean & David Blechman Cardiac and Vascular Center. The award-winning design pays close attention to such issues as patient flow, staffing needs and security. A visible outcome of this concern is the gracious environment, inspired by a hospitality design model.

The project includes the lobby, registration and resource areas, private and semi-private inpatient rooms, modalities for stress testing, echo-cardiogram facilities, cardiovascular testing room, vascular laboratory, and cardiac catheterization prep and recovery space. The use of sophisticated furnishings, subtle lighting design and original artwork allows the Center to put patients at ease the moment they enter the space.

Above: Examination rooms.

Left: Nurses station and recovery space.

Photography: Chuck Choi.

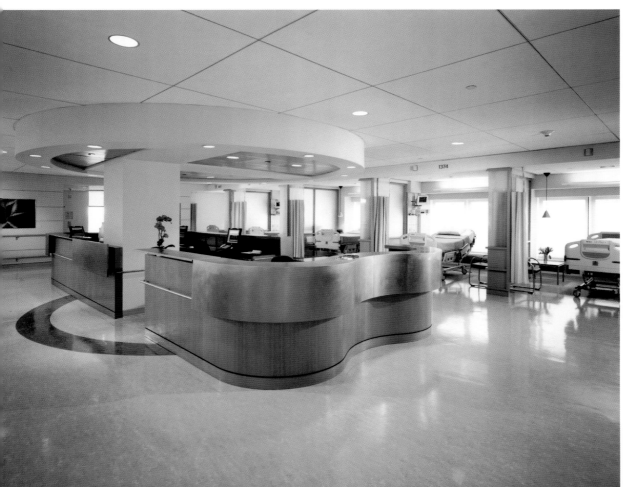

Above: Circulation spine.

Left: Stress testing room.

Below: Inpatient room.

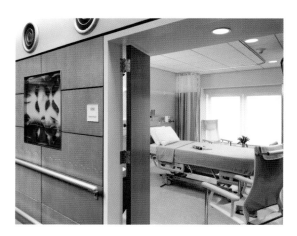

Perkins Eastman

Vassar Brothers Hospital
Comprehensive Cancer Center
Poughkeepsie, New York

Few centenarians may be as vivacious as Vassar Brothers Medical Center, founded in 1887 by the Vassar brothers, John Guy and Matthew Jr., in Poughkeepsie, New York. The regional medical center's current capital improvement program dates back to 1997, when the development of its expanded outpatient cancer treatment facility began. The program's goal, to provide Hudson Valley residents with the caliber of health services found at premier medical institutions, has been significantly advanced with the new, 32,000-square foot, three-story Dyson Center for Cancer Care, designed by Perkins Eastman Architects in association with Larsen Shein Ginsberg & Snyder. The award-winning ambulatory oncology pavilion comprises a generous atrium entrance and hospitality spaces, chemotherapy areas, patient examination and treatment areas, medical offices, conference facilities, cancer library and expansion space. Its hospitality-styled look sustains a positive, stress-reducing environment, reflecting research cited by Susan Davis, president of Vassar Brothers Medical Center, that patients heal more successfully in settings offering the physical and emotional support that the Dyson Center provides in abundance.

Above left: Lounge.
Left: Chemotherapy area.
Below: Exterior.
Opposite: Atrium entrance.
Photography: Chuck Choi

THE
DYSON CENTER
FOR
CANCER CARE

Hospitals may serve forever, but changing populations, medical discoveries, therapeutic innovations and technological advances all but ensure that their buildings have a life expectancy of about 60 years. For the M5 wing of New York Presbyterian Hospital, designed as a maternity ward in 1932 for one of the most comprehensive university hospitals in the world, its conversion to a 5,500-square foot executive suite, conference room/ library, residency administrator's facility, chief resident's office and a staff library, started with demolition that exposed the original concrete and steel structure. The new facility meets the client's desire for a unique space that meets hospital standards through a light-filled, airy milieu, characterized by stone paving, high ceilings, contemporary furnishings, glass clerestories, frosted glass sidelights and doors, and maple and mahogany millwork, all appropriate for an institution whose roots began with a Royal Charter granted by King George III of England in 1771 and the generosity of prominent New York philanthropist James Lenox in 1868.

Above: Conference room/ library.

Left, opposite above, opposite below: Corridor details.

Photography: by Chuck Choi and Walter Dufresne for the Department of Medicine

Perkins Eastman

New York University School of Medicine
Department of Medicine Laboratories
New York, New York

Above: Wet laboratory.

Below right: Corridor.

Photography: Chuck Choi.

To the physicians and scientists who frequently hear that laboratories must be bland and unexciting, New York University School of Medicine's Fisher Laboratories for the Department of Medicine stand as a shining contradiction. The newly renovated, 11,600-square foot space, designed by Perkins Eastman, houses three fully functioning wet laboratories and all necessary support spaces, such as an equipment room, tissue culture and microscopy laboratories, computer laboratory, darkroom, quiet room, offices, pantry and conference room. To give these facilities aesthetic form without loss of efficiency, the design reorganizes the typical wet laboratory to establish defined zones that differentiate the space. The effort has been noticed by faculty members like Glenn Fishman, M.D., F.A.C.C., who declared, "The Fisher Lab has really come together, and is looking terrific."

PERKINS & WILL

617 West 7th Street Suite 1200
Los Angeles CA 90017
213.270.8400
213.270.8410 (Fax)
www.perkinswill.com

Atlanta
Beijing
Boston
Charlotte/RTP
Chicago
Dallas
Houston
Los Angeles
Miami
Minneapolis
New York
Shanghai

PERKINS & WILL

Genesis Medical Center
Davenport, Iowa

How to get from A to B in a hospital becomes a serious challenge for patients, families and staff alike as it expands. However, when circulation problems are decisively resolved by design, the results can be dramatic as shown in Genesis Medical Center, a 502-bed, multiple campus complex in Davenport, Iowa. Over 450 physicians, 3,100 staff members and 1,000 volunteers serve the Quad Cities and surrounding areas. A 45,000-square foot renovation and addition, designed by Perkins & Will, has created a new building entrance for outpatient care separate from the inpatient entrance. This change connected the Center with two medical office buildings and provides updated and expanded facilities for outpatient surgery waiting, pre-operation holding, OR recovery, cancer center clinics, infusion and radiation therapy. Not only does the new entry's soaring, two-story lobby simplify wayfinding and access, it gives outpatient services a luminous new identity.

Above left: New entrance.

Above right: Patient room.

Right: Entrance corridor.

Far right: Neonatal ICU.

Opposite: Entry lobby.

Photography: George Laribos & Paul Schlisman.

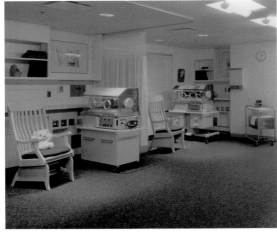

PERKINS & WILL

Greenwich Hospital
Greenwich, Ct

A dynamic alliance between visionaries and pragmatists has kept health care facilities up-to-date in Greenwich, Connecticut ever since a handful of citizens formed the Greenwich Hospital Association on March 2, 1902. Now, various moves and replacement hospitals later, the newest Greenwich Hospital welcomes residents of this historic town to a new era of patient-focused care, increased operating efficiency, expanded outpatient services and flexibility for growth. The handsome new,320,000-square foot, five-story, 160-bed facility, designed by Perkins & Will, includes medical/surgical patient care units, diagnostic and treatment services, clinical support services, patient services and administration /staff support in an out-standing environment that balances the needs of patients, families and staff with the cultural heritage, civic character and aesthetic context of the community. Indeed, the gracious brick, stone and cast stone architecture, landscaped grounds and residential-style interiors should go a long way towards smoothing the

transition towards increased ambulatory care in a town that has experienced numer-ous transitions in its 364 years.

Top right: LDRP room.

Upper right: Waiting room.

Right: Patient lounge.

Above: Semi-private patient room.

Opposite: Main Lobby.

Photography: Chuck Choi

PERKINS & WILL

Abott Northwestern Center for
Outpatient Care
Abbott Northwestern Medical Center
Edina, Minnesota

"Hotel-like" does not mean "hotel," as health care and design professionals rightly point out. What remains undeniable, nevertheless, is the power of hospitality- and residential-inspired design to transform health care's operations and perceptions. The impact is unmistakable inside the handsome Abbott Northwestern Center for Outpatient Care, a 32,000- square foot, two-story facility in Edina, Minnesota, with an interior design by Perkins & Will. Fitting out an advanced, patient-centered environment with nature- themed materials and furnishings keyed to an upscale market has produced an uncommonly attractive and relaxing facility housing ambulatory surgery, imaging suite, cardiology, timeshare clinic, internal medicine clinic, laboratory, physical therapy, administration and employee lounge. Denny DeNarvaez, president of Abbott Northwestern Medical Center, is hardly alone in praising "the calming atmosphere of a natural wetland" within the Center.

Above Left: Entry lobby.
Left: Recovery area.
Far left: Waiting room.
Photography: Dana Wheelock.

318

PERKINS & WILL

Saint Joseph's Hospital of Atlanta
Clinical Expansion
Atlanta, Georgia

To capitalize on its excellent cardio-vascular services, Saint Joseph's Hospital of Atlanta recently completed a 104,500-square foot, four level renovation/addition, designed by Perkins & Will, that enhances its capability in an interesting manner. The project, which provided attractively furnished new and remodeled space for inpatient beds, emergency department, OR suite and operating rooms dedicated to cardiology, special procedures rooms, endovascular treatment room, CT scan rooms and central energy plant, included a second patient entrance located off the red-line corridor of the surgical suite. This provision allows the new special procedures and endovascular treatment rooms to be turned into "operating rooms" if required, and is one of many reasons large and small why Saint Joseph's Hospital, a 346-bed, tertiary care institution, has remained a leading acute-care, specialty-referral hospital for the Southeast.

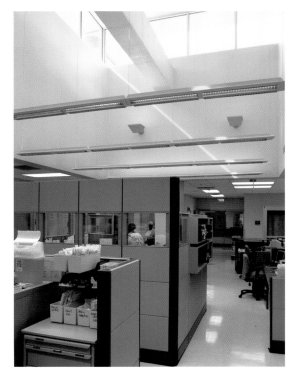

Top: Waiting room.
Center: Entrance.
Left: Laboratory.
Above right: Entry lobby.
Photography: Gary Knight.

PERKINS & WILL

Mayo Clinic
Cannaday Building
Jacksonville, Florida

Even since physicians and brothers Will and Charlie Mayo began practicing in Rochester, Minnesota at the dawn of the 20th century, the Mayo Clinic has developed a unique team approach to medical diagnosis, treatment and surgery that has attracted patients worldwide. In fact, since the charitable institution's tertiary-care center opened in Jacksonville, Florida in 1986, it has recorded some 610,000 patient registrations. Yet it strives tirelessly to improve its services, and the new, 103,040-square foot, three-story John and Lillian Cannaday Building, designed by Perkins & Will, typifies the outcome, combining a 250-seat auditorium for community education with medical offices for gynecological surgery on the second floor and primary care on the third floor. Says Dr. Bernd-Uwe Sevin, chair of Mayo's Department of Obstetrics and Gynecology, "We want this to be a place women of all ages and walks of life feel comfortable coming to for answers."

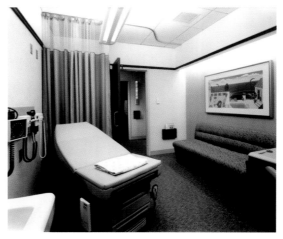

Top: Entry lobby.

Above left: Registration area.

Above right: Examination room.

Photography: Chuck Choi

RTKL Associates

Baltimore	Chicago	Tokyo
410.537.6000	312.704.9900	81.33583.3401
Dallas	Houston	Shanghai
214.871.8877	817.838.9200	86.21.6279.7657
Washington	Miami	Madrid
202.833.4400	786.268.3200	34.91.426.0980
Los Angelas	London	
213.627.7373	44.207.306.0404	www.rtkl.com

RTKL Associates

The Indiana Heart Hospital
Indianapolis, Indiana

What is the future of cardiovascular care, empowered by an all digital facility? Consider the remarkable new 210,000-square foot, four-story Indiana Heart Hospital in Indianapolis, designed by RTKL Associates with BSA LifeStructures. Conceived as a "center of excellence" with 56 inpatient and 32 day/outpatient beds, four operating suites, one endovascular suite, and six cardiac catheter laboratories, the award-winning facility is part of the Community Health Network. The total digitalization of information at Indiana Heart eliminates medical record storage, charting areas, and central nursing stations. The patient care unit is configured as a unique, three-arm spiral or "hurricane" shape where caregivers see and hear patients at all times from small, de-centralized care stations between every two patient rooms. CEO David Veillette is pleased to note, "RTKL realized from the beginning that supporting our technology and moving patient care back to the bedside was our primary goal.... They did an excellent job."

Left: Exterior view.

Right : Lobby.

Below left: Patient care unit.

Below right: Controlled access corridor linking the promenade to all diagnostics.

Photographer: Scott McDonald / Hedrich Blessing.

RTKL Associates

Florida Hospital Waterman
Tavares, Florida

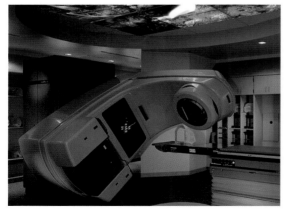

A tensile membrane roof stretching from the new Florida Hospital Waterman to an adjoining medical office building dramatically announces that the institution is ready for the 21st century. Indeed, the striking, 420,000-square foot, six-story, 204-bed replacement hospital in Tavares, just north of Orlando, significantly upgrades operations by incorporating the latest in medical technology and management. Its cloverleaf shaped patient tower wings maximize staff efficiency and patient care by replacing central nursing stations with multiple work zones, saving steps for care teams, establishing clear sightlines to patients, and improving infection control. Furthermore, the patientfriendly facility, designed by RTKL Associates with Jonathan Bailey Architects as associate architect, introduces a fresh, contemporary image. A highlight is its sunny central atrium that greatly enhances Waterman's appeal. Patient care manager De De Werts says, "The patients are the reason we're here, and the design of this hospital helps us provide better care."

Top: Patient room.

Above left: Exterior of main entry.

Left: Patient floor lounge.

Far left: Linear accelerator in Cancer Institute.

Opposite: Atrium.

Photography: © 2003 Gary Knight & Associates, Inc.

RTKL Associates

The Texas Heart Institute at St. Luke's Episcopal Hospital The Denton A. Cooley Building Houston, Texas

Research programs and educational activities at Texas Medical Center's Texas Heart Institute recently outgrew their 65,000 square feet within St. Luke's Episcopal Hospital. This should not surprise anyone familiar with the work of legendary heart surgeon Dr. Denton A. Cooley, the Institute's founder (1962) and president. The opening of the new, 327,000 square-foot, 10-story Denton A. Cooley Building, designed by RTKL Associates with Morris Architects, expands the Institute's horizons by creating much needed laboratory space along with a 12-room cardiovascular surgery suite, 93 patient rooms, pre- and post-operative clinics, a 521-seat auditorium, and a museum. The new facility does more than resolve old problems presented by a tight urban site, integration with an aging facility's floor plates and floor-to-floor heights, and overburdened circulation plans and support systems for staff, information and communication. It has enabled St. Luke's to rejuvenate its internal operations and has given the Institute a handsome public face.

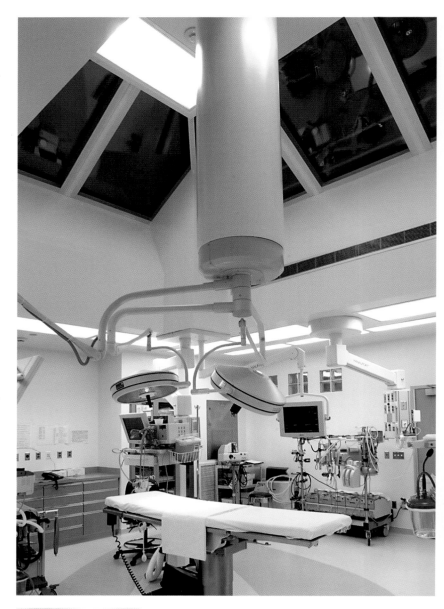

Above: Operating room with observation deck.

Left: Section.

Right: Exterior.

Photography: Ron St. Angelo Photography (interior) and Carl Mayfield Photography (exterior).

RTKL Associates

Memorial Hospital
Colorado Springs, Colorado

True or false: Healthcare institutions are never too old to grow. Memorial Hospital in Colorado Springs has never doubted its ability to keep pace with the vibrant Rocky Mountain region it has served during a century of medical care. Its esteemed reputation throughout southern Colorado is likely to grow with the addition of a new, 219,000-square foot, seven-story, 138-bed patient care tower, designed by RTKL Associates who also designed Memorial Hospital's off-campus outpatient facilities. The new tower supports and expands inpatient and ambulatory services. Since an existing tower maintains diagnostic / treatment services on level one, support services in the basement and on level two, and nursing units on levels three through seven,

the new tower adopts the same stacking plan. It groups the nursing units by specialty to allow municipally-owned Memorial to consolidate services for maximum efficiency as it grows. Considered the cornerstone of all future development, the attractively finished and landscaped new structure opens a promising gateway to Memorial's next century.

Above left: Pedestrian bridge between patient care towers.
Above right: Fountain.
Right: View from street.
Photography: Don Jones Photography.

Shepley Bulfinch Richardson and Abbott

40 Broad Street
Boston, MA 02109
617.423.1700
617.451.2420
www.sbra.com

Shepley Bulfinch Richardson and Abbott

Bronson Methodist Hospital
Kalamazoo, Michigan

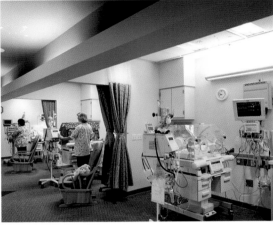

The new, full-service, 750,000 square-foot Bronson Methodist Hospital Replacement Campus is a paradigm of innovative healthcare design. Designed by Shepley Bulfinch Richardson and Abbott, the complex reflects the Hospital's new operational initiatives, is adaptable for future changes and creates a healing environment for the patient, family and community by integrating healthcare services, art and the natural environment. Adopting the consumer-driven model of "one-stop shopping," the design creates horizontal continuity for various medical specialties, so that each floor is self-sufficient with its own parking, beds and physicians' offices directly adjacent to treatment space. The "heart" of the Hospital is a Healing Garden, representing the institution's mission of connecting community, family and patients with the healing powers of art and nature. A leading participant in the Pebble Project, the 348-bed replacement Hospital uses evidence-based design to assess the impact of good design on positive patient outcomes. Evidence collected to date indicates that the design of the new facility has decreased patient stays, streamlined healthcare delivery and increased patient and physician satisfaction. "The New Bronson" has also become a significant center for healthcare resources serving the community at large.

Above left: Entry corridor.
Above right: NICU area.
Right: Atrium at night.
Opposite: Healing garden.
Photography: Peter Mauss/ Esto.

Shepley Bulfinch Richardson and Abbott

The Gateway Building
Virginia Commonwealth University Medical Center
Richmond, Virginia

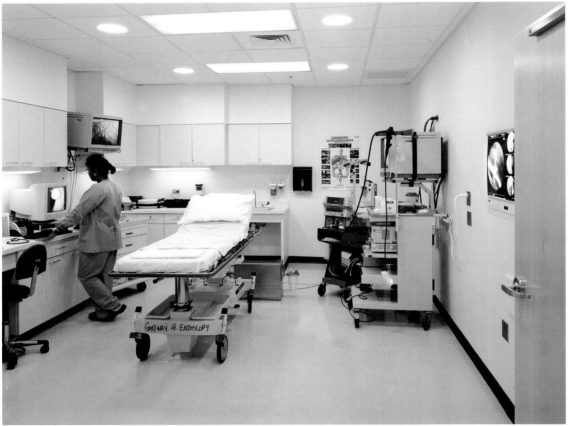

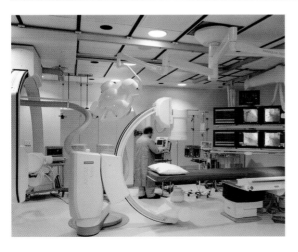

No institution stays on the forefront of healthcare without continuous effort, and the new Gateway Building on the campus of Virginia Commonwealth University Medical Center, the teaching hospital component of the Virginia Commonwealth University, helps to illustrate what must be done.

The 229,000-square foot, 10-story Gateway Building, designed by Shepley Bulfinch Richardson and Abbott in association with Baskervill & Son, collaborating Architect of Record, is an infill building that creates a new front door for the urban campus and connects existing inpatient and ambulatory facilities to one another.

The project establishes horizontal continuity between various medical specialties to facilitate the delivery of patient care and provides flexible space for formerly underserved diagnostic and clinical functions.

Shepley Bulfinch Richardson and Abbott

Bristol-Myers Squibb Children's Hospital
Robert Wood Johnson University Hospital
New Brunswick, New Jersey

Bristol-Myers Squibb Children's Hospital at Robert Wood Johnson University Hospital, designed by Shepley Bulfinch Richardson and Abbott, in collaboration with Hillier Architecture, is New Jersey's largest free-standing, state-designated acute care children's hospital. The goal of the 146,000-square foot, 38-patient bed, 24-peri-operative bed institution in New Brunswick is to establish a comfortable, family-centered atmosphere for state-of-the-art care. As a result, such functions as surgery, adolescent hematology and oncology, PICU, pediatric emergency department, level one trauma center and child life center display the benefits of sensitive planning, clear wayfinding, and patient-friendly amenities. Citing favorable public reaction, Stephen Jones, senior vice president, operations, for Robert Wood Johnson University Hospital, declares, "We love the design of the Hospital, which fosters our mission to provide family centered, child focused health care." Most recently, SBRA designed the exterior and Granary Associates designed the interiors for a new, three-story addition above the Phase One building just completed.

Above: Entrance.

Right: Same-day surgery entry.

Opposite top: Nurses station.

Opposite bottom: Waiting area.

Photography: Barry Halkin, Meg Shin for same-day surgery entry and waiting area.

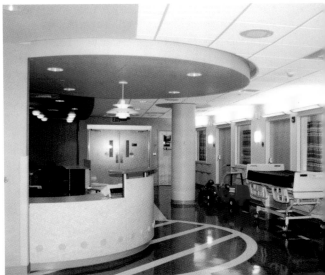

Shepley Bulfinch Richardson and Abbott

Norris Cotton Cancer Center
Dartmouth-Hitchcock Medical Center
Lebanon, New Hampshire

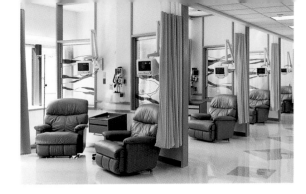

With a 120,000-square foot, three-story addition and 30,000 square feet of remodeled space, the existing building for Dartmouth-Hitchcock Medical Center's renowned Norris Cotton Cancer Center has been transformed into a comprehensive, integrated medical center for cancer clinical care and research. The new scheme for the Cancer Center, designed by Shepley Bulfinch Richardson and Abbott, supports the institutional mission of integrating the highest level of patient-centered health care with advanced research activities to facilitate innovative strategies for the treatment and cure of cancer. "The new facility has had an immediate impact, providing a beautiful and energized environment for interaction and collaboration," says Cancer Center Director Dr. Mark Israel. "The expansion of our facilities has brought about a fundamental change in the way we operate. The building is a winner." In the infusion center and hematology/oncology clinics, patients are treated in a comfortable, reassuring healing environment brightened by stained glass artwork and warmly colored interiors. The user-friendly, high-efficiency lab space is designed with maximum flexibility, including moveable casework, to facilitate multidisciplinary and evolving research. The sun-filled atrium of the Cancer Center offers a restful space for informal gathering or contemplation. Interactive teaching spaces and conference rooms are gathered at the atrium, where shared resources ensure that all users interact and appreciate the interconnected nature of the entire facility.

Top: Infusion center.

Above right middle : Glass "waterfall" in atrium.

Above right bottom: Research lab.

Above left : Balcony in atrium.

Photography: Richard Mandelkorn.

Sizeler Architects

300 Lafayette Street, Ste. 200
New Orleans, LA 70130
www.sizeler.com

Sizeler Architects

New Orleans Cancer Institute
Memorial Medical Center
New Orleans, Louisiana

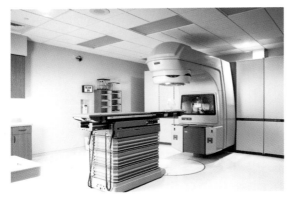

Though its roots go back to the founding of its two campuses, Mercy Hospital (1896) and Southern Baptist Hospital (1917), which merged in 1994, Memorial Medical Center prides itself on providing modern health care to the people of New Orleans. The new, 30,000-square foot, two-story New Orleans Cancer Institute, designed by Sizeler Architects, demonstrates how Memorial continually improves its services. Though the Center maintained a wide range of oncology programs, they were scattered around the campus. Not only does the new Institute gather together such facilities as linear accelerators, oncology services, doctors' offices and examination/treatment areas, its clear spatial organization and attractive interiors are developed around patient flow from initial registration and examination or treatment to check out, making patient experience as pleasant and comfortable as possible. Larry Walker, director of operations for the Institute, reports the design "allows us to function more effectively."

New Orleans Cancer Institute
Memorial Medical Center
Tenet Health System

Above: Waiting room.

Right: Core area.

Opposite upper left: Linear accelerator.

Opposite upper right: Public education room.

Opposite center: Exterior.

Photography: David Richmond.

339

Sizeler Architects

Wellness Center
East Jefferson General Hospital
Metairie, Louisiana

Baby Boomers have entered middle age determined to maintain their physical well-being. In response to this, facilities like the new, 39,589-square foot, two-story Wellness Center at East Jefferson General Hospital, in Metairie, Louisiana, are likely to become community magnets for them. Accordingly, the award-winning, free-standing facility, designed by Sizeler Architects, houses a cardiovascular fitness room with overhead walking track, multi-purpose exercise room, natatorium with warm water therapy pool, lap pool and garden whirlpool, fitness assessment and education classrooms, locker rooms and administrative offices. The designers made skillful use of traditional architecture to evoke a handsome country club. Daylight, exterior views to landscaped courtyards and green spaces, and interiors appointed in such timeless materials as brick, mahogany, granite and slate, complete the impression that the Wellness Center will respond with grace and charm to users' needs in Metropolitan New Orleans.

Above: Entrance.

Right: Garden Whirlpool.

Far right: Exercise room.

Opposite above: Multi-purpose exercise room

Opposite center: Atrium entrance.

Photography: David Richmond.

Sizeler Architects

Joseph C. Domino Healthcare Pavilion
East Jefferson General Hospital
Metairie, Louisiana

Below left: Atrium.

Below right: Main lobby.

Bottom left: Entrance.

Opposite above left: Waiting area.

Opposite above right: Recovery room.

Photography: David Richmond. (Glade Bilby II- Bottom Right & Top Right Photos Only)

How has competition affected health care in America? The people of Metairie, Louisiana, are delighted with the new, 219,000-square foot, four-story Joseph C. Domino Healthcare Pavilion, an addition to East Jefferson General Hospital designed by Sizeler Architects in association with FKP Architects, to dramatize the Hospital's introduction to the out-patient market. The award-winning Domino Pavilion encloses same day surgery, outpatient imaging, GI/endoscopy, admissions, pre-admit testing, lobby, gift shop and chapel in a modern, patient-friendly environment that acts as a "front door" to the adjacent acute care facility and a focal point for a growing campus. Since opening day, Bruce Curson, former COO of the Hospital observes, "there have been nothing but rave reviews from our staff, doctors and most importantly, our patients and families."

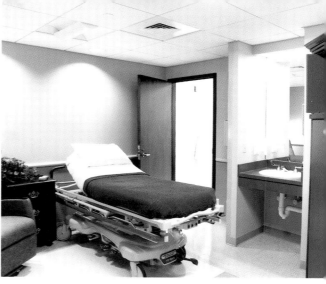

Sizeler Architects

Emergency Department Expansion
Terrebonne General Medical Center
Houma, Louisiana

When Terrebonne General Medical Center recently decided to expand and remodel its overcrowded emergency department, there was no doubt the 304-bed facility in Houma, Louisiana, would seek a progressive solution. Terrebonne is Louisiana's only hospital to receive the United States Senate Award for Innovation, and its new, 22,000-square foot, one-story, 28-bed emergency department, designed by Sizeler Architects, has established a unique patient flow based on the patient's perspective. Patients who drive up to the covered entrance are greeted as they enter the open waiting area, proceed from triage directly to treatment rooms large enough to accommodate the family groups who typically accompany loved ones, and leave via a rear exit. While such facilities as the trauma rooms, cardiac rooms, pediatric fast-track area,

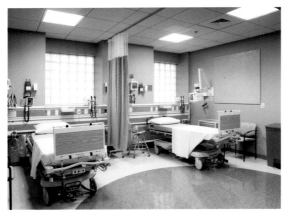

OB/GYN rooms and family counseling rooms are state-of-the-art, the colors, lighting, furnishings and original art, including a commissioned mural depicting marine life in the nearby Gulf of Mexico, are part of a patient-focused and hospitality-inspired environment that reaches out to patients and families living in the heart of "Bayou Country."

Top: Waiting room.
Above left: Observation unit.
Above right: Nurses' station.
Right: Cardiac room.
Photography: David Richmond.

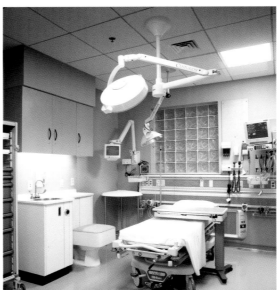

The S/L/A/M Collaborative

Glastonbury, CT
Atlanta, GA
Cambridge, MA
www.slamcoll.com

The S/L/A/M Collaborative

Hospital for Special Care
New Britain, Connecticut

Was there a restorative quality to the dairy pasture where the City of New Britain erected a "Temporary Rest Home for Tuberculosis Sufferers" in 1938? The Hospital for Special Care has certainly flourished there since 1941, becoming a respected, not-for-profit, 200-bed rehabilitation and chronic disease hospital that specializes in rehabilitating people who have had a stroke, spinal cord injury, brain injury or other complex orthopedic need. Not content to rest on its laurels, the hospital recently completed a 112,000-square foot renovation and 90,000-square foot addition, designed by The S/L/A/M Collaborative, combining state-of-the-art medical facilities with courtyards, gardens and other public areas that promote patient socialization among its chronic care population. The sleek, modern-style transformation is dramatic in such diverse areas as outpatient examination and treatment, gymnasiums, aqua therapy, physical therapy, chronic disease and pulmonary unit, 27- bed pediatric unit, and 36-bed rehabilitation unit. The hospital reports that virtually every prospective patient who visits seeks treatment there.

Top right: Pediatric activity room.

Left: Exterior of addition.

Middle right: Interior courtyard.

Bottom right: Chapel.

Opposite: Entry lobby.

Photography: Esto Photographics, Nick Wheeler.

The S/L/A/M Collaborative

Hartford Hospital C.O.R.E.
Hartford, Connecticut

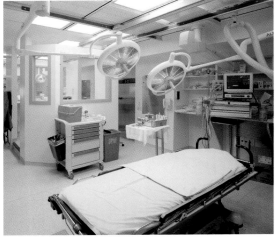

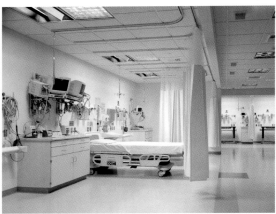

Urban tertiary care hospitals often find that they must undertake a major upgrade of essential clinical facilities without disrupting critical operations. Hartford Hospital, the largest medical center in Connecticut, needed to renovate three adjacent clinical buildings that were failing to meet current technological and clinical demands, at the same time that it needed to expand its imaging, emergency and surgical services. The recently finished 72,000 sq. ft. renovation and 113,000 sq. ft. new construction, designed by The S/L/A/M Collaborative, solved these challenges by inserting a new addition between the three outmoded buildings, providing efficient organization of clinical services while significantly improving the delivery of care, circulation, access and adjacencies. The project includes new clinical support spaces; a 10-room universal operating suite that unbundles OR case scheduling; and a new emergency department designed as versatile private rooms that can flex between trauma, observation and examination/treatment areas. The new construction required the demolition of the hospital's old chapel, which was relocated within the interior of the new facility, using artificial light for dramatic effect.

Top left: Chapel.

Right: Operating room.

Bottom right: Emergency department.

Opposite: Exterior of clinical addition.

Photography: Woodruff/Brown Photography.

The S/L/A/M Collaborative

Lakeland Health Park
Lakeland Regional Healthcare System
St. Joseph, Michigan

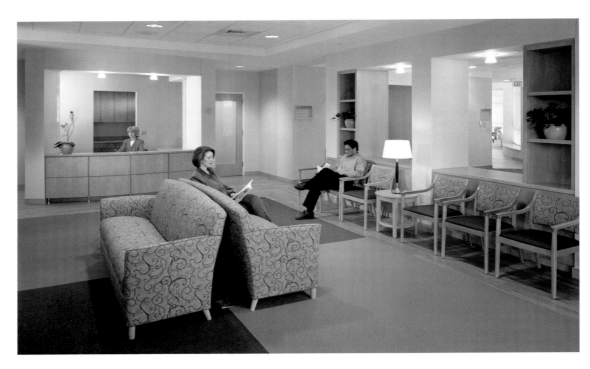

With the need to consolidate outpatient services from three crowded hospitals and a desire to embody the ideals of patient centered care, Lakeland Regional Healthcare System, working with The S/L/A/M Collaborative, developed its first free-standing ambulatory care center. Visitors are welcomed by an airy double height entry arcade that orients and directs them to surgery/imaging services, and includes a unique set of functions (a health resource library, quiet room, education space, and café) to support patients and family as they prepare for a procedure. Generous interior gardens, an internalized courtyard, along with double height corridors and ample skylighting introduce elements of the landscape and daylight deep into the 67,500 s.f. footprint creating bright, uplifting spaces that help promote restoration and healing.

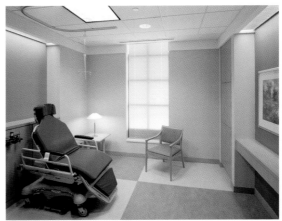

Top: Waiting room.

Upper right: Sub-waiting

Bottom left: Recovery corridor.

Bottom right: Recovery room

Opposite: Entry Arcade.

Photography: Woodruff/Brown Photography.

The S/L/A/M Collaborative

Miriam Hospital
Cardiovascular Thoracic Intensive Care Unit
Providence, Rhode Island

Right: Central nursing station for consultation and overflow work.

Below: Vision panels for visual access to patient rooms.

Photography: Woodruff/Brown Photography.

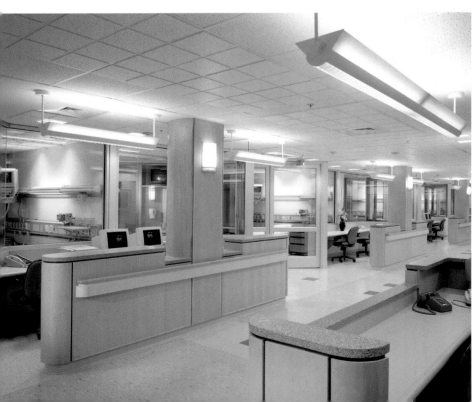

In response to increased community demand, the 247-bed Miriam Hospital, a not-for-profit acute care general hospital founded in 1926, needed to renovate an inpatient care wing into a 10-bed cardiovascular thoracic intensive care unit, consisting of two five-bed units, each with its own nursing station. The award-winning 5,000 sq. ft. renovation was designed by The S/L/A/M Collaborative and not only improves integrated care management but creates a supportive environment featuring wood cabinetry, glass doors and vision panels, artwork and soothing colors and finishes.

SmithGroup

SmithGroup
1825 Eye Street, NW
Suite 250
Wasington, DC 20006
202.842.2100
202.974.4500 (Fax)
www.smithgroup.com

Ann Arbor
Chicago
Detroit
Los Angeles
Madison
Phoenix
San Francisco
Washington, DC

SmithGroup

Fran + Ray Stark Assisted Living Villa
Woodland Hills, California

Where do the people who illuminate our cinema and television screens go when the lights dim on their careers? One appealing destination is the Wasserman campus in Woodland Hills, California, where an assisted-living facility, residential cottages, hospital, chapel, theater, and activity center have covered half of the Motion Picture & Television Fund's 46-acre site since the 1940s. Now, the new, 63,000-square -foot, three-story Fran & Ray Stark Assisted Living Villa, a residence for up to 90 retirees designed by SmithGroup, marks a milestone for the campus. As phase one in the

implementation of a master plan for the undeveloped campus acreage, also created by SmithGroup, the Villa transcends senior housing stereotypes by providing an imaginative, stimulating and attractive "home" to nurture daily interaction among residents. The building's stucco, stone and slate exterior, whose extended elevations and barrel-vaulted roofs recall old Hollywood studios, encloses an upscale, residential-style interior of major public areas and multiple smaller ones, oriented around gardens, where residents can socialize at varying distances from their private units in two residential "arms." Settings ranging from the main living room and main dining room to such smaller-scale spaces as the computer/business center, residents' kitchen garden with potting room, juice bar, spa, outdoor dining room and koi pond encourage all residents to step into the spotlight.

Above: Entrance.

Left: Main dining room.

Far left: Koi pond.

Lower left: Computer/business center.

Opposite: Entry hall.

Photography: John Edward Linden, Tom Bonner.

SmithGroup

Nanticoke Cancer Care Center
Seaford, Delaware

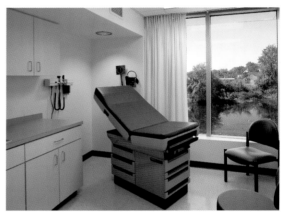

Armed with studies showing that patients who experience a direct connection to nature require less narcotic pain medication and may respond better to treatment, Smith-Group worked with Nanticoke Memorial Hospital in Seaford, Delaware, to ensure that the Nanticoke River would be a focal point for the new, 22,000-square- foot, two-story Nanticoke Cancer Care Center and a key part of the patient experience. Thus, the Center's curved glass and metal curtainwall "floats" above the water, and the main lobby and all patient treatment, examination and meeting rooms enjoy calming river views. This distinctive orientation is just one of numerous design features, such as good circulation and efficient space utilization, that make the facility'scancer treatment departments, including the first floor's radiation treatment and chemotherapy and the second floor's ancillary services, so effective. Barbara Young, a Nanticoke administrative director, praises its "serene and comfortable atmosphere conducive to healing."

Above left: River elevation.

Top right: Cuning exxterior facade.

Above right: Examination room.

Right: Radiation room.

Photography: Prakash Patel

SmithGroup

Shanghai Traditional Chinese Medicine University Shunguang Hospital
Shanghai, China

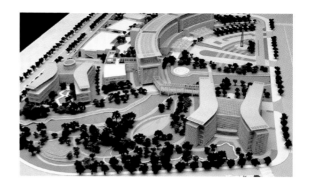

Right: Site plan.

Below: Entrance.

Bottom: Skylit atrium.

Illustration: Courtesy of SmithGroup.

Traditional Chinese medicine, ignored for much of the 20th Century despite centuries of practice, has recently regained its importance in Chinese culture while attracting the interest and respect of health care professionals worldwide. Today, for the first time, Chinese medical students can study both traditional Chinese medicine and orthodox Western medicine and major in the teaching and practice of either system in a new state-of-the-art medical campus, Shanghai Traditional Chinese Medicine University/ Shuguang Hospital Replacement, due in 2006. The design of the 882,641-square-foot, 7-story, 720-bed hospital, designed by SmithGroup, is as unique as its function, embodying multiple concepts drawn from traditional Chinese medical practice and spiritual ideas as well as emerging concepts of healing gardens and other elements of Western therapeutic environments in a technically advanced facility.

SmithGroup

Walt Comprehensive Breast Center
Karmanos Cancer Institute
Detroit, Michigan

Women too busy or afraid to have mammograms are the focus for the Alexander J. Walt Comprehensive Breast Center at Detroit Medical Center's respected Barbara Ann Karmanos Cancer Institute. Formidable as the challenges proved to be, the Karmanos Institute and SmithGroup interior designers enthusiastically developed the 10,000-square-foot infill project using a spa-like design. The fresh ideas at the

Walt Center, named for the late Dr. Walt, a tireless advocate of compassionate cancer care, are particularly noticeable in the changing space and examination rooms, where patients are pampered with privacy, soothing music and soft lighting and in interiors where carpet, wood, mosaic tile and decorative lighting replace the clinical appearance patients typically encounter.

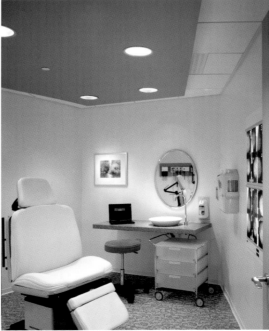

Above: Waiting room.

Left: Examination room.

Far left: Changing space.

Photography: Jason Maconochie/Hedrich Blessing.

SmithGroup

Kaiser Permanente Los Angeles Medical Center
Los Angeles, California

Right: North elevation.

Below left: Glazed stair towers.

Below right: Sunset Boulevard elevation.

Illustration: Courtesy of SmithGroup.

Kaiser Permanente's largest acute care medical center appears to enjoy the best of two worlds — the tranquillity of formal landscape and the bustle of city life on its three city blocks in Los Angeles along Sunset Boulevard, bordered by historic Barnsdall Park and the mid-Sunset urban cityscape. However, limited area and height restrictions on those same blocks have decisively shaped the new, one million-square-foot, seven-story, 456-bed tertiary care hospital, designed by SmithGroup with Gordon H. Chong & Partners to replace

the existing main hospital and service buildings by 2007, in order to bring it in compliance with updated seismic codes. Kaiser chose to stay and rebuild only after conducting a thorough review of its options with SmithGroup. Not surprisingly, the new Kaiser Permanente Los Angeles Medical Center will exploit the site intensively with a design that optimizes horizontal adjacencies for functions that relate strongly and have a high degree of cross-traffic. Organizing floors by treatment categories effectively creates a series of small, dedicated "mini-hospitals" that should greatly reduce patient and staff traveling distances and promote shared support services for integrated approaches to care. In another break from its past, the new Center will respond warmly to its neighborhood with entrances and landscaping, something the old Center never attempted.

SmithGroup

North Building
Providence Holy Cross Medical Center
Mission Hills, California

Heavy damage to a key support building at Providence Holy Cross Medical Center in Mission Hills, California, during the 1994 Northridge earthquake cleared the way for the new, 24,300-square-foot, one-story North Building, designed by SmithGroup. The new facility is more than a replacement, however. Besides housing the older structure's medical records and administrative functions, the new space incorporates an outpatient rehabilitation facility previously located in an adjacent building, adds a new, 2,500-square-foot meeting hall for conferences and community gatherings, and features a semi-enclosed courtyard beside the meeting hall as a public, outdoor extension of interior space. In fact, the interplay of building and open space

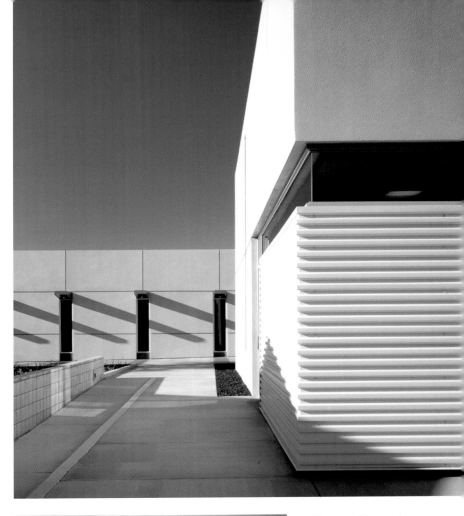

addresses widespread concern that the site – a cherished, grassy knoll after the existing structure was demolished—would remain a place of meeting and relaxation. For the only California community hospital named as one of America's 50 best by U.S. News & World Report, little matters can make a big difference.

Above: View towards meeting hall.

Left: Landscaping and architectural details.

Photography: Charles Sanchez.

The Stein-Cox Group

821 North Central Avenue
Phoenix, AZ 85004
602.462.0966
602.462.9495 (Fax)
www.stein-cox.com
sally@stein-cox.com

The Stein-Cox Group

Phoenix Children's Hospital
Phoenix, Arizona

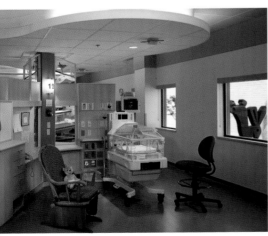

Designing a children's hospital is always a challenge, but the new, 410,000-square foot, five-story, 307-bed Phoenix Children's Hospital was especially so. Designed by Karlsberger in association with the Stein-Cox Group, the complex project transformed a 40-year-old general hospital into a state-of-the-art pediatric facility where interior function and flow are completely new. A new entrance plaza connects three major campus buildings and parking, and natural light appears extensively throughout public and patient spaces, complementing the bold use of color and texture on exterior and interior surfaces. Everything in this hospital was considered with children in mind to create a healing environment celebrating nature and architecture of the Southwest. In fact, the design process regularly involved asking children how to improve the design, which resulted in the Hospital's special collection of art created by children, as well as a full-service children's library. Children refer to Phoenix Children's as a "happy place," while parents find ease in knowing it is so special.

Above: Entrance.

Right: Overall campus.

Opposite upper left: Plaza.

Opposite lower left: NICU.

Photography: Gary Knight.

Aerial Photo: Value Productions.

The Stein-Cox Group

Nebraska Heart Hospital
Lincoln, Nebraska

If the new, 90,000-square foot, two-story, 63-bed Nebraska Heart Hospital, in Lincoln, designed by The Stein-Cox Group, does not look or feel like other hospitals in the Cornhusker State, that's because it was planned that way. Before any work began, surgeons and cardiologists agreed this would be a place like no other; an efficient, user-friendly hospital patients and families would choose over others. Careful placement of nursing and clinical functions, maintaining patient proximity to services, provides convenience for patients, families and staff. The environment is patient-focused at every entry level, including the extensive use of natural day lighting for environment and way finding. Home-like colors, materials, and art promote calmness and well being, despite rigid technical requirements. Large, private rooms allow families to gather and one member to stay overnight. Nebraska's first specialty hospital has set a standard of care worth emulating.

Above: Hopsitality entry.

Right: Patient room.

Far right: Family space.

Opposite left: Lobby.

Photography: Paul Brokering.

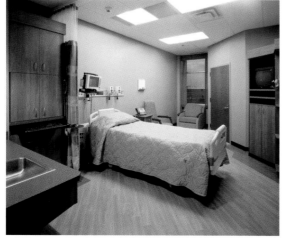

The Stein-Cox Group

SimonMed Imaging Center
Scottsdale, Arizona

Right: Lobby and reception room.

Lower right: CT exam.

Bottom right: MRI exam.

Photography: Mark Boisclair.

What are European-style furnishings that would look appropriate in a five-star hotel doing alongside state-of-the-art imaging equipment for such procedures as CT, MRI, ultrasound, RF and digital mammography? At Simon-Med Imaging, a 6,000-square foot imaging center established in Scottsdale, Arizona by Dr. John Simon, the goal was to create an intimate, residential-style, upscale atmosphere in an efficient high-technology facility. A critical goal of The Stein-Cox Group's design was to provide a comfortable setting for all patients and families, and a supportive workplace for staff. Patients consistently report that the distinctive environment restores composure and eases anxiety.

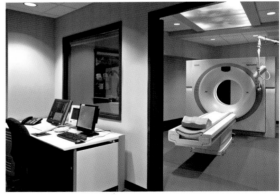

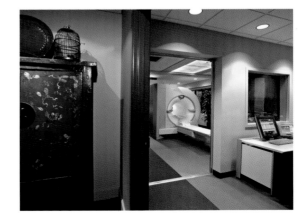

The Stein-Cox Group

Fresh Start Women's Resource Center
Phoenix, Arizona

"A glimmer of hope can open the door to a lifetime of happiness." The Fresh Start Women's Foundation creed became a reality when donations by the Phoenix community funded the construction of the Fresh Start Women's Resource Center. The Stein-Cox Group participated by donating architectural and interior design services, creating the Center as the first facility of its kind for the Fresh Start Women's Foundation, a not-for-profit organization formed in 1992 to help fill gaps in women's support services. The 22,000-square foot, two-story center houses counseling services, professional support for employment and legal services, a library, child watch areas, and meeting spaces that accommodate 14-190 people. Every facet of the Center breathes warmth and security, starting with the entry through the center courtyard, which illuminates the entire building with natural light.

Top: Courtyard entrance.

Above left: Street image.

Above far left: Lobby atrium.

Photography: Mark Boisclair.

The Stein-Cox Group

Advanced Medical Plaza
Chandler, Arizona

Having created flexible, integrated patient-care environments for 17 years, The Stein-Cox Group used its experience to design Advanced Medical Plaza, a 30,000-square foot, two-story medical office building for the Arizona Heart Institute, one of the state's leading cardiovascular care providers. This award-winning structure was developed for optimal efficiencies in leasing and circulation, making it suitable for any tenant, from a radiology suite to an outpatient cath lab for the Institute itself. The building compensates for its desert climate with concrete block, copper, aluminum and insulated glass construction. To gain contemporary flair and reduce anxiety for patients and visitors, interior common areas are appointed in wood, stone and textiles, establishing a true oasis in the desert.

Above: Building entry.
Photography: Mark Boisclair.

The Stichler Group

9655 Granite Ridge Dr. #400
San Diego, CA 92123
858.565.4440
858.569.3440 (Fax)
www.stichler.com
info@stichler.com

The Stichler Group Inc.

Harris Methodist Fort Worth
David E. Bloxom Tower
Fort Worth, Texas

Top: Patient floor lounge.

Above: ICU corridor.

Left: Nurses station.

Lower left: ICU patient room. with articulating arms.

Photography: Michael Lyon.

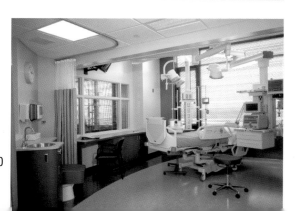

Harris Methodist Forth Worth Hospital, the flagship of Harris Methodist Hospitals, has provided advanced medical services to people of Tarrant County, Texas for over seventy years. Having introduced specialized care in such areas as oncology, trauma, cardiology, and women's services, the hospital now adds a new 64-bed critical care tower. The new ICU rooms feature ceiling-mounted articulating booms that eliminate traditional headwalls and provide maximum flexibility and 360 degree access to patients. Universal patient rooms service all types of patients, and a nursing station between each 2—patient room creates high visibility of each patient. Patient room lighting is operable by the patient, family, and nurses, and physician offices and surgical rooms are tied to the PACS system for digital viewing of x-rays. This quiet and unassuming facility consistently wins high scores from nursing and patients, and has recently won the prestigious ICU Design Citation award from The Society of Critical Care Medicine, American Association of Critical Care Nursing, and the AIA.

EMERGENCY
LABOR DELIVERY
KLABZUBA PARKING
KLABZUBA TOWER

DO NOT
ENTER

The Stichler Group Inc.

Sioux Valley Hospital
Ortho/Neuro/Rehab Center
Sioux Falls, South Dakota

Bigger isn't necessarily better. However, 476-bed Sioux Valley Hospital USD Medical Center, the largest facility of Sioux Valley Hospitals & Health System, a regional partnership of over 140 facilities in South Dakota, Minnesota, Iowa and Nebraska, provides numerous services at a level of quality that wins awards. It's concern for the needs of patients and staff, dating back to its founding in 1894, is evident in its new, 128,905-square foot, four-story outpatient Ortho/Neuro/Rehab Center, designed by The Stichler Group. Because the structure occupies a sloping site, there are two main entrances, as well as an underground tunnel to the Center's main building. From the lower level entrance for rehabilitation, featuring a 2-1/2-story rotunda, to the ground level entrance for orthopedics and neurology, at the opposite end of the building, the Center surrounds patients and staff with an efficient yet caring environment.

Above: Exterior.

Right: Registration and main lobby.

Far right: MRI.

Lower right: Patient examination room.

Lower far right: Rehabilitation pool.

Opposite: Rotunda at rehab entrance lobby.

Photography: Jeff Veire/Imagery.

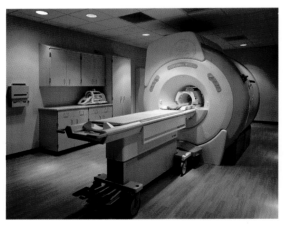

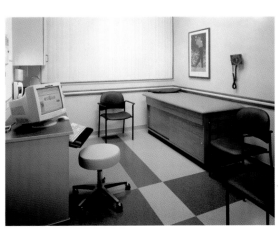

372

The Stichler Group Inc.

Scottsdale Healthcare Shea
Women's Center
Scottsdale, Arizona

What a difference four decades have meant for Scottsdale, Arizona. When Scottsdale Healthcare opened in 1962 as the 120-bed City Hospital of Scottsdale, this Arizona community had 10,000 residents. Today, the population exceeds 215,000, the city is a popular vacation destination, and Scottsdale Healthcare thrives as a not-for-profit community health system with top-ranked institutions like 305-bed Scottsdale Healthcare Shea recently developed a 180,000-square foot, five-story, 28-bed Women's Center, designed by The Stichler Group. The Center continues Scottsdale Healthcare's award-winning designs making a large-scale facility feel much smaller through six-room patient "neighborhoods," and attracting women of all ages with an imaging center offering mammography, healing spa, health resource library, and health conference and education center, all within a healing environment that resembles a five-star hotel.

The Stichler Group Inc.

Sioux Valley Hospital
Women's Pavilion and Family Suite
Sioux Falls, South Dakota

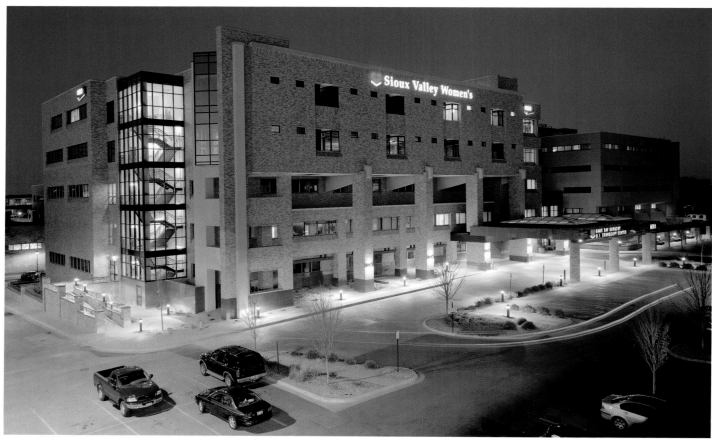

Above: Exterior.

Top right: Entry lobby.

Upper right: Nursery.

Right: LDRP room.

Photography: Imagery/Jeff Veire.

Despite predictions that it couldn't be done, Sioux Valley Hospital USD Medical Center has successfully completed the new, 52,000-square foot, two-story, 28-30-bed Women's Pavilion and Post-Partum Family Center Addition, designed by The Stichler Group. By converting an existing medical office building into outpatient services for women and adding two floors of in/patient beds, the new Women's Pavilion was created. The construction benefited from such ingenuity as cantilering one side of the addition 14-16 feet and extending the front facade of the upper levels approximatly eight feet with new columns. Equally important, the heart of the handsome interior of wood, crown moldings and custom carpet and upholstery features four family centered patient rooms clustering around a mini-nursing station for maximum patient security and enhanced nurse/patient interaction. That's why Georgia Stern, Manager of women's health services, reports patient response has been overwhelmingly positive.

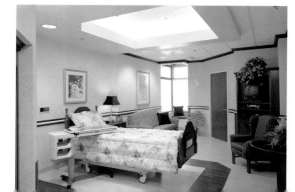

Taylor & Associates Architects

2220 North University Drive
Newport Beach, CA 92660
949.574.1325
949.574.1338 (Fax)
www.taa1.com
info@taa1.com

Taylor & Associates Architects

Kaiser Permanente East Los Angeles
Medical Office Building
East Los Angeles, California

How do you create a new, 50,000-square foot, two-story medical office building for the primarily Latino and Asian neighborhood of East Los Angeles, California, to suit the nation's largest non-profit health plan? When Taylor & Associates Architects was asked by Kaiser Permanente to create its East Los Angeles Medical Office Building, the goal was a facility that would provide quality medical care and establish an environment that the service area population would find culturally familiar and inviting. The design simultaneously establishes a distinctive environment that speaks to local residents while maintaining the prescribed budget. The design solution incorporates attractive cultural motifs in key locations within the facility. The exterior's bold colors and cleanly detailed architecture are reminiscent of Mexico's Ricardo Legorreto. The interior includes a distinctive water feature at the entrance, decorative pots from around the world, and specially commissioned artwork from local artists. The building floor plan is based on a standard "provider module" used throughout the Kaiser Permanente system. Each module contains 12 physician offices and 24 examination rooms arranged in a U-shaped configuration for easy, efficient flow of patients and staff. While the second floor contains two opposing modules, the first floor provides such support functions as pharmacy, imaging, vision services, laboratory and registration. Confirming the value of this design approach, Kaiser has warmly praised the improved therapeutic outcomes and enhanced staff performance in the new building.

Top right: Entry reception area.
Upper right: South entry.
Right: Water feature at entry.
Far right: North entry.
Photography: Assassi Productions.

378

Taylor & Associates Architects
In Association with
Questar Engineering, Inc.

Saddleback Memorial Medical Center
Meiklejohn Critical Care Pavilion
Laguna Hills, California

Having Leisure World, a large, planned community for senior residents, as a next door neighbor has significantly defined the mission of 252-bed Saddleback Memorial Medical Center, in Laguna Hills, California, which otherwise services young families in the surrounding community of expanding Orange County. For this reason, the three-decade-old institution recently completed their new, 55,000-square foot, three-level, 22-bed Meiklejohn Critical Care Pavilion, designed by Taylor & Associates Architects, to provide intensive care and emergency services for the entire community, with a special consideration for the needs of the elderly. The first floor emergency care unit more than doubles the size of the old ECU, including an 11-bed, 23-hour stay unit to accommodate the high volume of cardiac observation patients. The unit is designed so the various levels of acuity are separate but still in close proximity to nursing stations and the central command hub to maximize flexibility during high patient volume periods. The intensive care floor is comprised of two 11-bed units, including four

isolation rooms and shared service core, arranged in an efficient configuration that minimizes travel distance for nursing staff. An inviting environment of natural illumination and openness is complemented by an interior design that incorporates soothing neutral colors, carpeting, TVs in patient rooms, comfortable furniture, and such amenities as a Serenity Room for families and friends. A Physicians' Library offers the latest medical journals and Internet service which is appreciated by staff as well as patient and visitors. With the opening of the Meiklejohn Critical Care Pavilion, Saddleback Memorial now has a modern emergency facility that is capably of treating nearly 2,500 patients and 500 paramedic calls each month.

Upper left: Reception and waiting area.

Left: Emergency entry.

Opposite: Intensive care unit nursing station.

Photography: Assassi Productions.

Taylor & Associates Architects

Hoag Memorial Hospital Presbyterian
East Tower - Women's Pavilion
Newport Beach, California

Due for completion in 2005, the East Tower-Women's Pavilion will be the cornerstone of Hoag Memorial Hospital Presbyterian's 10-year facility master plan. Providing both a replacement for an outdated building, as well as a significant enhancement to this established Southern California landmark, this project will become the new gateway to the entire acute care campus. The 320,000-square foot, seven-story East Tower will accommodate both inpatient and outpatient components of women's health services. This building will house the programs of breast care and imaging services, a comprehensive ambulatory services center, and two 41-bed nursing floors including short stay, extended recovery and med-ical/surgical swing space. The new facility has also been specially designed to maintain a patient-focused environment for women and their new babies. The post-partum patient rooms, which are sized to allow space for newborn infants to stay with their mothers also provides overnight daybed accommodations for their fathers. The first floor will provide such welcoming and hospitality functions as an information center, health resource center, café, gift shop and various visitor lounges and waiting areas.

Above: Exterior.

Right: Compass rose at entry plaza.

Opposite center: Lobby/waiting area.

Illustrations: Taylor & Associates Architects.

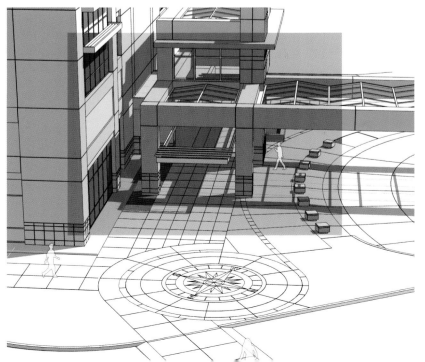

Taylor & Associates Architects

Kaiser Permanente Harbor-MacArthur Medical Office Building
Santa Ana, California

Below right: Reception lobby.

Below left: Exterior.

Photography: Assassi Productions.

Kaiser Permanente may be America's largest non-profit health plan with 8.2 million members, but it strives to serve communities at a personal level, as exemplified by their new 80,000-square foot, three-story Kaiser Permanente Harbor-MacArthur Medical Office Building, in Santa Ana, California. Designed by Taylor & Associates Architects, there is no question that this new medical office building has an ambitious program, including family practice, physical therapy, pharmacy, imaging center, acute care services, laboratory and blood draw, and vision services. The structure was designed with facades that are reminiscent of the early 20th-century California Craftsman style, as evidence by the main entry which was designed with a low pitched roof and exposed framework. Thoughtful detailing, specially selected building materials and beautiful landscaping also enhance the building and the site location which is orientated to take advantage of the spectacular views of the San Gabriel Mountains.

URS

227 West Nationwide Blvd.
Columbus, OH 43215
614.464.4500
614.464.0588 (Fax)

3950 Sparks Drive, S.E.
Grand Rapids, MI 49546
616.574.8500
616.574.8542 (Fax)

www.urscorp.com

Cleveland
Denver
Indianapolis
New York
Tampa
Toronto
Washington, DC
Dallas
Cincinnati
Detroit
San Francisco
Seattle

URS Health

Indiana Surgery Center
Howard Community Hospital
Kokoma, Indiana

Among the best qualities of outpatient surgery are efficiency and economy, but successful surgery centers embody other virtues that are clearly displayed in the handsome, new, 36,000-square foot, two-level Indiana Surgery Center at Howard Community Hospital, in Kokomo, Indiana. The freestanding facility, designed by URS Corporation to incorporate five operating rooms, 15 private patient rooms and other staff and support spaces as well as office space for individual physicians, connects to the Hospital via an enclosed walkway. Its design is based on using an attractive environment to comfort patients during surgery, accommodating intensive family support, configuring space for efficient operations, including prompt patient turn rates, and maintaining private patient rooms where all patient preparation and recovery occur, rather than in open cubicle bays. A sign of outpatient surgery's growing popularity here is the facility's readiness to expand with two operating rooms, 10 patient rooms and additional support space.

Above: Patient care team center.

Left: Care giver sub-station and patient room.

Below: Operating room.

Opposite: Entrance lobby.

Photography: Justin Maconochie/Hedrich Blessing.

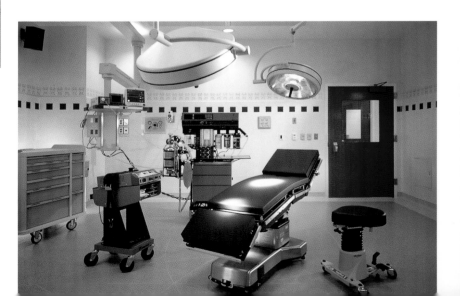

URS Health

Patient Care Services Plan
Spectrum Health
Grand Rapids, Michigan

A merger by 529-bed Butterworth Hospital and 410-bed Blodgett Memorial Medical Center, both in Grand Rapids, Michigan, in 1997 created Spectrum Health, a major regional health care provider serving western Michigan with nine hospitals, a 548-bed continuing care division and numerous ambulatory services. Spectrum subsequently initiated a strategy to consolidate all acute care and key clinical services on the Butterworth campus, and retained URS to provide master facility planning and architect-of-record services. Accordingly, URS has designed a new, 308,142-square foot, 10-level Heart Center, a 48,000-square foot, three-story addition to the existing South Tower including adult and pediatric medical/surgical patient care, a renovation and expansion of the level I emergency services facility from 25,000 to 48,000 square feet, and a new Pediatric Radiology Department at DeVos Children's Hospital in the Phase I implementation of the Patient Care Services Plan.

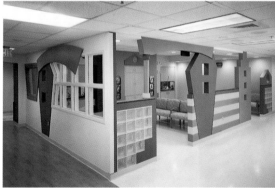

Top: South Tower VIP suite.

Left: Pediatric radiology waiting room.

Above right: Pediatric emergency waiting room.

Opposite: South Tower patient care floor team center.

Photography: Justin Maconochie/Hedrich Blessing.

URS Health

North Colorado Medical Center
Greeley, Colorado

Old, undersized surgical suites, undersized, non ADA compliant inpatient beds, growing cardiac and women's services programs, and a desire to maximize light, natural elements and patient amenities provided motivation for the upcoming, 248,000-square foot addition and renovation at North Colorado Medical Center in Greeley, designed by URS. Among the facilities resulting from the project will be 15 new OR surgery suites with designated general and cardiac ORs and 34 private pre and post recovery rooms, new and remodeled Monfort Family Birth Center with 10 LDRs,

26 postpartum rooms, 10-bed level II NICU and 14-bed well baby nursery, new Heart Center with diagnostic and interventional cardiology services, new 16-bed critical care unit and new 60-bed cardiovascular care unit. Distinctive features will include new ground-floor surgery suites adjacent to new and renovated central sterile facilities, a sunken garden for pre- and post-operative surgery patients, a central atrium, private, acuity-adaptable patient rooms, numerous family waiting and gathering spaces, cafe, gift shop and community resource center.

Top: Exterior of addition.

Above left, above right, left: Waiting areas and lounges.

Illustration: Courtesy of URS Health.

URS Health

Grant Medical Center
Columbus, Ohio

People are increasingly turning to Grant Medical Center a 640-bed institution in downtown Columbus, Ohio respected for its advances in heart care for surgery and other procedures. To upgrade its surgical facilities, patient access and public amenities, the Grant Medical Center is working with URS to develop a 154,000-square foot new building and expansion program in which an existing and underutilized structure on campus will be imploded and removed to create a site for the project. The completed facility, housing an 18-OR surgery department, pre/post operative areas, PACU, pre-procedure testing, sterile processing, non-invasive cardiology, MRI suite, main entrance and lobby, retail court, ambulance drop-off and parking, will create state-of-the-art medical facilities and public accommodations that patients, families and staff will find convenient and reassuring to use, from new, larger and well equipped ORs to a soaring, two-story entrance atrium.

Top left: New addition/expansion.

Far left: Phase one, new MOB.

Left: MOB lobby.

Illustration: Courtesy of URS Health.

391

Top right: Medical office building.

Above left: Ambulatory care center.

Below right: Medical mall corridor.

Right: Waiting area.

Photography: Lux Studios.

Laying the groundwork for what will ultimately be a 150-bed acute care hospital, several physician office buildings and a comprehensive outpatient services diagnostic center in upscale Dublin, Ohio, OhioHealth, a not-for-profit health care organization serving 46 Ohio counties, and URS, which provided master planning, design and engineering services, faced an interesting siting challenge. The first facilities on site for Dublin Health Center, comprising a 35,000-square foot, one story ambulatory care facility and a 40,000-square foot, two story medical office building, would face an Interstate Highway on the back side and several multi-use developments, including retailing, offices and housing, on the front side. Thus, not only would the new buildings be patientfriendly, offering densely landscaped grounds, covered drop-offs and an easily accessible medical mall corridor along the front of the ambulatory facility, all sides of both buildings would be handsomely detailed in brick. The diligence is already paying dividends. Favorable community response has encouraged Ohio Health to proceed with the inpatient hospital.

VOA Associates Incorporated

224 So. Michigan Avenue
Chicago, IL 60604
312.554.1400
312.554.1412
www.voa.com

VOA Associates Incorporated

Outpatient Center
Suburban Chicago, Illinois

Can architecture exemplify a hospital's commitment to holistic care? That intent and the requirements for a modern, 224,000-square foot, four-story Outpatient Center on a 73-acre academic medical center in suburban Chicago constituted a recent response by VOA Associates. The new facility, combining 14 multidisciplinary care centers, day surgery and outpatient cancer care as a "one-stop" ambulatory solution exemplifies both a healing environment and communicates "best practices" in contemporary healthcare delivery. Patients, families and staff benefit from such features as separate staff/service zones and patient/family zones; a comfortable environment featuring an exterior healing garden, central interior Winter Garden, and scenic views in clinical waiting areas; and efficient and flexible floor plans, all within a radiant space organized around a two-story, light-filled atrium.

Above left: Exterior.

Left: Clinic waiting area.

Far left: Staff/service corridor.

Right: Winter garden atrium.

Photography: Nick Merrick /Hedrich Blessing.

VOA Associates Incorporated

Little Company of Mary Hospital
Regional Cancer Center
Evergreen Park, Illinois

Demonstrating how an addition can complement existing architecture, the 35,000-square foot, three-level addition to Little Company of Mary Hospital in Evergreen Park, Illinois expands and consolidates services at the not-for-profit Catholic community hospital's Regional Cancer Center with a pre-cast and tile roofed structure that simultaneously respects the existing building's heritage and introduces a new level of spatial sophistication. The new construction accommodates chemotherapy treatment, radiation therapy, a learning resource center, meeting rooms for support groups and other amenities in a healing environment where a new octagonal tower, clerestory windows, and a skylighted main entrance flood the Hospital in daylight with views as never before. VOA Associates' use of natural materials like stone and wood, as well as a light palette, creates a calming environment focused on the patient's experience.

Above: Octagonal tower.
Right: Main entrance lobby.
Far right: Lobby reception.
Opposite: Chemotherapy area.
Photography: Scott McDonald /Hedrich Blessing.

VOA Associates Incorporated

La Rabida Children's Hospital
Inpatient Addition
Chicago, Illinois

Above: Elevator lobby.

Left: Rooftop addition, new arcade and campanile for mechanical equipment.

Below: Patient room.

Opposite: Pick Building lobby.

Photography: Scott McDonald/Hedrich Blessing.

Visitors to Chicago's Columbian Exposition of 1893 who admired the Spanish Pavilion, a replica of the La Rabida monastery from which Columbus embarked on his epic voyage, would recognize the new 16,500-square foot Inpatient Addition to La Rabida Children's Hospital, designed by VOA Associates. The hospital for chronically ill and disabled children began as a children's fresh air sanitarium when Spain donated the Pavilion to the City of Chicago, and the Pavilion was the model for the building it soon constructed to the south. A century later, the Inpatient Addition honors the Pavilion by restoring a harmony disturbed when a 1960 building to the north ignored its style. Besides creating the child-friendly, nautical-themed "S.S. La Rabida" with 37 inpatient acute care beds, the addition to the 1960 building adds arcades on each side of the building that mirror the Pavilion.

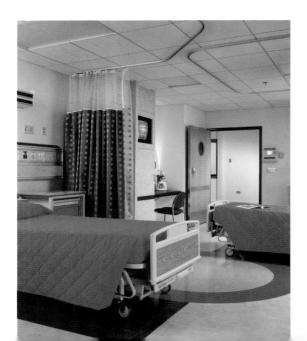

VOA Associates Incorporated

New Prentice Women's Hospital
Northwestern Memorial Healthcare
Chicago, Illinois

When it opens in 2007, the new Prentice Women's Hospital will be a world-class facility designed to meet women's healthcare needs throughout all stages of life. The new 18-floor, 256-bed facility will have 10 operating rooms and encompass 938,792 square feet. Designed jointly with OWP/P, the new hospital will feature artwork, roof-top and street-level landscaping, interior greenery and views of Lake Michigan and natural light to support its goal of creating a warm, healing environment. The state-of-the-art facility will feature all private rooms designed to be family-friendly with convertible window seats to daybeds for overnight guests and space for in-room dining. Retail spaces will represent the specific needs of women and their families. A women's health learning center will offer the latest health information along with a comprehensive array of classes, health screenings and medical referrals. To support the needs associated with childbirth, the new facility will have the capacity for 13,600 deliveries per year and will offer one of the largest centers for special-care infants in the country. The new Prentice Women's Hospital also will house one of the largest comprehensive breast centers for women's health in the region and its women's programs will extend across the Northwestern Memorial campus and into the community.

Watkins Hamilton Ross Architects, Inc.

20 Greenway Plaza
Suite 450
Houston, TX 77046
713.665.5665
713.655.6213 (Fax)
www.whrarchitects.com

Watkins Hamilton Ross Architects   Oklahoma Heart Hospital
Oklahoma City, Oklahoma

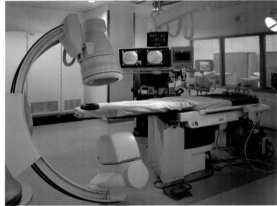

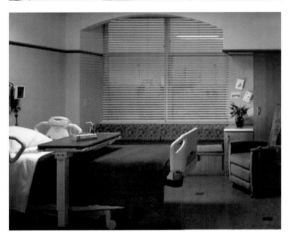

Patients and families often feel the anxiety mount as they enter a hospital unless they're visiting Oklahoma Heart Hospital, part of Mercy Health Center in Oklahoma City. The goal of this impressive, new, 234,000 -square foot, three-story, 64 bed facility, designed by Watkins Hamilton Ross Architects, is to create an exceptional unity of care through a critical path patients follow to minimize waiting times and transfers. As a result, all outpatient services and pre-admission testing are concentrated near the front door; imaging, diagnostics, pathology and pharmacy departments conveniently share the second floor with patient rooms (patients can be x-rayed in bed if necessary); every patient room in an eight-bed cluster or pod is convertible to a critical care room; a chair /folding bed and window seat/bed in each patient room accommodate overnight stays; and family members can accompany patients to admissions and waiting areas, or relax in the A la Heart Cafe and the chapel. In addition, a third-floor open-plan clinical practice with private examination rooms lets physicians work here rather than in an adjacent medical office building.

Top left: Exterior.

Top right: Corridor.

Left: Cath lab.

Below left: Patient room.

Opposite: Atrium lobby.

Photography: Gary Knight & Associate.

402

Watkins Hamilton Ross Architects

Goryeb Children's Center
Morristown Memorial Hospital
Morristown, New Jersey

Do you know how a hospital looks to a youngster? Children may not comprehend the philosophy behind the innovative, new, 86,000-square foot, three-story, 26-bed Goryeb Children's Center at Morristown Memorial Hospital, in Morristown, New Jersey, but they appear to embrace the facility spontaneously. When 642-bed Morristown Memorial Hospital started developing a separate hospital for children, the century-plus-old institution sought a family-focused environment that could alleviate children's feelings of isolation, disorientation and helplessness by giving patients and families a new, participatory view of health care. Watkins Hamilton Ross Architects actually created the design with the active involvement of groups representing children, families and care givers and it shows. For example, oversized private and semi-private patient rooms have private bathrooms with

Above: Entry.

Right: Main waiting area.

Far right: Exterior.

Photography: Gary Knight & Associates.

showers, windows with views to nature, built-in beds, recliners and multi-purpose custom light fixtures above beds. Elsewhere, patients and families will find built-in banquettes in examination rooms for parents and siblings, family great rooms with daylight, TV lounge, computer ports, kitchen, washers and dryers, and separate overnight sleeping rooms, oversized windows overlooking attractive vistas in chemotherapy, and such "positive distractions" in the main waiting area as a large, fresh-water aquarium, patterned hand-painted ceiling tiles, large "trees," daylight and views, video

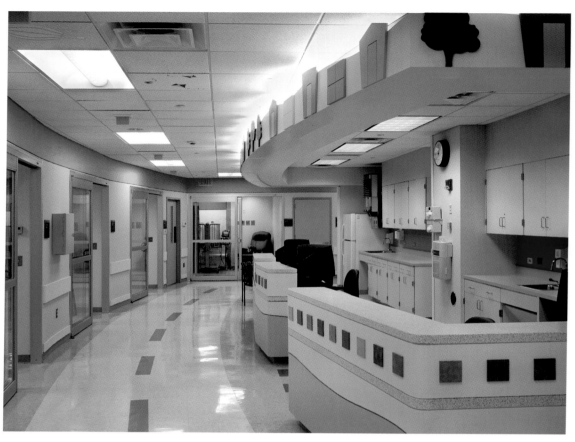

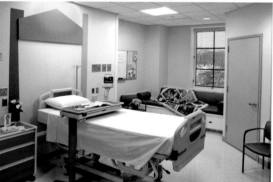

Above: Nursing station in clinical unit.

Left: Private patient room.

Far left: Chemo room.

Below left: Family great room.

Opposite: Waiting area.

game area and a blinking cityscape on a wall. Care givers are also acknowedged with such features as U-shaped clinical units in the special care unit and day hospital designed so nurses have visual access to patients, offices for physicians located in the sub-specialty areas, and clinical examination and consultation areas that are similar in design so staff can flow from one area to the next as the patient population dictates. Furthermore, the Center is a good neighbor on the Morristown Memorial campus, offering convenient connections to the main hospital from the lobby and clinical floors, distinctive entry portico, two-story atrium lobby and other-wayfinding cues, exterior building materials that complement the main hospital, constructed in 1948, and room for an adjacent children's emergency center and future expansion. No wonder Richard Lillo, physician services manager, reports that pediatric patient satisfaction is at an all-time high, and Dr.Leonard G. Feld, chairman of the Department of Pediatrics, happily proclaims, "The Children's Center is a kid-friendly and family sensitive hospital."

Left: Inpatient corridor.

Above: Waiting area.

Below: Examination room.

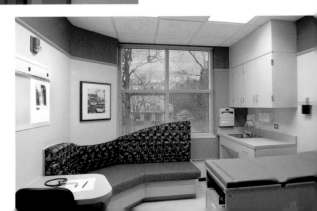

KI healthcare solutions. Comfort, quality, and function.

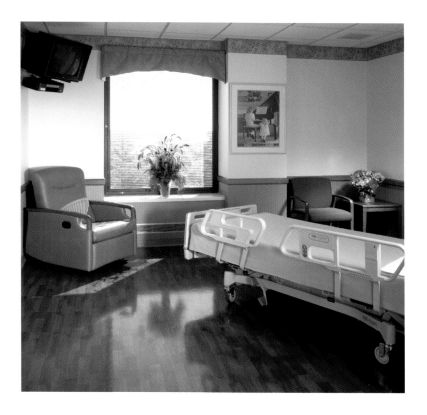

Whether helping hospital staff work more efficiently, patients heal faster, or family members rest easier, KI leads the way with award winning healthcare furniture solutions. The KI family of companies — AGI™, Period™, Spacesaver®, and Pallas® — offer truly unique solutions for patient room and lobby/waiting room seating, administrative office furniture, site furnishings, high-density healthcare supply storage, and textiles that are hygienic, washable, and breathable. We'll improve the quality of life at your facility! KI...your source for innovative healthcare solutions!

Call 1-800-424-2432. Or visit www.ki.com.

KI WORKING FOR YOU

No Waiting Room

As demand for health care soars across the United States, healthcare institutions must develop new facilities to deal with situations no one has faced before.

Residents of Oklahoma needn't panic. However, they may be wondering why state officials had to intervene in the autumn of 2003, when Oklahoma City's respected OU Medical Center, a merger between state-operated University and Children's Hospitals and privately-owned Presbyterian Hospital, declared it could no longer be the only hospital providing emergency care for the Sooner State's most critically injured trauma patients. According to the General Accounting Office, fewer than half of the approximately 100 specialty hospitals in Oklahoma and other states provide emergency care, particularly trauma care, placing the burden firmly on the shoulders of general hospitals. It's just one factor in the dynamic and evolving state of healthcare in the United States that is dramatically illustrated in the latest wave of remodeled and new healthcare facilities.

Soaring demand for healthcare by an aging population, relentless pressure for cost containment, ongoing industry consolidation and specialization, growing numbers of uninsured and underinsured patients, chronic staff shortages, changing medical technologies and practices, and increasing acceptance of the benefits of patient-focused environments are some of the key trends driving the development of today's healthcare facilities. How successfully these hospitals, clinics, medical office buildings, senior residences and other institutions resolve the healthcare problems in their regions will have to be played out over time. For all the talk about hospital closings due to declining utilization rates and population shifts, the American Hospital Association (AHA) reports in its 2002 survey that the nation had 5,794 registered hospitals with 975,962 staffed beds that reported 36,325,693 total admissions.

Readers of Healthcare Spaces No. 2 will be pleased to note that the recently-completed healthcare facilities featured in these pages frequently stand out as effective, flexible and user-friendly healing environments that please patients, families and staff alike. Obviously, America's 21st-century healthcare architecture has historic precedents reaching back to the 19th century. Even so, the newest generation of buildings and interiors is unmistakably different from its predecessors. The modern healthcare environment is now designed to satisfy the needs of patients and families as well as staff, anticipates change with flexible, modular construction, and uses its resources, including people as well as materials and energy, as sparingly as possible.

Why inpatient days and admissions are rising again.

Healthcare's impact on the nation's economy has not been as benign as its effect on architecture, to be sure. The numbers of hospitals and hospital beds were

A critical shortage of health care professionals, particularly pharmacists, nurses and imaging and laboratory technicians, puts staff under non-stop pressure.

steadily declining as little as five years ago, due to falling utilization rates. Countering a growing population's tendency to require more inpatient services, the healthcare industry developed innovative and cost-effective ways to minimize inpatient stays and reorient healthcare delivery towards ambulatory care over the last two decades. As noted by the AHA, the number of community hospitals decreased by 8.7 percent between 1990 and 2000. Of course, hospital capacity varied considerably by region, with such high growth states as Nevada, Arizona and Colorado having to raise inpatient capacity. Now, hospital inpatient days and

admissions are increasing along with outpatient volume. For example, over 60 percent of hospitals included in a recent AHA nationwide survey reported that their emergency departments were "at" or "over" capacity, and over 30 percent admitted to diverting ambulances. Capacity constraints are thus a prime reason for the ongoing development of space for healthcare.

If the demographics of the American people are reflected in their health-care facilities, what do the latest facilities say about us? The pages of Healthcare Spaces No. 2 are filled with independent and affiliated heart hospitals, oncology facilities at existing hospitals, birthing centers in general hospitals and women's hospitals, dedicated children's hospitals within larger medical centers, expanded emergency departments and ambulatory care centers within general hospitals, independent ambulatory surgery centers, and replacement hospitals. Perhaps the most important demographic factors highlighted by the new construction are the swelling ranks of senior citizens and their health problems, and growing uncertainty over how patients will pay their healthcare providers.

Designing healthcare facilities for reimbursement?

While the United States is not aging as fast as Japan or such Western European countries as Italy, France or Germany, its elderly are quickly assuming a larger percentage of the total population. The nation added about 33 million people or 13.1 percent to its population from 1990-2000, of which 1.2 million were the very oldest citizens, over age 85, a gain of 40.3 percent during the decade. Looking ahead, the nation will find the number of Americans age 65 and older doubling in the next 30 reinre

reinforced by aging Baby Boomers, to swell the ranks of the elderly to about 20 percent of the population. Advancing age is already powering the surge in cancer care centers, heart hospitals and senior housing for residents with varying degrees of disability and dementia.

Will these aging patients be able to pay for the treatment they seek? Prospects for a nation that currently spends some $1.4 trillion a year on healthcare could be better. Federal Reserve Bank chairman Alan Greenspan has suggested that future Social Security and Medicare benefits be reduced to meet a coming shortfall that the Treasury Department and the Congressional Budget Office estimate at a staggering $18-44 trillion over the next 75 years. For now, trustees of the Medicare and Social Security funds predict that the two funds will generate annual surpluses of over $200 billion a year to sustain them through this decade. But unless the American people and their leaders

Over 60 percent of hospitals reported that their emergency departments were "at" or "over" capacity and over 30 percent even sent ambulances elsewhere.

take drastic action soon, Medicare and Social Security will reach respective inflection points in 2013 and 2018, when both start paying out more than they take in.

Meanwhile, the healthcare industry is busy positioning itself to deal with current financial problems, which are formidable enough. For example, the growing ranks of uninsured Americans, whom the Census Bureau counted at 43.6 million in 2002, has inspired hospitals to expand emergency departments and streamline emergency care operations to process more patients faster, better and at lower cost. In addition, hospitals and group medical practices are specializing to focus on providing the most lucrative procedures, namely those that Medicare and private insurers are most willing to reimburse, such as cardiac care, cancer care and imaging. Yet the consequences of this targeting may result in excessive demand for treatment rather than

better care, with scant attention paid to such vital services as preventive care and case management.

As for the cost-cutting efforts demanded by health maintenance organizations and other third-party payers, the drastic staff reductions and other economies of the 1990s have left existing resources stretched to their limits. It's true that the newest facilities are designed to let fewer personnel do more work with greater effectiveness. But it's also true that fewer personnel can oblige patients to wait longer to address non-life-threatening conditions.

Healing environments are good medicine.

Happily, the design of new healthcare facilities makes them better equipped to deal with the physical and emotional needs of patients, families and staff as well as the operational needs of staff, equipment and the volatile medical and business conditions of the 21st century. Since physicians, nurses and healthcare administrators increasingly accept the emotional well-being of patients as a factor in therapeutic outcomes, largely through advances in psychoneuroimmunology, the study of the role that emotions play in the pathogenesis of physical diseases associated with immunological dysfunctions, the role of the healthcare environment as a source of the patient's stress or tranquillity is now openly acknowledged in healthcare architecture and interior design. This means creating a home-like or hospitality-inspired "healing environment" is not just good intentions, it's good medicine.

For patients and families, the impact of a patient focused setting can be dramatic. Patients retain more of their autonomy, orientation and sense of normalcy when they occupy patient rooms with patient-operated controls and facilities, move through public and private spaces equipped with

subtle lighting, outdoor views and attractive furnishings, and have space to receive family members and store or display personal objects. Family members are encouraged to provide personal care to patients and to participate actively in their treatment when there are patient rooms with daybeds for overnight stays and desks with Internet service, family counseling rooms where physicians and families can speak without patients overhearing, resource centers where families can conduct their own research, laundries, kitchenettes and sleeping areas dedicated to family use, and such amenities as cafeterias, gift shops and public education classrooms.

Yet the new healing environment rightly embraces the staff of healthcare facilities as well. A critical shortage of healthcare professionals, particularly pharmacists, nurses and imaging and laboratory technicians, puts staff under non-stop pressure to perform at optimum levels. Healthcare facilities can compensate for stressful conditions with efficient spaces that are easy to operate and maintain, state-of-the-art technologies that save time and effort, and dedicated lounges and other refuges where relaxation and counseling are available away from patients and families.

Americans age 65 and older will double in the next 30 years as Baby Boomers swell the ranks of the elderly to about 20 percent of the population.

Of course, healthcare design can only accomplish what healthcare institutions and society want them to. Yet heightened expectations for the performance of hospitals, clinics and the like is causing the architects of these facilities to rise confidently to the challenge. If today's best healing environments are a foretaste of what's to come, tomorrow's patients, families and staff could begin to feel better just by checking into the right space at the right time. Is there an architect in the house?

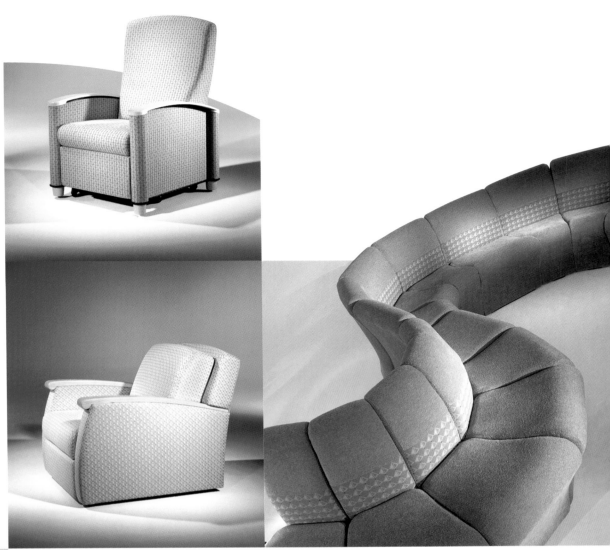

The cure for the common area.

Imaginative styling. Rugged durability. Easy maintenance. From the first impression of public areas to the lasting impression of patient rooms, Wieland Furniture is setting the standard for health care seating.

WIELAND · FURNITURE

WIELAND FURNITURE.COM

888.WIELAND

NeoCon®
World's Trade Fair 2004

June 14-16, 2004
The Merchandise Mart • Chicago, Ill. USA

1,200 EXHIBITORS

100 CEU SEMINARS

KEYNOTE SPEAKER SERIES

EXCLUSIVE TOURS

PHOTOS (FROM LEFT TO RIGHT): TEKNION, BENTLEY PRINCE STREET, HELLER, SKB ARCHITECTURE & DESIGN, RSP, BESTAR, NBBJ.

SOLUTIONS FOR THE DESIGN & MANAGEMENT OF THE BUILT ENVIRONMENT

NeoCon® Leads — Business Follows

Revered as the premier event of the year by the contract industry, NeoCon® World's Trade Fair offers three days of exhibits, education, networking, special events and awards. Be there to expand your design perspective and uncover the hottest trends and products that will impact our industry.

For more information or to request a brochure,
visit www.merchandisemart.com or call 800.677.6278.

FEATURING: Buildings Show® • Office Expo By OFDA • TechnoCon™ •
Fine Design Residential Furnishings Show™ • NEWHospitality • GREEN*life*™

photography: R. Wes Brown

The Natural Solution.

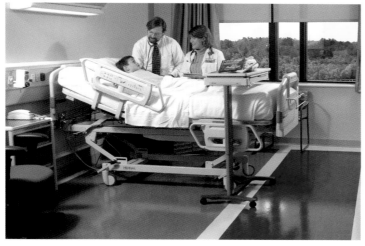

photography: Randy Hadaway, Greenville Hospital System

ETERNAL® wood & form

Designed to compliment Marmoleum, Forbo also offers Eternal, a uniquely constructed vinyl sheet collection.

Eternal is extremely hardwearing, resistant to most chemicals, comfortable to stand on, and virtually maintenance free. Eternal is ideal for surgery areas, operating rooms, pharmacies and more.

Marmoleum offers a natural solution to the demanding needs of healthcare facilities.

Made from natural ingredients, Marmoleum is available in a wide range of colors to match any decor and provide patients with the most comfortable, uplifting environment possible.

Marmoleum's naturally occuring anti-microbial properties make it an ideal floor where respiratory concerns are present, as the surface can easily be kept dust-free. Plus, it has bactericidal properties that actually halt the breeding of certain micro-organisms.

A simple, low chemical usage, recommended maintenance system makes Marmoleum one of the lowest cost of ownership resilient floors available.

Time-tested durability and reparability, combined with one of the quietest and most comfortable underfoot floors, make Marmoleum the natural solution for healthcare applications.

MARMOLEUM®
naturally™

Forbo Linoleum
6 Maplewood Drive
Humboldt Industrial Park
Hazleton, PA 18201

T: 1-800-842-7839/570-459-0771
F: 570-450-0258
info@fL-NA.com
www.forboLinoleumNA.com

Seating ■ **Casegoods** ■ **Tables** ■ **Wall Protection Systems**

You're in Good Hands...

At Kwalu, each order passes through 47 pairs of skillful hands, from the time you place your order, to the moment it is delivered. With over 20 quality control check points, it becomes easy to understand why we offer the industry's only 10 year warranty on the construction and finish of our casegoods, tables, seating and wall protection systems. Like all committed healthcare professionals, our dedication to a healthy environment goes beyond mere words. Our furniture is both waterproof and impervious to the harsh effects of disinfectants. They won't split, swell, or contribute to the transmission of nosocomial infections. Available in over dozens of wood-grained polymer finishes, our virtually indestructible products preserve internal air quality, as they don't release VOC's. And best of all, they can be fully recycled when no longer required. Our scuff-resistant finish makes in-field repair simple, leaving you with time on your hands to focus on what's important – your patients. With Kwalu, your furniture remains as impressive as the quality of care you provide. *Kwalu – there really is no replacement.*

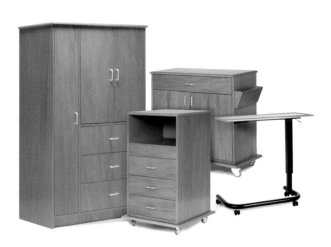

800.405.3441
www.kwalu.com

Resources*

Advanced Medical Plaza
Design Firm: The Stein-Cox Group, Inc.
General Contractors: Wespac Construction

Ambulatory Health Care Center - McGuire Air Force Base
Design Firm: EwingCole
Carpets & Flooring: Tate
Lighting: Architectural Area Lighting, Bronzelite, DAC Lighting, GE, Hadco, Lighting Services, Lightolier, Neoray, Newstamp Lighting, Pathway, Starfire, Sylvania, Visa Lighting
Window Treatments: Levolor
General Contractors: Terminal Construction Co.

Arkansas Children's Hospital - Pediatric Intensive Care Unit
Design Firm: Cromwell Architects Engineers
Carpets & Flooring: Armstrong, Collins & Aikman, DalTile, Milliken
Ceilings: Armstrong
Wallcoverings: ICI, JM Lynne, Maharam, Nevamar, Pionite, Vycon, Wilsonart
Window Treatments: ArcCom, MechoShade
General Contractors: Nabholz

Ball Memorial Hospital Emergency Department
Design Firm: BSA LifeStructures
Carpets & Flooring: Lees, Marmoleum
Fabrics: Designtex, Maharam
Ceilings: Armstrong
Wallcoverings: MDC
General Contractors: Hagerman Construction

Bachelor Children's Research Institute - University of Miami School of Medicine
Design Firm: Karlsberger Companies
Furniture: Haworth, Herman Miller
Carpets & Flooring: Armstrong, Collins & Aikman
Ceilings: Armstrong
General Contractors: Bovis Lend Lease

Beth Israel Medical Center
Design Firm: Guenther 5 Architects
Furniture: HBF, Herman Miller
Carpets & Flooring: Forbo, Karastan, Paris Ceramics
Fabrics: Designtex
Lighting: Artemide, Edison Price, Lightolier
Ceilings: Tectum
Wallcoverings: Conrad
Window Treatments: Conrad
General Contractors: Gazetten Construction

Brementon Naval Hospital
Design Firm: NBBJ
Furniture: Steelcase Carpets & Flooring: American Olean, Armstrong, Harbinger, Interface, Mannington
Lighting: Louis Poulsen
Ceilings: USG
Window Treatments: MechoShade
General Contractors: Harper/Nielsen Dillingham Builders

Bristol-Myers Squibb Children's Hospital at Robert Wood Johnson University Hospital - phase one and two
Design Firm: Shepley Bulfinch Richardson and Abbott
Furniture: AGI, Brayton, Carnegie, Cramer, David Edward, Fixtures and Furniture, Gunlocke, Harpers/Kimble, Herman Miller, Intrex, KI-ADD, Nemschoff, Office Ritter, Specialty, Softcare, Steelcase

Carpets & Flooring: American Olean, Armstrong, Forbo, Interface, Mannington
Fabrics: ArcCom, Architex, Carnegie, Cramer, Designtex, Herman Miller, KI, Maharam, Momentum, Pallas
Lighting: Bega, Color Kinetics, Louis Poulsen, Nessen, Wynona, Zumtobel
Ceilings: Armstrong, Hunter Douglas
Wallcoverings: American Olean, Carnegie, Chromtech, Formica, Koroseal, Marlite, Wilsonart
Window Treatments: MechoShade, Techstyle
General Contractors: William Blanchard Co.

Bronson Methodist Hospital
Design Firm: Shepley Bulfinch Richardson and Abbott
Carpets & Flooring: American Olean, Shaw
Lighting: Alkco, Columbia, Illumination Concepts, Lightolier, Prescolite
Ceilings: Armstrong
Wallcoverings: Benjamin Moore, CS Acrovyn
General Contractors: Barton Malow / CSM

The Busse Center for Specialty Medicine - Northwest Community Hospital
Design Firm: Marshall Erdman & Associates
Furniture: AGI, David Edward, Herman Miller, KI
Carpets & Flooring: Armstrong, Lees
Fabrics: Architex, Designtex, Maharam, Westbury Frost
Lighting: Boyd Lighting, Eureka, Lithonia, Visa
Wallcoverings: Bolta, Lentex, Stafford, Vycon
Window Treatments: Nanik
General Contractors: MEA

Cache Valley Specialty Hospital and Medical Office Building
Design Firm: Architectural Nexus
Furniture: AGI, Lowenstein, Nemschoff, Thonet
Carpets & Flooring: Lees, Mannington, Perma Grain, Shaw, Toli
Fabrics: ArcCom, Architex, Designtex
Lighting: LBL
Ceilings: USG
Wallcoverings: JM Lynne
General Contractors: Jacobsen Construction Company

Cancer Prevention Pavilion - Fox Chase Cancer Center
Design Firm: EwingCole
Carpets & Flooring: DalTile, Endura, Forbo, Karastan, Mannington, Monterey, Toli
Fabrics: Carnegie, Maharam
Ceilings: Armstrong
Wallcoverings: MAB
General Contractors: Nason and Cullen

The Cardiac and Vascular Institute at NYU Medical Center
Design Firm: Perkins Eastman Architects
Furniture: Herman Miller, ICF, KI, Kron, Vitra
Carpets & Flooring: Pacificrest
Fabrics: Designtex, Herman Miller, ICF, Luna, Paul Brayton
Lighting: Tango Lighting
Ceilings: Armstrong
Window Treatments: Sol-R-Shade
General Contractors: HRH Construction Corp.

Cedars Sinai Medical Center - Outpatient Care Unit
Design Firm: HMC Architects

Furniture: Herman Miller, Johnson Tables, Midmark, Peter Pepper
Carpets & Flooring: Armstrong, Cross Ceramics
Fabrics: Designtex, Knoll
Lighting: PM Lighting
Ceilings: Armstrong, Conwed
Wallcoverings: Acrovyn, Formica, Nevamar, Wilsonart
Window Treatments: Hunter Douglas
General Contractors: Turner Construction

Center for Advanced Medicine - Washington University Medical Center
Design Firm: HOK
Furniture: Bernhardt, David Edward, Teknion, Weiland
Carpets & Flooring: Collins & Aikman, Design Weave, Lees, Monterey
Fabrics: Designtex, Momentum
Lighting: Elliptipar, Kramer Lighting, Light Pipe, Linear, Lithonia
Ceilings: Armstrong
Window Treatments: MechoShade
General Contractors: Alberici Construction, McGrath & Associates

CentraCare Health Plaza
Design Firm: HGA
Furniture: AGI, Carolina, Fixtures, Nemschoff
Carpets & Flooring: Atlas, DalTile, Mannington
Fabrics: Anzea, ArcCom, Architex, Fantagraph, Knoll, Momentum
Lighting: Lightsource
Ceilings: Celotex
Wallcoverings: Benjamin Moore
Window Treatments: Graber 2, Wausau
General Contractors: PCL Construction Services

Central Indiana Orthopedics
Design Firm: BSA LifeStructures
Carpets & Flooring: Shaw
Fabrics: Architex
General Contractors: Lauth Property Group

Chandler Regional Hospital
Design Firm: Moon Mayoras Architects, Inc.
General Contractors: DPR Construction, Inc.

Children's Hospital
Design Firm: HDR
Furniture: ADD, Berco Seating, Magnus, Olefson, Steelcase
Carpets & Flooring: Armstrong, Collins & Aikman
Fabrics: Anzea, ArcCom, Brentano, Steelcase
Lighting: Eliptipar, Visa
Ceilings: Armstrong, Decoustics
Window Treatments: Levolor
General Contractors: Peter Kiewit Construction Co.

Children's Hospital of Philadelphia
Design Firm: Karlsberger Companies
Carpets & Flooring: Forbo, Mannington
Wallcoverings: Vycon
General Contractors: L.F. Driscoll

Children's Medical Center of Dallas
Design Firm: Mitchell Associates
Furniture: AGI, Epic, Herman Miller, Johnson Tables, KI, Nucraft, Thonet, Versteel
Carpets & Flooring: Armstrong, Boylu, DalTile, Mannington, Toli
Fabrics: Designtex, Herman Miller, Momentum
Lighting: ALS, Fiberstar, Lite Control, Lithonia, Zumtobel

Ceilings: USG
Wallcoverings: Eykon
Window Treatments: MechoShade
General Contractors: Centrex Construction Company

Children's Memorial Hospital - Surgical Short
Stay Observation Unit
Design Firm: Anderson Mikos Architects ltd.
Furniture: Allsteel, Fixtures, KI-ADD, Memschoff, Wieland
Carpets & Flooring: Mannington, Marley Floors,
Toli, VPI
Fabrics: ArcCom, Maharam, Momentum
Lighting: Lightolier, Metalux
Ceilings: Armstrong
Wallcoverings: Benjamin Moore, JM Lynne
General Contractors: Krahl Construction

Christ Hospital - Reception and Public Space
Modernization
Design Firm: Champlin/Haupt Architects
Furniture: Charles Alan, Herman Miller, Nemschoff,
Source International
Carpets & Flooring: Armstrong, DalTile, Lees,
Masland, Milliken, Pacificrest
Fabrics: Architex, Liz Jordan-Hill, Maharam,
Momentum, Pallas
Lighting: American Glass Light, Celestial Lighting,
Focal Point, Lightolier, Prescolite, Zumtobel
Ceilings: Armstrong
Wallcoverings: Blumenthal
Window Treatments: MechoShade
General Contractors: Messer Construction Company

Christ Hospital - School of Nursing
Design Firm: Champlin/Haupt Architects
Furniture: Herman Miller, KI
Carpets & Flooring: Armstrong, Bruce, Lees,
Mannington, Nora
Fabrics: Deepa, Maharam, Momentum
Lighting: ALFA, Capri, Davis/Muller, Day-Brite, Insight,
Kim, Mark, Precision Architectural Lighting, Vantage
Ceilings: Armstrong
Wallcoverings: Guard, Tower Contract
Window Treatments: Hunter Douglas
General Contractors: Messer Construction Company

Christ Hospital - Special Care Nursery
Design Firm: Champlin/Haupt Architects+ Brandrud,
Herman Miller, IOA, Nemschoff, Versteel
Carpets & Flooring: Amtico, Atlas, Forbo, Mannington
Fabrics: Knoll, Momentum, Unika Vaev
Lighting: Bruck, Lithonia, Targetti, S.P.I.
Ceilings: Armstrong
Wallcoverings: JM Lynne, Knoll, Wolf Gordon
Window Treatments: MechoShade
General Contractors: Denis Construction Company

Cleveland Clinic Florida - Naples Hospital
Design Firm: Marshall Erdman & Associates
Furniture: David Edward, Herman Miller, Nemschoff,
Techline
Carpets & Flooring: Armstrong, Collins & Aikman,
Crossville, Forbo, Mannington
Fabrics: Anzea, Brunschwig & Fils, Designtex,
Donghia, Maharam, Momentum, Pallas, Robert Allen
Lighting: SPI
Ceilings: Armstrong
Wallcoverings: Essex, Genon, Vycon
General Contractors: MEA

Contra Costa County Regional Medical Center -
Ambulatory Care Clinic
Design Firm: Anshen+Allen

Carpets & Flooring: Armstrong, Bentley, Dupont
Antron, Mannington
Fabrics: Architex
Lighting: Litecontrol, Louis Poulsen, Zumtobel
Ceilings: Armstrong, Hunter Douglas
Window Treatments: Carnegie, Levolor, MechoShade
General Contractors: Lathrop

Cuthbertson Village at Aldersgate
Design Firm: FreemanWhite, Inc.
Furniture: Hickory, Nemschoff, St. Timothy
Carpets & Flooring: Collins & Aikman, Pacific
Crest, Shaw
Fabrics: Duralee, Pindler & Pindler, Robert Allen,
Schumacher
Lighting: Progress, Visa
Ceilings: Armstrong
Wallcoverings: Brunschwig & Fils, Koroseal, Olney
Window Treatments: John E. Hinkel, Inc.
General Contractors: Bovis Lend Lease

David C. Pratt Cancer Center - St. John's Mercy
Medical Center
Design Firm: Christner, Inc.
Furniture: Allsteel, First Office, Howe, Nemschoff
Carpets & Flooring: Armstrong, Collins & Aikman,
Constantine, DalTile, Interstyle, Mannington
Fabrics: ArcCom, Interspec
Ceilings: Armstrong, Decoustics
Wallcoverings: Carnegie, Gilford of Maine, InPro Corp.
Window Treatments: MechoShade
General Contractors: McCarthy

Drake Center, Inc.
Design Firm: Champlin/Haupt Architects
Furniture: Brandrud, David Edward
Carpets & Flooring: Invision, Interface, Mannington
Fabrics: Architex, Designtex, Liz Jordan-Hill, Maharam
Lighting: Beta-Calco, Lightolier
Wallcoverings: Guard, JM Lynne, Koroseal
Window Treatments: Levolor
General Contractors: Turner Construction, Special
Projects Division

Duke University Children's Health Center
Design Firm: KMD
Furniture: Herman Miller, Price Modern, Wieland
Fabrics: Herman Miller
Lighting: Light Control, Zumtobel
General Contractors: Bovis Lend Lease

DuPont at Jefferson Pediatrics - Thomas
Jefferson University Hospital
Design Firm: Francis Cauffman Foley Hoffmann
Architects
Furniture: Thonet
Carpets & Flooring: Armstrong, Interface
Fabrics: Designtex, Maharam
Lighting: Lightolier
Ceilings: Armstrong
General Contractors: C. Erickson

Eccles Critical Care Pavilion - University of Utah
Medical Center
Design Firm: Architectural Nexus
Furniture: Nemschoff
Carpets & Flooring: Collins & Aikman, Forbo
Fabrics: ArcCom, Architex, Robert Allen
Lighting: Beta Celco
Ceilings: Armstrong
Window Treatments: MechoShade
General Contractors: Layton Construction Company

Edward Heart Hospital
Design Firm: Matthei & Colin Associates
Furniture: AGI, Allsteel, Bernhardt, Carolina, David
Edward, Jofco, Kimball
Carpets & Flooring: Lees, Lonseal, Shaw
Fabrics: Architex, HBF
Lighting: Metalux
Ceilings: USG
Wallcoverings: D.L. Couch
Window Treatments: Pallas
General Contractors: Pepper Construction

Emergency & Ambulatory Surgery Addition -
Lincoln County Hospital
Design Firm: Christner, Inc.
Furniture: AGI, Hallmark, Peter Pepper, Thonet
Carpets & Flooring: Armstrong, Carnegie, DalTile,
Interface, Monterey
Fabrics: ArcCom
Ceilings: Armstrong
Wallcoverings: Carnegie, Designtex, JM Lynne
General Contractors: Murray Company

Emergency Department Expansion - Terrebonne
General Medical Center
Design Firm: Sizeler Architects
Furniture: AGI, David Edward, KI, Shelby Williams,
Steelcase
Carpets & Flooring: American Olean, Armstrong,
Collins & Aikman
Fabrics: Designtex, Maharam, Steelcase
Lighting: Columbia, Forecast, Lightolier, Prescolite
Ceilings: USG
Wallcoverings: Maharam
Window Treatments: Designtex
General Contractors: TCC (Thompson Construction
Contractors)

Flagstaff Medical Center
Design Firm: Devenney Group Architects
General Contractors: Kitchell Contractors

Florida Hospital Waterman
Design Firm: RTKL Associates Inc.
Furniture: Arconas, Bola, Brayton, Donovan, ERG,
Equinox, Falcon, Gunlocke, Howe, Johnson Tables,
Knoll, Nemschoff, Nucraft, Peter Pepper, Wieland
Carpets & Flooring: Armstrong, DalTile, Interface,
Mannington, Terrazzo
Fabrics: Designtex, Maharam
Ceilings: Armstrong
Wallcoverings: Acrovyn, Benjamin Moore, ICI,
Lanark, MDC, Symphony
Window Treatments: Maharam
General Contractors: Brasfield & Gorrie, LLC

Forum at Carle
Design Firm: HDR
Furniture: Allsteel, KI
Carpets & Flooring: American Olean, Armstrong,
Bentley, Roppe
Fabrics: Designtex, Maharam
Lighting: Lithonia, Visa
Ceilings: Armstrong
Wallcoverings: Essex, Koroseal
Window Treatments: Levolor
General Contractors: McCarthy Construction Co.

The Fran + Ray Start Assisted Living Villa
Design Firm: SmithGroup
Furniture: David Edward, ERG, Forms and Services,
HBF, Salman
Carpets & Flooring: Invision, Karastan, Permagrain

softcare

innovative healthcare solutions

Lighting: Modernica, Shaper Lighting
Ceilings: Benjamin Moore
General Contractors: Millie & Severson

Fresh Start Women's Resource Center
Design Firm: The Stein-Cox Group, Inc.
Carpets & Flooring: Armstrong, Interface, Mannington, Prince Street, Roppe
Fabrics: Guilford of Maine, Reflections
Wallcoverings: ICI, Pittsburgh Paints
General Contractors: Chancen Construction

Grossmont Spring Valley Family Health Center
Design Firm: Moon Mayoras Architects, Inc.
General Contractors: Greer Construction Company

Goryeb Children's Center - Morristown Memorial Hospital
Design Firm: Watkins Hamilton Ross Architects, Inc.
Furniture: Bradley, Childcraft, Cramer, David Edward, Davis, Gressco, Inscape, Intrex, Johnson Tables, Keystone Ridge, Kidzspace Interactives, Kron, National, Nucraft, People Friendly Places, Peter Pepper, Playscapes, Steelcase, Thomasville, United Chair, Vecta
Carpets & Flooring: Armstrong, Bonar, DalTile, Johnsonite, Lees, Mannington, Shaw, Tarkett, Toli
Fabrics: Anzea, ArcCom, Architex, Designtex, Guilford of Maine, Maharam, Mayer, Momemtum, Paul Brayton, Sina Pearson
Lighting: Hallmark
Wallcoverings: Abet Laminati, Acrovyn, Benjamin Moore, Brewster, Corian, Formica, Korogard, Permatone, Seabrook, Sherwin Williams
General Contractors: William Blanchard Company

Harris Methodist Fort Worth - David E. Bloxom Tower
Design Firm: The Stichler Group, Inc.
General Contractors: Centex

Harrison Silverdale Healthcare Campus
Design Firm: KMD
Carpets & Flooring: Interspace
Ceilings: Armstrong
Wallcoverings: Designtex
General Contractors: Sellen Construction

Hartford Hospital C.O.R.E.
Design Firm: The S/L/A/M Collaborative
Furniture: David Edward
Carpets & Flooring: Bentley, Lees, Mannington, Nova
Fabrics: Architex
Ceilings: Armstrong, USG
Wallcoverings: Glidden/ICI Paint, J. Josephson, Koroseal

The Health & Wellness Center by Doylestown Hospital
Design Firm: Marshall Erdman & Associates
Furniture: AGI, KI, La-Z-Boy
Carpets & Flooring: Armstrong, Crossville, DalTile, Lees
Fabrics: ArcCom, Designtex, Maharam, Momentum, Pallas
Lighting: Visa
Ceilings: USG
Wallcoverings: Genon, Sherwin Williams
Window Treatments: Nanik
General Contractors: MEA

The Health Park at WakeMed
Design Firm: FreemanWhite, Inc.
Furniture: Herman Miller, Kimball, Landscape Forms
Carpets & Flooring: American Olean, Lees, Toli
Fabrics: Herman Miller, Montana, Thonet

Ceilings: USG
Wallcoverings: American Olean
General Contractors: T.A. Loving

Heart Clinic Arkansas
Design Firm: Cromwell Architects Engineers
Carpets & Flooring: American Olean, Bolyu, Collins & Aikman, DalTile
Ceilings: Armstrong
Wallcoverings: Formica, JM Lynne, Johnsonite, Koroseal, Nevamar, Sherwin Williams, Willsonart
General Contractors: CDI Contractors, Inc.

The Heart Hospital at Geisinger Wyoming Valley
Design Firm: Francis Cauffman Foley Hoffmann Architects
Furniture: Carolina, David Edward, Herman Miller, Thonet
Carpets & Flooring: Antico, Armstrong, Collins & Aikman, Constantine, DalTile
Fabrics: Herman Miller, Knoll, Maharam, Pallas
Lighting: Eureka, Metalux, Neoray, Portfolio, Zumtobel
Ceilings: Armstrong, Decoustics
Wallcoverings: Acrovyn
Window Treatments: Pallas, Vimco
General Contractors: Geisinger Facilities Department

Hinsdale Hospital - Koplin Family Endoscopy Center
Design Firm: Anderson Mikos Architects Ltd.
Furniture: Herman Miller, Peter Pepper, Sit-On-It, Wieland
Carpets & Flooring: Bentley, Bolyu, Mannington, Tarkett
Fabrics: Knoll, Maharam, Paul Brayton, Unika Vaev
Lighting: Columbia, Delray, Lite Control, Louis Poulsen, Nessen
Ceilings: Armstrong, USG
Wallcoverings: Benjamin Moore, JM Lynne, Seabrook, Vicrtex, Xorel
Window Treatments: Architex
General Contractors: Hinsdale Hospital Construction Dept.

Hoag Hospital East Tower - Women's Pavilion
Design Firm: Taylor & Associates Architects
General Contractors: McCarthy Building Co., Inc.

Hoag Memorial Hospital-Presbyterian - Kitchen & Cafeteria Upgrade
Design Firm: Caruana & Associates
Furniture: ERG, Fixtures Furniture
Carpets & Flooring: Bentley, Summitville
Fabrics: Maharam, Luna
Lighting: Prudential
Ceilings: Armstrong
Wallcoverings: Corian, Maharam, Marlite
General Contractors: Norm Wilson & Sons

Hospital for Special Care
Design Firm: The S/L/A/M Collaborative
Furniture: Brayton, Intrex, Wieland
Carpets & Flooring: Amtico, Armstrong, Atlas, Azrock, US Axminster
Wallcoverings: Arcmitex, Benjamin Moore, Carnegie, Knoll, Zolatone
General Contractors: Downes Construction

Huntsman Cancer Institute Research Hospital - University of Utah Medical Center
Design Firm: Architectural Nexus
Furniture: AGI, Martin Brattrud, Steelcase, Wieland
Carpets & Flooring: Collins & Aikman, Forbo,

Mannington, Shaw
Fabrics: ArcCom, Designtex, Maharam, Paul Brayton
Lighting: LBL, Leucos, Shaper, Visa
Ceilings: Armstrong, USG
Window Treatments: MechoShade
General Contractors: Layton Construction Company

The Indiana Heart Hospital
Design Firm: RTKL Associates Inc.
Furniture: Brayton, Falcon, Kimball, Knoll, Peter Pepper, Task, Thonet, Wieland
Carpets & Flooring: Armstrong, DalTile, Forbo, Interface, Mannington, Terrazzo
Fabrics: ArcCom, Designtex, Maharam
Ceilings: USG
Wallcoverings: Benjamin Moore, Colour & Design, ICI
Window Treatments: MechoShade
General Contractors: Summit Construction

Institute for Orthopaedics & Neurosurgery, Bend, OR
Design Firm: Marshall Erdman & Associates
Furniture: KI, Nemschoff, Techline, Via
Carpets & Flooring: Armstrong, Crossville, Lees, Mannington
Fabrics: ArcCom, Architex, Maharam
Ceilings: USG
Wallcoverings: Bolta, Lentex
Window Treatments: Nanik

Jackson T. Stephens Spine and Neurosciences Institute - University of Arkansas for MedicalSciences
Design Firm: Cromwell Architects Engineers
Furniture: Brayton, David Edward, Steelcase, Vecta
Carpets & Flooring: Collins & Aikman, DalTile, Johnsonite, Mannnington
Fabrics: Nevamar
Ceilings: Armstrong
Wallcoverings: JM Lynne, MDC Wallcovering
Window Treatments: Interspec
General Contractors: CDI Contractors, Inc.

Jonesboro Ambulatory Surgery Center
Design Firm: Cromwell Architects Engineers
Furniture: Haworth, Nemschoff
Carpets & Flooring: Collins & Aikman, Johnsonite, Mannington
Ceilings: Armstrong
Wallcoverings: Acrovyn, Pionite, Sherwin Williams, Symphony, Vycon
Window Treatments: Levolor, Maharam

Joseph D. Domino Healthcare Pavilion - East Jefferson General Hospital
Design Firm: Sizeler Architects
Carpets & Flooring: Collins & Aikman, Durkan, Lees, Permagrain
Lighting: Columbia, Lithonia, Omega, Prescolite, Visa
Ceilings: USG
Wallcoverings: Guard, Innovations, Koroseal, Maharam, Maya Romanoff
General Contractors: Manhattan Gibbs Construction

Kaiser Downey Medical Center
Design Firm: HMC Architects
Carpets & Flooring: Azrock, Collins & Aikman, Mannington
Fabrics: Maharam
Ceilings: Armstrong
Wallcoverings: Scuffmaster, Wolf Gordon
Window Treatments: MechoShade
General Contractors: McCarthy Construction

Kaiser Permanente East Los Angeles Medical

Design Firm: Taylor & Associates Architects
Furniture: Brandrud, Harter, Steelcase, Thonet, Versteel
Carpets & Flooring: Collins & Aikman
Fabrics: Maharam
General Contractors: Kaiser Permanente Construction Services

Design Firm: Taylor & Associates Architects
Furniture: Haworth, Nemschoff, Peter Pepper, Steelcase, Thonet
Carpets & Flooring: Collins & Aikman, DalTile, Innovative, Mannington
Fabrics: Architex, Designtex
Ceilings: Armstrong
General Contractors: McCarthy Building Co. Inc.

Design Firm: SmithGroup
General Contractors: Rudolph & Sletten

Design Firm: HMC Architects
Carpets & Flooring: Armstrong, Collins & Aikman, Spec Ceramics
Fabrics: Architex, Maharam
Ceilings: Armstrong
Wallcoverings: Scuffmaster, Wolf Gordon
Window Treatments: MechoShade
General Contractors: McCarthy Construction

Design Firm: Bradley-Brewster & Associates
Furniture: Corian, Falcon, Martin Brattrud, Nemschoff, Teknion
Carpets & Flooring: American Olean, Armstrong, Atlas, Crossville, Johnsonite, Mannington
Fabrics: Designtex, Maharam
Lighting: Halo, Lithonia, Prescolite, Visa, Winona
Ceilings: Armstrong
Wallcoverings: Eykon, Genon, Koroseal, Maharam, Sherwin Williams
General Contractors: Milton J. Womack, Inc.

Design Firm: The S/L/A/M Collaborative
Furniture: Bernhardt, Bright, HBE
Carpets & Flooring: Atlas, Bolyu, DalTile, Forbo, Permagrain
Fabrics: ArcCom, Bernhardt, Carnegie, HBF, Knoll, Liz Jordan-Hill, Maharam, Paul Brayton
Lighting: Architectural Area Lighting, Edison Price, Lightolier, Louis Poulsen
Ceilings: Armstrong, Hunter Douglas
Wallcoverings: Koroseal, Pittsburgh Paints, Wolf Gordon
Window Treatments: Levolor
General Contractors: Turnek/Shelton

Design Firm: Francis Cauffman Foley Hoffmann Architects
Furniture: David Edward, Kimball, Office Specialty, Patrician
Carpets & Flooring: Armstrong, Collins & Aikman
Fabrics: Designtex, Maharam
Ceilings: Armstrong
Wallcoverings: MAB Paints
General Contractors: P. Agnes

Design Firm: BSA LifeStructures
Carpets & Flooring: American Art and Mosaic
Lighting: Lithonia
General Contractors: Hannig Construction

Design Firm: FreemanWhite, Inc.
Fabrics: Designtex
Lighting: Color Kinetics Inc.
General Contractors: ECI Inc.

Design Firm: KMD (Seattle Group)
Furniture: KI, Knoll, Lowenstein, Touhy
Carpets & Flooring: Interface, Mannington, Terrazo
Fabrics: Knoll
Ceilings: USG
Wallcoverings: Koroseal
Window Treatments: Knoll
General Contractors: McCarthy

Design Firm: Caruana & Associates
Furniture: Gunlocke, Leland, Krug, Nemschoff, Softcare, Via
Carpets & Flooring: Armstrong, Designweave
Fabrics: ArcCom, Architex, Maharam
Lighting: Lithonia
Ceilings: Armstrong
General Contractors: Millie & Seversy

Design Firm: Anderson Mikos Architects Ltd.
Furniture: Allsteel, Brayton, David Edward, Fixtures
Carpets & Flooring: Tarkett, Terrazzo
Fabrics: ArcCom, Designtex, Maharam, Paul Brayton
Lighting: Boyd Lighting, Leucos, Lightolier, Lithonia
Ceilings: Armstrong
Wallcoverings: Benjamin Moore, JM Lynne, Pratt & Lambert
Window Treatments: MechoShade
General Contractors: Fred Berglund & Sons

Design Firm: HKS, Inc.
Carpets & Flooring: Azrock, Forbo, Mannington, Mohawk
Lighting: Lightolier, Prescolite
Ceilings: USG

Design Firm: Mitchell Associates
Furniture: AGI, David Edward, Falcon, Jofco, KI, Nemschoff
Carpets & Flooring: Amtico, Forbo, Karastan Bigelow, Kentile, Mannington, Mohawk, Patcraft
Fabrics: ArcCom, Carnegie, Designtex, Fantagraph, Liz-Jordan-Hill, Momentum
Lighting: ALS, Baldinger, Bruck, Edison Price, Lightolier, Lithonia, Neoray, Nessen
Ceilings: USG
Window Treatments: MechoShade
General Contractors: W.M. Jordan Company

Design Firm: Moon Mayoras Architects, Inc.
General Contractors: WDL Construction

Furniture: Bernhardt, Boyd, Brandrud, Brayton, Cabot Wren, Falcon, FCI, Gunlocke, Lowenstein, Metro, Nemschoff, Nessen, Nucraft, Peter Pepper, Steelcase, Thonet, Tuohy, Vecta
Carpets & Flooring: DalTile, Mannington, Tarkett, Toli
Fabrics: Maharam
Wallcoverings: Corian, Laminart, Nevamar, Pionite, Wilsonart, Zolatone

Design Firm: Bradley-Brewster & Associates
Carpets & Flooring: Armstrong, Belvedere, Endura, Excelon, Factor, Mannington, Permatage
Lighting: Alkco, Hubbell, Lightolier, Lithonia, Omega, Prescolite
Ceilings: Armstrong
Wallcoverings: Essex, Grennon
General Contractors: Milton J. Womack, Inc.

Design Firm: RTKL Associates Inc.
General Contractors: PCL Construction

Design Firm: EwingCole
Carpets & Flooring: American Olean, Armstrong, Atlas, Azrock, Constantine, Forbo, Mannington, Masland, Monterey
Fabrics: Architex, Carnegie, Maharam
Ceilings: Armstrong
Wallcoverings: Blumenthal, JM Lynne
Window Treatments: Solar Shades
General Contractors: Barr and Barr

Design Firm: Champlin/Haupt Architects
Furniture: Brandrud, Kimball, National, Nemschoff, Patrician, Softcare
Carpets & Flooring: Armstrong, Constantine, DalTile, Designweave, Forbo, Mannington, Nora
Fabrics: Carnegie, Knoll, Maharam, Pallas
Lighting: Beta-Calco, Energie, Sistemalux
Ceilings: Armstrong
Wallcoverings: Denova, Designtex, Maharam, Versa
Window Treatments: MechoShade
General Contractors: Danis Building Company

Design Firm: Architectural Nexus
Carpets & Flooring: Forbo, Patcraft, Shaw, Tarkett
Lighting: LBL, Lightolier, Shaper, Scott
Ceilings: Armstrong
Wallcoverings: Maharam
Window Treatments: MechoShade
General Contractors: Layton Construction Company

Design Firm: HDR
Carpets & Flooring: Forbo, Shaw
Ceilings: Armstrong
Wallcoverings: Sherwin Williams
General Contractors: Turner-Christman Construction

Design Firm: HGA
Carpets & Flooring: Bentley, Lees
Wallcoverings: Maharam
Window Treatments: Walters and Wolf

An
important
difference
you can't
see.

Introducing environmentally friendly
C/S Acrovyn® 3000.

New PVC-Free Acrovyn® 3000 performs better than traditional Acrovyn Wall Protection. **It has the same outstanding impact resistance, Class I fire rating, universal code compliance and comprehensive color range.** But the important difference you can't see with Acrovyn 3000 is its built-in protection for our environment. For literature detailing the comprehensive Acrovyn 3000 line – including Wall Covering – and its timely, exciting benefits, **call 1-888-621-3344 or visit www.c-sgroup.com.**

Miriam Hospital - Cardiovascular Thoracic Intensive Care Unit
Design Firm: The S/L/A/M Collaborative
Carpets & Flooring: Armstrong, Collins & Aikman, Tarkett, Toli
Fabrics: Maharam
Lighting: Linear, Winona
Ceilings: Armstrong
Wallcoverings: Acronyn, Benjamin Moore
Window Treatments: Maharam
General Contractors: Designer Built

Missouri Baptist Medical Center (exterior only)
Design Firm: Christner, Inc.
General Contractors: Alberki

Monroe Carell, Jr. Children's Hospital at Vanderbilt - Vanderbilt University Medical Center
Design Firm: Earl Swensson Associates
Furniture: AGI, Brayton, Chromcraft, Egan Visual, Falcon, MTS, Nemschoff, Nova Solutions, Peter Pepper, Steelcase, Stow Davis, Thonet Johnson
Carpets & Flooring: Altro, Amtico, Armstrong, Collins & Aikman, DalTile, Interface, Johnsonite, Nora, Roppe, Toli
Fabrics: Anzea, ArcCom, Architex, Carnegie, Designtex, Duralee, Knoll
Lighting: Artemide, Challenger Lighting, Hampstead, Uni Lights, Winona
Ceilings: Armstrong
Wallcoverings: Abet Laminati, Chemetal, Corian, Formica, Koroseal, Lentex, Maharam, MechoShade, Nevamar, Versa, Vycon, Wilsonart
General Contractors: Centex Rodgers, Inc.

Morgan Stanley Children's Hospital of New York-Presbyterian
Design Firm: EwingCole
Furniture: Bernhardt, Brandrud, Brayton, Carnegie, David Edward, Glen, Harter, Hill-Rom, Humanscale, Metro, Midlands, Peterson Geller Spurge, SoftCare, Steelcase, Vecta
Carpets & Flooring: Armstrong, Atlas, Dupont Antron, Toli
Fabrics: ArcCom, Carnegie, Designtex, Momentum
Lighting: Kirlin, Kurt Versen, Shaper, Zumtobel
Ceilings: Armstrong
Wallcoverings: Abet Laminati, Benjamin Moore, Formica, Pionite, Wilsonart
Window Treatments: MechoShade
General Contractors: Bovis Lend Lease

Mount Sinai Medical Center - Lauder Center for Maternity Care
Design Firm: Guenther 5 Architects
Furniture: Brayton, Hillrom, Knoll, Nucraft
Carpets & Flooring: Amtico, Fritz Tile, Nora
Fabrics: Designtex
Lighting: Artemide, Floss
Ceilings: Simplex
Wallcoverings: Alchemy, Benjamin Moore, Bisazza, Innovations, Interstyle
Window Treatments: Phifer SheerWeave
General Contractors: Morgan Contracting

Nanticoke Cancer Care Center
Design Firm: SmithGroup
Carpets & Flooring: Armstrong, Lees, Toli
Lighting: H.E. Williams, Hubbell, Infinity, Lightech, LSI, Poles, Simkar, W.F. Harris
Ceilings: Armstrong, Tectum
Wallcoverings: CS Group, ICI, Roppe, USG
Window Treatments: MechoShade

General Contractors: Nason Construction, Inc.

Nebraska Heart Hospital
Design Firm: The Stein-Cox Group, Inc.
Furniture: Brandrud, Carolina, Children's Furniture, David Edward, Design Links, Epic, KI, Krug, Nucraft, Sit-On-It, Spec, Thonet
Carpets & Flooring: American Olean, Armstrong, Bentley, Crossville, Interface, Mannington, Patcraft, Roppe, Stonehard, Toli
Fabrics: Architex, Coral, Designtex, Knoll, Liz Jordan-Hill, Maharam, Momentum
Wallcoverings: Benjamin Moore, IPC, Versa
General Contractors: Weitz Construction

New Orleans Cancer Institute Memorial Medical Center
Design Firm: Sizeler Architects
Furniture: Carolina Business Furniture, National
Carpets & Flooring: American Olean, Armstrong, Collins & Aikman, Tarkett
Fabrics: ArcCom
Lighting: Lightolier, Translight Sonoma
Ceilings: USG
Window Treatments: MechoShade
General Contractors: Landis Construction Company

New York Presbyterian Hospital - Office for the Department of Medicine
Design Firm: Perkins Eastman Architects
Furniture: Steelcase
Carpets & Flooring: Innovative Marble, Toli, World Contract
Lighting: Kurt Versen, Linear
Ceilings: Armstrong, Ceilings Plus
General Contractors: Gazetten Contracting

New York Presbyterian Medical Center
Design Firm: Guenther 5 Architects
Furniture: AllSeating, Breuton, Metro, Steelcase
Carpets & Flooring: Fritz Tile, Harbinger
Fabrics: Deepa, Maharam, Paul Brayton, Pollack, Sina Pearson
Lighting: Columbia, Neoray
Ceilings: Simplex
General Contractors: West Contracting Corp.

NYU School of Medicine - Department of Medicine Laboratories
Design Firm: Perkins Eastman Architects
Furniture: Herman Miller, Steelcase
Carpets & Flooring: Azrock, Collins & Aikman
Lighting: Aleria Lighting, Lightolier, Neoray, Zumtobel
Ceilings: Armstrong
Wallcoverings: Benjamin Moore
Window Treatments: MechoShade
General Contractors: Marco Martelli Assoc.

Oklahoma Heart Hospital
Design Firm: Watkins Hamilton Ross Architects, Inc.
Furniture: Brandrud, Charlotte, Haworth, Herman Miller, Krug, Nemschoff
Carpets & Flooring: Armstrong, DalTile, Durkan, Interface, Mannington, Patcraft
Lighting: Scott Architectural Lighting, Visa
Wallcoverings: DuPont, Formica, Maharam, Nevamar, Pionite, Victrex, Wolf Gordon
Window Treatments: Echo Etching
General Contractors: Flintco

Outpatient Diagnostic & Treatment Pavilion - Union Regional Medical Center
Design Firm: FreemanWhite, Inc.
Fabrics: Knoll

Lighting: Alera, Winona
Ceilings: Armstrong
Wallcoverings: Nova Solutions
General Contractors: Rodgers Builders

Parkland Health Center - Bonne Terre
Design Firm: Christner, Inc.
Furniture: Thonet
Carpets & Flooring: Armstrong
Ceilings: Armstrong
Wallcoverings: Johnsonite
General Contractors: S.M. Wilson

Parrish Medical Center
Design Firm: Earl Swensson Associates
Furniture: ERG International, Falcon, Nemschoff, Steelcase, Vecta
Carpets & Flooring: Shaw
Fabrics: ArcCom, Architex, Maharam
Lighting: GE Supply, Illuminations Atlanta
Ceilings: USG
Wallcoverings: JM Lynne, Koroseal, Maharam
Window Treatments: Kirsh, Levolor, Standard Textile
General Contractors: Skanska Building USA, Inc.

Patient Care Wing - SSM Cardinal Glenron Children's Hospital
Design Firm: Christner, Inc.
Furniture: KI, Kimball, Nemschoff, Peter Pepper, RPI, Sit-On-It, Softcare
Carpets & Flooring: Collins & Aikman, DalTile, Interface, Mannington, Missouri Terrazzo, Nevamar, Pionite, Wilsonart
Fabrics: Anzea, Designtex, Interspec, Momentum
Lighting: Alkco, Lightolier, Metalux, Tech-Lighting
Ceilings: Armstrong
Wallcoverings: Baumann, Genon
Window Treatments: Designtex, Levolor, Louver Drape, Rockland Mills
General Contractors: Alberki

Patrick H. Dollard Discovery Health Center
Design Firm: Guenther 5 Architects
Furniture: Bernhardt, HBF, Herman Miller, ICK, Keilhauer, Neinkamper
Carpets & Flooring: Amtico, Forbo, Interface, Stratica
Fabrics: Designtex, Maharam, Unika Vaev
Lighting: Bega, Flos, Lightolier, Louis Poulsen, Zumtobel
Ceilings: Armstrong
Wallcoverings: Benjamin Moore
General Contractors: Storm King Contracting

The Peaks at Flagstaff
Design Firm: Devenney Group Architects
General Contractors: Kitchell Contractors

Phoenix Children's Hospital
Design Firm: Karlsberger Companies
Furniture: Brayton, Fixtures, Spec, Steelcase
Carpets & Flooring: Armstrong, Atlas, Interface
Fabrics: Anzea, Architex, Boltatex, Designtex
Ceilings: Armstrong
General Contractors: Hunt Construction Group

Phoenix Children's Hospital
Design Firm: The Smith-Cox Group, Inc.
Furniture: US Business Interiors
Carpets & Flooring: Armstrong, Atlas, Interface, Prince Street
Lighting: Light Source
Wallcoverings: ICI
Window Treatments: MechoShade
General Contractors: Hunt Construction Group

Design Firm: BSA LifeStructures
Furniture: Martin Brattrud
Carpets & Flooring: Interface, Terrazzo
Fabrics: Momentum
Ceilings: Armstrong
Wallcoverings: Symphony
General Contractors: Shiel Sexton

Design Firm: NBBJ
Furniture: Children's Furniture Co., David Edward, Gunlocke, Knoll, Nemschoff, Steelcase
Carpets & Flooring: American Olean, Armstrong, Bentley, Crossville, Constantine, Durken, Interface, Shaw, Toli
Fabrics: ArcCom, Deepa, HBJ, Knoll, Unika Vaev
Ceilings: Armstrong
Wallcoverings: Innovations, JM Lynne, Knoll
General Contractors: Bostleman Corporation

Design Firm: NBBJ
Furniture: Children's Furniture Co., David Edward, Gunlocke, Knoll, Nemschoff, Steelcase
Carpets & Flooring: American Olean, Armstrong, Bentley, Constantine, Crossville, Interface, Shaw, Toli
Fabrics: ArcCom, Deepa, HBJ, Knoll, Unika Vaev
Ceilings: Armstrong
Wallcoverings: Innovations, JM Lynne, Knoll
General Contractors: Lathrop

Design Firm: SmithGroup
Carpets & Flooring: Armstrong, Mannington
Lighting: Prescolite
Ceilings: Armstrong
Window Treatments: Levolor
General Contractors: OC American Construction, Inc.

Design Firm: Earl Swensson Associates
Furniture: Adden, Hillrom, La-Z-Boy
Carpets & Flooring: American Olean, Armstrong, Bolyu, Collins & Aikman, Crossville, Roppe, Toli
Fabrics: Architex, Brayton, Designtex, Interspec, La-Z-Boy Vinyls, Maharam, Paoli
Lighting: Fine Arts Lamps, Lightolier, Lithonia, Morlite, Winona
Ceilings: Armstrong, USG
Wallcoverings: Acrovyn, American Olean, Designtex, Essex, JM Lynne, Koroseal, Maharam, MDC, Seabrook, Sherwin Williams
Window Treatments: Standard Textiles
General Contractors: Bovis Lend Lease

Design Firm: BLM Architects (interiors), Gresham Smith (architecture)
Furniture: ADD, Hillrom, Nemschoff
Carpets & Flooring: Bentley, Bolyu, DalTile, Interface, Mannington, Prince Street, Shaw, Toli
Fabrics: ArcCom, Architex, Designtex, Interspec
Lighting: ALS, Baldinger, Boyd, Nessen, Starfire, Translite
Ceilings: Armstrong
Wallcoverings: Blumenthal, Essex, JM Lynne, Zolatone
Window Treatments: MechoShade
General Contractors: Greenhut Construction Co.

Design Firm: Taylor & Associates Architects

Furniture: ADD, HON, KI, Kimball, Nemschoff, Peter Pepper
Carpets & Flooring: Armstrong, Bentley, DalTile, Interface, Mannington
Fabrics: ArcCom, Fantagraph, Momentum
Ceilings: Armstrong
General Contractors: Questar Engineering, Inc.

Design Firm: The Stichler Group, Inc.
Furniture: David Edward, Gunlocke
Carpets & Flooring: Mannington, Shaw
Fabrics: Boltaflex, Guilford of Maine, Momentum
Ceilings: Armstrong
Window Treatments: MechoShade
General Contractors: Kitchell Contractors

Design Firm: The Stein-Cox Group, Inc.
Carpets & Flooring: DalTile, IMC, Lees, Lonseal, Mannington, Roppe
Fabrics: Knoll
Wallcoverings: Benjamin Moore
Window Treatments: MechoShade
General Contractors: Rowlands-Cox Construction

Design Firm: The Stitchler Group, Inc.
Carpets & Flooring: Collins & Aikman, Mannington
Wallcoverings: Gilman, Guilford of Maine, JM Lynne, Versa, Vycon
General Contractors: Henry Carlson Co.

Design Firm: The Stichler Group, Inc.
General Contractors: Henry Carlson Co.

Design Firm: Caruana & Associates
Furniture: Via
Carpets & Flooring: Armstrong
Fabrics: Maharam
Lighting: Lightolier, Visual Therapy
Wallcoverings: Maharam
General Contractors: Callison Building Services, Inc.

Design Firm: NBBJ
Furniture: ISA International, Steelcase
Carpets & Flooring: Lees, Van Dijk
Fabrics: Maharam, Sunbrella
Lighting: Illuminating Experiences, Wila Lighting
Ceilings: Interior Environments
General Contractors: Nesser Construction

Design Firm: Champlin/Haupt Architects
Furniture: Herman Miller, Sauder
Carpets & Flooring: Armstrong, Cambridge, Forbo, Shaw
Fabrics: Maharam, Momentum
Lighting: ITRE USA, Prescolite
Ceilings: Armstrong
Wallcoverings: Designtex, DL Couch, Koroseal, MDC, Symphony, York
Window Treatments: MechoShade
General Contractors: Messer Construction Company

Design Firm: BLM Architects
Furniture: AGI, Architectural Supplements, Fixtures Furniture, KI, Kimball, National Office, Peter Pepper, Wieland

Carpets & Flooring: Atlas, Bentley, Blueridge, Bolyu, Designweave, Durkan, Philadelphia Carpet, Prince Street
Fabrics: Anzea, ArcCom, Architex, Carnegie, Designtex, Pallas, Robert Allen Contract, Sina Pearson
Lighting: Capri, Day-Brite, Halo, Lithonia, Omega, Scott, Visa
Ceilings: Armstrong
Wallcoverings: Essex, Genon, JM Lynne, Seabrook, Typhony
Window Treatments: MechoShade, Tivoli
General Contractors: Hunzinger

Design Firm: BLM Architects
Furniture: AGI, Nemschoff
Carpets & Flooring: Bentley, Interface Mannnington, Monterey, Patcraft, Prince Street, Toli
Fabrics: ArcCom, Architex, Designtex, Maharam
Lighting: Baldinger, Blauet, Nessen
Ceilings: Armstrong
Wallcoverings: Blumenthal, Designtex, Innovations, Koroseal, Maharam, Vycon, Wolf Gordon
Window Treatments: MechoShade
General Contractors: Huntzinger

Design Firm: HGA
Furniture: Bernhardt, Cabott Wren, HBF, IOA, KI, Softcare, Steelcase
Carpets & Flooring: Armstrong, Collins & Aikman, Mannington, Monterey
Fabrics: Architex, Designtex, Maharam, Pallas
Ceilings: USG
Wallcoverings: JM Lynne, LinTex, Metro
Window Treatments: Graber
General Contractors: Linbeck

Design Firm: HKS, Inc.
Carpets & Flooring: Armstrong, Karastan, Permagrain
Wallcoverings: Benjamin Moore, Wilsonart
Window Treatments: MechoShade

Design Firm: BSA LifeStructures
Furniture: David Edward
Carpets & Flooring: Gemtec Flooring, Shaw
Fabrics: Architex, Designtex, Maharam
Lighting: G Lighting
Ceilings: Armstrong
General Contractors: Summit Construction

Design Firm: Karlsberger Companies
Carpets & Flooring: Eco, Marley
Ceilings: Armstrong
General Contractors: Pepper Construction

Design Firm: BSA LifeStructures
Furniture: Haworth, Thonet, Versteel, Wieland
Carpets & Flooring: Atlas, Shaw
Fabrics: Designtex
Ceilings: Armstrong
Wallcoverings: Seabrook, Versa
General Contractors: Dunlap & Company, Inc.

Design Firm: BSA LifeStructures
Furniture: AGI
Carpets & Flooring: Lees
Fabrics: Maharam
General Contractors: Wurster Construction Co.

St. Vincent Randolph Hospital
Design Firm: BSA LifeStructures
Furniture: Brattrud, Brayton, Davis, Haworth, Keilhauer, Lowenstein, Nemschoff, Romweber, Sauder, Steelcase, Versteel, Wieland
Carpets & Flooring: Armstrong, Atlas, DalTile, Interface, Mannington, Metropolitan, Technostone
Fabrics: ArcCom, Architex, Brayton, Designtex, Haworth, Keilhauer, Knoll, Maharam
Ceilings: Armstrong
Wallcoverings: JM Lynne, Lanark, Versa, Vycor
General Contractors: Meijer Najemxs

Sutter Maternity and Surgery Center - Santa Cruz
Design Firm: KMD
General Contractors: Bogard Construction

Swedish Covenant Hospital - Acuity-Adaptable Inpatient Unit
Design Firm: Anderson Mikos Architects ltd.
Furniture: KI-ADD, Nemschoff, Sit-On-It, Trendway
Carpets & Flooring: Bigelow, Forbo
Fabrics: ArcCom, Knoll, Maharam, Momentum
Lighting: Halo, Leucos, Linear, Louis Poulsen, Metalux
Ceilings: Armstrong
Wallcoverings: Blumenthal, JM Lynne, Vescom
Window Treatments: Levolor
General Contractors: Pepper Construction

Swedish Medical Center, Cancer Institute
Design Firm: NBBJ
Furniture: Bernhardt, Brandrud, Brayton, Davis, Herman Miller, Keilhauer, KI
Carpets & Flooring: Ann Sacks, Atlas, Design Weave
Fabrics: ArcCom, Carnegie, Knoll, Sina Pearson
Ceilings: USG
Wallcoverings: Carnegie
General Contractors: Sellen Construction

Texas Chilldren's Hospital - Abercrombie Backfil - Phase I
Design Firm: FKP Architects, Inc.
General Contractors: W.S. Bellows Construction Corp.

Texas Chilldren's Hospital - Feigin Research Center
Design Firm: FKP Architects, Inc.
General Contractors: W.S. Bellows Construction Corp.

Texas Chilldren's Hospital - Clinical Care Center
Design Firm: FKP Architects, Inc.
Wallcoverings: Wallcoverings International
General Contractors: W.S. Bellows Construction Corp.

Texas Children's Hospital - West Tower Expansion and Renovation
Design Firm: FKP Architects, Inc.
Wallcoverings: Wallcoverings International
General Contractors: W.S. Bellows Construction Corp.

The Texas Heart Institute at St. Luke's Episcopal Hospital - The Denton A. Cooley Building
Design Firm: RTKL Associates, Inc.
Furniture: Bernhardt, Brandrud, Cramer, Egan, Epic, Falcon, Gunlocke, HBF, Howe, Images of America, Metro, Steelcase
Carpets & Flooring: American Marble, Atlas, DuPont, Interface, Mannington
Fabrics: Anzea, Architex, Jhane Barnes, Spinneybeck

Lighting: Cooper Lighting
Ceilings: Armstrong
Wallcoverings: ICI, Pionite, Wilsonart
Window Treatments: Levolor, MechoShade
General Contractors: Linbeck Construction

Three Rivers Hospital & Health Center
Design Firm: Moon Mayoras Architects, Inc.
General Contractors: Anderson Construction Company Inc.

Torrance Memorial Medical Center - Family Medicine Center
Design Firm: Caruana & Associates
Carpets & Flooring: Interface
Fabrics: Architex
Ceilings: Armstrong
Wallcoverings: Maharam
General Contractors: Callison Building Services, Inc.

UCSF Children's Hospital Ambulatory Care Center, Pediatrics Clinic
Design Firm: Anshen+Allen
Furniture: Fixtures Furniture, KI, Nemschoff, Steelcase, West Coast Industries
Carpets & Flooring: Armstrong, Dupont, Lees, Toli
Fabrics: Architex, Maharam
Lighting: Flos, Lite Control, Prescolite, Zumtobel
Ceilings: Armstrong
Wallcoverings: Abet Laminati, ICL, Innovations, Maharam, Nevamar, Pionite, Sherwin Williams, Zolatone
General Contractors: Lem Construction

University of North Carolina Hospitals
Design Firm: HKS, Inc.
Carpets & Flooring: Amtico, Armstrong, DalTile
Lighting: Daybrite, Kirlin, Omega, Targetti
Wallcoverings: Benjamin Moore, Corian, Sherwin Williams
Window Treatments: MechoShade

UPMC Cancer Center - John. P. Murtha Pavilion
Design Firm: Burt Hill Kosar Rittelmann Associates
Furniture: Bernhardt
Carpets & Flooring: Atlas
Fabrics: ArcCom
Lighting: Leucos
Ceilings: Armstrong
Wallcoverings: Lentex, Maharam
General Contractors: Dick Corporation

UPMC Lee Regional Patient Care Facility
Design Firm: Burt Hill Kosar Rittelmann Associates
Furniture: National, Nemschoff
Carpets & Flooring: Tarkett, Toli
Fabrics: ArcCom, Crypton, Maharam
Lighting: Advent, Eureka
Ceilings: Armstrong
Wallcoverings: Maharam, Zolatone
Window Treatments: ArcCom
General Contractors: Dick Corporation

Upper Chesapeake Medical Center
Design Firm: Mitchell Associates
Furniture: David Edward, Gregson, Haworth, KI, Peter Pepper, Thonet
Carpets & Flooring: Amtico, Lees, Mannington
Fabrics: ArcCom, Designtex, Maharam, Pallas
Lighting: Leucos
Ceilings: USG
Wallcoverings: JM Lynne, Vycon
Window Treatments: MechoShade
General Contractors: Turner Construction

Vassar Brothers Hospital - Comprehensive

Cancer Center
Design Firm: Perkins Eastman Architects w/Larsen Shein Ginsberg Snyder
Furniture: Brandrud, Images of America
Carpets & Flooring: Armstrong, Prince Street
Fabrics: Maharam
Ceilings: Armstrong
Wallcoverings: Benjamin Moore, Donghia
Window Treatments: Sol-R-Shade
General Contractors: Barr & Barr

Villages Regional Hospital
Design Firm: Earl Swensson Associates
Furniture: Bryan Ashley, Janus Et Cie, Kimball, Lifestyles Contract, Nemschoff, Spec, Woodard
Carpets & Flooring: Armstrong, DalTile, Permagrain, Shaw
Fabrics: Anzea, ArcCom, Carnegie, Designtex, Fabricut, Fantagraph, Knoll, Kravet, Maharam, P. Kaufman, Schumacher
Lighting: Architectural Details, Arte De Mexico, Corbett, Sea Gull Lighting
Ceilings: Armstrong, Cirrus
Wallcoverings: Koroseal, Len-Tex, Maharam, MDC, Versa
General Contractors: Skanska Building USA, Inc.

Virginia Commonwealth University Medical Center - Gateway Building
Design Firm: Shepley Bulfinch Richardson and Abbott
Furniture: David Edward, Herman Miller, Milcare
Carpets & Flooring: Armstrong, Collins & Aikman, DalTile, Manningtn, Tarkett, Terrazzo
Fabrics: Designtex
Lighting: Advent, Columbia, Leucos, Prescolite
Ceilings: Armstrong
Wallcoverings: Duron, JM Lynne, Koroseal, Wolf Gordon
Window Treatments: MechoShade
General Contractors: Gilbane Building Company

Virginia G. Piper Cancer Center - Scottsdale Healthcare
Design Firm: Devenney Group Architects
General Contractors: Hunt Construction

Walt Comprehensive Breast Center - Karmanos Cancer Institute
Design Firm: SmithGroup
Furniture: Brattrud, Brayton, Kartell, Knoll, Peter Pepper
Carpets & Flooring: Ann Sacks, Collins & Aikman, Constantine
Fabrics: Designtex, Knoll
Ceilings: Armstrong
Wallcoverings: Acrovyn, Construction Specialities, Hastings, ICI Paints, Maharam, Pittsburgh Paints, Scuffmaster

Washoe Medical Center - Smith Meadows Diagnostic and Treatment Pavilion
Design Firm: HMC Architects
Furniture: KI, Thonet
Carpets & Flooring: Mannington, Milliken, Quartzitec, Tarkett
Fabrics: Maharam
Lighting: Aleva, Focal Point, Louis Poulsen, Nelson, Prudential
Ceilings: Armstrong
Window Treatments: MechoShade
General Contractors: Shaven Construction

Wellness Center - East Jefferson General Hospital
Design Firm: Sizeler Architects
Carpets & Flooring: American Olean, Permagrain, Shaw
Lighting: Kim Lighting
Ceilings: Armstrong
Wallcoverings: Maharam
General Contractors: GCI Construction, Inc.

Advertisers Index

Index by Projects